# Stones the Builders Rejected

# Stones the Builders Rejected

*The Jewish Jesus, His Jewish Disciples, and the Culmination of History*

MARK S. KINZER

*Edited and with an Introduction by* Jennifer M. Rosner

CASCADE *Books* • Eugene, Oregon

STONES THE BUILDERS REJECTED
The Jewish Jesus, His Jewish Disciples, and the Culmination of History

Copyright © 2024 Mark S. Kinzer. All rights reserved. Except for brief quotations in critical publications or reviews, no part of this book may be reproduced in any manner without prior written permission from the publisher. Write: Permissions, Wipf and Stock Publishers, 199 W. 8th Ave., Suite 3, Eugene, OR 97401.

Cascade Books
An Imprint of Wipf and Stock Publishers
199 W. 8th Ave., Suite 3
Eugene, OR 97401

www.wipfandstock.com

PAPERBACK ISBN: 978-1-6667-7860-1
HARDCOVER ISBN: 978-1-6667-7861-8
EBOOK ISBN: 978-1-6667-7862-5

*Cataloguing-in-Publication data:*

Names: Kinzer, Mark S. [author] | Rosner, Jennifer M. [editor].

Title: Stones the Builders Rejected: The Jewish Jesus, His Jewish Disciples, and the Culmination of History / Mark S. Kinzer.

Description: Eugene, OR: Cascade Books, 2024 | Includes bibliographical references and index.

Identifiers: ISBN 978-1-6667-7860-1 (paperback) | ISBN 978-1-6667-7861-8 (hardcover) | ISBN 978-1-6667-7862-5 (ebook)

Subjects: LCSH: Messianic Judaism. | Christianity and antisemitism. | Judaism (Christian theology)—Biblical teaching. | Judaism—Relations—Christianity.

Classification: BR158 K56 2024 (print) | BR158 (ebook)

Unless otherwise indicated, all Scripture quotations are from the New Revised Standard Version Bible, copyright © 1989 the Division of Christian Education of the National Council of the Churches of Christ in the United States of America. Used by permission. All rights reserved.

Scripture quotations marked (RSV) are from the Revised Standard Version of the Bible, copyright © 1946, 1952, and 1971 National Council of the Churches of Christ in the United States of America. Used by permission. All rights reserved worldwide.

Scripture quotations marked (NASB) are from the New American Standard Bible. Copyright © 1960, 1971, 1977, 1995, 2020 by The Lockman Foundation. Used by permission. All rights reserved. lockman.org.

Scripture quotations marked (TLV) are from the Holy Scriptures, Tree of Life Version. Copyright © 2014, 2016 by the Tree of Life Bible Society. Used by permission of the Tree of Life Bible Society.

Versions of chapters 1 and 12 in this volume were previously published in German in *Jesus der Messias Israels? Messianisches Judentum und christliche Theologie im Gespräch*, edited by Mark S. Kinzer, Thomas Schumacher, and Jan-Heiner Tück (Freiburg: Herder, 2023), and are to be published in English in *Jesus—the Messiah of Israel? Messianic Judaism and Christian Theology in Conversation*, edited by Mark S. Kinzer, Thomas Schumacher, and Jan-Heiner Tück (New York: Crossroad, 2024).

A version of chapter 2 of this volume was previously published in *Kesher* 24 (2010) 29–52. In 2012, the *Kesher* article was translated into Italian and appeared in the Jesuit theological journal *Rassegna Di Teologia* ("Nicea e la divinità di Yeshua," 601–24). Finally, it was published as appendix 4 in Mark S. Kinzer, *Searching Her Own Mystery: Nostra Aetate, the Jewish People, and the Identity of the Church* (Eugene, OR: Cascade, 2015).

A version of chapter 3 of this volume was previously published in *Upholding God's Word, Reaching God's Chosen: A Festschrift in Honor of Dr. Mitchell L. Glaser*, edited by Jim Melnick et al. (New York: KIFM, 2022).

A version of chapter 4 in this volume is also to be published in the forthcoming volume *Israel as a Hermeneutical Challenge*, edited by Michael Mulder, Koert van Bekkum, and Arco den Heijer (Leiden, Netherlands: Brill).

A version of chapter 5 of this volume was previously published in *Understanding the Jewish Roots of Christianity: Biblical, Theological & Historical Essays on the Relationship between Christianity & Judaism*, edited by Gerald R. McDermott (Bellingham, WA: Lexham, 2021).

A version of chapter 6 of this volume was previously published in *Kesher* 28 (2014) 79–101.

A version of chapter 11 in this volume was previously published in *The New Christian Zionism*, edited by Gerald R. McDermott. Copyright (c) 2016 by Gerald R. McDermott. Used by permission of InterVarsity Press, P.O. Box 1400, Downers Grove, IL 60515, USA. www.ivpress.com.

To my comrades in the grand adventure that was the Helsinki Consultation, and especially to Boris Balter (1952–2020), z"l.

*The stone that the builders rejected has become the chief cornerstone . . .
Blessed is the one who comes in the name of the L*ORD*.
We bless you from the house of the L*ORD*.*
~Psalm 118:22, 26

# Contents

*Acknowledgments xi*

Introduction: The Thought and Theology of Mark Kinzer—
A Decade Later *by Jennifer M. Rosner* xv

## I. CHRISTOLOGY AS MESSIANOLOGY: THE JEWISH JESUS, YESTERDAY, TODAY, AND FOREVER

1. Post-Supersessionist Messianology:
   The Present and Future Jewish King  3
2. Finding Our Way through Nicaea: The Deity of Jesus, Bilateral Ecclesiology, and Redemptive Encounter with the Living God  15
3. Judaism and the Divine-Human Jesus  40

## II. ECCLESIOLOGY AS ISRAELOLOGY: JEWISH DISCIPLES OF JESUS AND THE TWOFOLD PEOPLE OF GOD

4. Israel Within: Jewish Ecclesial Communities as Prophetic Sign and Theological Challenge  51
5. Recovering the Jewish Character of the *Ekklēsia*: Jewish Disciples of Jesus and the Jewish-Christian Schism  72
6. The Community of Jewish Disciples of Jesus: Standing and Serving as a Priestly Remnant  88
7. The Torah and Jews in the Christian Church: Covenantal Calling and Pragmatic Practice  112

8. Jewish Disciples of Jesus and the Healing of the Twofold Tradition: Eight Theses  122

9. Jewish Disciples of Jesus: The Sacrament of Messianic Communion  131

10. "Physician, Heal Yourself": Baptized Jews and the Wounded People of God  140

## III. ESCHATOLOGY AS ZIONOLOGY: THE JEWISH JESUS AND THE CULMINATION OF HISTORY

11. The People and Land of Israel in Lukan Eschatology  151

12. Post-Supersessionist Eschatology: Welcoming Jesus at the Mount of Olives  176

Appendix A. The Messianic Jewish Rabbinical Council's Vision for Messianic Judaism  189

Appendix B. Collected Statements of the Helsinki Consultation on Jewish Continuity in the Body of Messiah  196

Bibliography  203
Name/Subject Index  211
Ancient Document Index  213

# Acknowledgments

THE PRESENT VOLUME IS a successor to a 2011 collection of essays, also edited and introduced by Jennifer Rosner. Most of the articles included in that earlier volume originated in presentations delivered at Messianic Jewish conferences in North America. However, the final two chapters consisted of material initially directed to more diverse audiences in Vienna and Jerusalem.

As it turned out, the shift in originating contexts for the essays in *Israel's Messiah and the People of God* accurately charted the trajectory of my work over the past two and a half decades. My primary aim in the early 2000s was to strengthen the Messianic Jewish community in North America. But as the first decade of the new millennium was ending, new opportunities led providentially to a reconfiguration of the audiences I addressed and the issues I considered. I spent far more time in Europe, and, when in North America, the settings in which I spoke were usually ecumenical in composition. I focused less on speaking *to* the Messianic Jewish world, and more on speaking to others *on its behalf*.

The dedication of *Stones the Builders Rejected*, and the acknowledgements that follow, reflect this shift. To begin, I must thank Fr. Antoine Lévy, co-chair of the Helsinki Consultation on Jewish Continuity in the Body of Messiah, and all the members of the Consultation, for a decade of friendship and intense theological engagement that widened my heart and my vision. The Helsinki Consultation gave birth in 2019 to Yachad BeYeshua, an international ecumenical fellowship of Jewish disciples of Jesus. This young fellowship seeks to embody many of the ideas contained in these essays, and I cherish it as a hopeful foretaste of good things to come.

Among the founders of the Helsinki Consultation and Yachad BeYeshua was Boris Balter. Boris was a Russian Jew, an Orthodox Christian, and a physicist in the Space Research Institute of the Russian Academy of Sciences. He was also a Bible teacher, a connoisseur of fine music, poetry, and art, and a true mystic. I knew that Boris was brilliant even though I understood little of his highly abstract oral and written communication. That was not due to inadequacies in his English, for he was more articulate than many gifted native speakers. (When I first met him, I asked why and how he learned to speak such beautiful English. His answer: "How else could I read Emily Dickenson?")

Boris was born in 1952, the same year that I entered the world. He died of Covid at the beginning of the pandemic in 2020. We were as different as two people could be, yet we both sensed that our lives were mysteriously intertwined. May his memory be a blessing in the world.

I also wish to thank other European friends who have encouraged my theological endeavors and provided settings in which I could share their fruit. In the context of the present volume, deserving of special mention are His Eminence, Christoph Cardinal Schönborn and Johannes Fichtenbauer from Vienna, and Michael Mulder and Jeroen Bol from the Netherlands.

A few of the chapters in *Stones the Builders Rejected* derive from North American presentations, though from settings far different from those underlying *Israel's Messiah and the People of God*. I thank my friend and esteemed colleague Gerald McDermott for organizing ecumenical theological conferences (and editing books) in which two of these chapters first reached the light of day. I also thank my two friends and sparring partners, Zev Garber and Kenneth Hansen, for kindly inviting me to review their volume, *Judaism and Jesus*, at the 2020 annual convention of the Society for Biblical Literature and American Academy of Religion. Their invitation required courage, for it is still uncommon among Jewish scholars to welcome Messianic Jewish voices in such discussions. Their decision also showed prophetic foresight, as will become evident when this tacit communal ban comes to its inevitable end.

Last but certainly not least, I thank my dear friend and colleague Jennifer Rosner for once again undertaking a joint publication project with me. My wife and I consider Jen, her husband, and their children to be members of our own family. She is a jewel, both as a human being (a *mensch*), and as a scholar and spiritual leader. She was a leading figure in the Helsinki Consultation and now occupies a prominent role in the ecumenical fellowship springing from Helsinki. I am honored to once again have her name linked with mine.

May these essays glorify the Blessed Holy One, and aid all "builders" in reclaiming stones essential to the holy temple that is the twofold messianic people of God.

# Introduction
## The Thought and Theology of Mark Kinzer— A Decade Later

In November 2022, I sat across a table from Mark Kinzer in Denver, Colorado, as we shared a meal and discussed the intricacies of Jewish observance amidst the ongoing balancing of complex, life-defining, and often conflicting commitments. What struck me that evening is what has always struck me about Kinzer's thought—his ideas, while theologically sophisticated and intellectually rigorous, are firmly grounded in the real lives that we live with the real obligations and limitations that daily confront us. There is a profound humanity to Kinzer's vision and theology, and this robust humanity arguably anchors the entirety of his theological paradigm. For Kinzer, it is never about black-and-white answers that ignore the particulars of context and calling; rather, it is about the intricate negotiation of faith and practice amid the multifaceted nuances of identity and community.

While this feature of Kinzer's thought has always been central to his unique theological perspective, it has arguably become sharpened and deepened over the past ten years. The essays in this volume were born out of engagement with concrete sociological contexts that have provided the forum for Kinzer's ongoing theological reflection, building upon the trajectory of his unfolding biography in conversation with his distinctive theological commitments. In this introductory essay, my goal is to frame Kinzer's thought vis-à-vis the particular endeavors in Kinzer's personal and professional life that have nurtured his theology over the past decade and highlight significant distinctives that define his ongoing work.

This volume can be seen as a companion and follow-up to *Israel's Messiah and the People of God*, a collection of Kinzer's essays that was published in 2011. As Kinzer notes in his acknowledgments, the audiences and aims of those earlier essays already pointed in the direction of Kinzer's future work and thought. The first six chapters of that book emerged from discussions internal to the Messianic Jewish community and reflected the primary focus of Kinzer's energies in the first ten years of the new millennium. But the seventh chapter ("*Lumen Gentium* through Messianic Jewish Eyes") was written for the 2008 meeting of the Roman Catholic–Messianic Jewish Dialogue Group in Vienna and contained the seeds of Kinzer's 2015 volume addressed to a Catholic audience.[1]

The epilogue of *Israel's Messiah* ("*Postmissionary Messianic Judaism*, Three Years Later") was also first presented in 2008 outside North America, at the Baptist House in Jerusalem. Among other things, Kinzer considered in that piece the practical outworking of bilateral ecclesiology.[2] He suggested that Messianic Jews and Protestant Christians had much to learn from "the wisdom of the Catholic tradition" when it came to "incorporating new communities and movements into its institutional life without fragmentation."[3] This epilogue also acknowledged the role of Christian leaders in supporting the Jewish identity of Jews within their pastoral orbit.[4] Kinzer thereby opened the door to a form of bilateral ecclesiology that included not only Messianic Jewish congregations but also new modes of Jewish expression within existing Christian church structures. Thus, the final two articles in *Israel's Messiah and the People of God* serve as a bridge between Kinzer's earlier engagement with the internal direction of the Messianic Jewish community and his later efforts to represent the perspectives and concerns of that community to the world beyond its borders.

In the present successor volume to *Israel's Messiah*, we see the trajectory of Kinzer's work and thought extended into the second and third decades of the new millennium. Kinzer here expands upon the foundational concepts that characterized his earlier work and homes in on additional foci that further flesh out the depth and breadth of his theological vision. In this way, Kinzer's thought has become more refined over the

---

1. See Kinzer, *Searching Her Own Mystery*.

2. Bilateral ecclesiology is a key theological pillar in Kinzer's thought, referring to the twofold character of the one people of God. This concept is unpacked in great detail in Kinzer, *Postmissionary Messianic Judaism*.

3. Kinzer, *Israel's Messiah and the People of God*, 189.

4. Kinzer, *Israel's Messiah and the People of God*, 194.

years, continually being influenced by the real-life tensions and pressing theological needs of those in his academic and personal circles.

Here we will approach Kinzer's thought from three distinct angles which, together, offer us a helpful window into the contents that follow. The first two angles are particular communities that have served as primary audiences of and catalysts for Kinzer's ongoing theological work, namely the Catholic (and, to some extent, Eastern Orthodox) Church and a widened circle of Jewish followers of Jesus. The final angle is a particular theological topic: eschatology in conversation with land theology. We will look at each of these topics on its own as well as how they overlap with and mutually inform one another in Kinzer's thought. Finally, we will offer an overview of the chapters that follow.

## ENGAGEMENT WITH THE CATHOLIC WORLD

The Catholic Church has led the way in terms of post-Holocaust Christian reflection on Judaism and the Jewish people, and Kinzer has been an important voice assessing the impact of this new chapter in Jewish-Christian relations, perhaps especially as it relates to Messianic Jewish theology. However, as Kinzer recounts in *Searching Her Own Mystery: Nostra Aetate, the Jewish People, and the Identity of the Church*, the influence of the Catholic Church on his own theology and spirituality predates his theological work related to it. Kinzer describes a freshman history class that profoundly impacted his religious imagination and how this influence deepened during a transformative European backpacking trip the following summer.

Kinzer writes about how, at the time, he was aware of the long legacy of Christian anti-Judaism but was not overly bothered by it on account of having "little affection for Jewish life myself." Kinzer's coming to faith in Jesus ignited a deeper passion for his Jewish identity and thus made this aspect of Christian history more troubling to him. As Kinzer explains, "it was only after I had received the gift of faith that my identity as a Jew became a pressing issue for me. In an ironic twist, Jesus kindled in me for the first time a love for Judaism and a commitment to the Jewish people. . . . I could no longer minimize the history of Catholic anti-Judaism as a minor blemish on the achievements of the High Middle Ages."[5]

---

5. Kinzer, *Searching Her Own Mystery*, 28.

Kinzer goes on to describe his involvement with and eventual leadership of the Word of God community in Ann Arbor, Michigan, an ecumenical community fueled by the Catholic Charismatic Renewal and deeply informed by the Second Vatican Council. Kinzer worked to develop a Messianic Jewish neighborhood group within the Word of God and through this community he built relationships with key Catholic figures who would have a profound influence on his theological development. In this way, Kinzer's involvement in and contribution to the Catholic community and the Messianic Jewish community went hand in hand. The Catholic Charismatic Renewal emerged during the same era as the Messianic Jewish movement, which increasingly replaced the phenomenon of Hebrew Christianity.[6] Kinzer's involvement in these two communities both informed and flowed from his own ongoing search for how to live authentically as a Jewish follower of Jesus. Kinzer increasingly saw the deep resonances between Judaism and Catholicism as his involvement with each deepened.

As Kinzer explains, his appearance on the scene of Messianic Judaism was met with some suspicion on the part of the extant leaders. "My theological framework and idiom appeared strange to my new community, and many suspected that I was not quite 'orthodox' in my doctrine. I leaned too much on tradition—Jewish and Christian—in my interpretation of Scripture; embraced ritual as an integral expression of a life of faith; and highlighted the significance of community as a check on unfettered American individualism."[7] Kinzer's spiritual formation had taken place in a different theological and sociological matrix than the mostly evangelical milieu that largely characterized (and, to a large extent, still characterizes) the Messianic Jewish movement.

While the influence of Catholicism on Kinzer's thought has always been significant, this aspect of his work has become more visible over the past ten years. Clearly indicative of this is Kinzer's ongoing involvement in the Roman Catholic–Messianic Jewish dialogue group and the publication of *Searching Her Own Mystery: Nostra Aetate, the Jewish People, and the Identity of the Church* (2015), which has since been translated into French, Polish, Italian, and Spanish.

---

6. For a more detailed overview of this shift, see Kinzer, *Postmissionary Messianic Judaism*, ch. 8.

7. Kinzer, *Searching Her Own Mystery*, 35.

Also noteworthy in this regard is Kinzer's engagement with Roch Kereszty on Messianic Jews and the Catholic Church,[8] and Tom Weinandy (as well Gerald McDermott and Gavin D'Costa) on the topic of the Jews and the body of Christ.[9] Finally, Kinzer's friendship, collaboration, and academic engagement[10] with Fr. Antoine Lévy reveals the overlap between Kinzer's deep connection with the Catholic Church and the shift in his focus from Messianic Jews to Jewish followers of Jesus more broadly. It is to this latter shift that we now turn.

## JEWISH FOLLOWERS OF JESUS: WIDENING THE CIRCLE

Kinzer's life and community have always been characterized by a certain ecclesial diversity, and while this is still very much the case, a primary element of Kinzer's core community over the past decade has been Jewish disciples of Jesus from a wide cross-section of ecclesial affiliations, spanning from historic Christian denominations to the mainstream Jewish world. Many of the individuals representing this diverse array of Jewish followers of Jesus have served as both the audience of and the occasion for a number of essays included here.

One large subset of this group is Catholic Jews, and here Kinzer's thought overlaps significantly with his engagement with the Catholic Church more broadly. While part of the impetus for that work is helping the Catholic Church to think more deeply and more clearly about Judaism and the Jewish people, it is also focused upon the very specific life and existence of Catholic Jews. As discussed above, Kinzer's relationship to and work with Fr. Antoine Lévy (a French Jewish Dominican priest) has been central in this regard and is clearly on display in Kinzer's engagement with Lévy's book *Jewish Church: A Catholic Approach to Messianic Judaism* (2021).[11]

Kinzer's early work tends to focus more explicitly on Messianic Jews and the Messianic Jewish movement. In his first book, *Postmissionary Messianic Judaism* (2005), Kinzer establishes the framework for a Torah-observant Messianic Judaism based upon covenant fidelity rather than

---

8. See *Communio* 42.3 (Fall 2015).
9. See *Pro Ecclesia* 27.4 (2018), 412–50.
10. See *Pro Ecclesia* 31.3 (2022), 350–428. Also of note is Coolman, "Jewish Church."
11. Lévy, *Jewish Church*.

missionary expediency. He argues that the New Testament presumes ongoing Torah observance for Jewish followers of Jesus and he explains how the early church precipitates a departure from this framework as hostility builds between the now gentile-majority Christian community and the increasingly Jesus-averse Jewish community. In this book, Kinzer coins the term "bilateral ecclesiology," which points toward a reality whereby Jewish followers of Jesus maintain their Jewish identity (rooted in the practice of Torah) while gentile followers of Jesus are joined to the commonwealth of Israel without being obligated to take on Jewish practice. In other words, according to this model, discipleship looks different for Jews than it does for non-Jews.

Kinzer's second book, *Israel's Messiah and the People of God* (2011), continues to flesh out the concrete contours of Messianic Jewish covenant fidelity. Here he offers a vision for Messianic Judaism that builds upon a uniquely Messianic perspective on core tenets of traditional Judaism as well as a uniquely Jewish perspective on core tenets of Christian faith.

As stated above, *Searching Her Own Mystery* (2015) addresses theological concerns related to the Catholic Church's post-Holocaust reappraisal of Judaism and the Jewish people, and as we will discuss in the next section, both *Jerusalem Crucified, Jerusalem Risen* (2018) and its trade companion *Besorah* (2021) focus on eschatology and land theology.

The essays in the present volume represent a widening of the circle in which Kinzer's primary focus and audience is not exclusively those who self-identify as Messianic Jews (or those interested in Messianic Judaism), but rather Jewish followers of Jesus more broadly, including those who find their ecclesial home in the historic Christian churches and denominations.

Central to the essays in this volume is the historical emergence of the Helsinki Consultation on Jewish Continuity in the Body of Messiah, which later evolved into the organization Yachad BeYeshua.[12] The Helsinki Consultation grew out of Kinzer's friendship with Fr. Antoine Lévy. Underlining the proleptic significance of the epilogue to *Israel's Messiah and the People of God*, this French Jewish Catholic theologian first met Kinzer while attending his 2008 lecture at the Baptist House in Jerusalem, whose text became the epilogue. Lévy was intrigued by this American Messianic Jewish theologian whose presentation displayed an ecumenical vision and appreciation for the Catholic tradition, and he requested a

---

12. See www.yachad-beyeshua.org.

meeting. At a Jerusalem café, they spoke of the value of forging relationships among Jewish disciples of Jesus across the ecclesial spectrum. As a first step, they discussed convening a high-level theological consultation that would include Messianic Jews, Jewish Catholics, Jewish Protestants, and Jews from the Russian Orthodox Church. They then invited a group of such scholars to Helsinki, Finland, in 2010 for both a public conference and a set of private meetings.

Already at this first meeting, the group felt a strong bond and sense of solidarity and began to envision a larger community comprised of a wide swath of Jewish followers of Jesus. The Helsinki Consultation met annually in different European cities for the next eight years, and chapters 6–10 in this volume are modified versions of Kinzer's presentations at these conferences. Each year, the Helsinki Consultation endeavored to create a statement relevant to that year's particular conference theme, and these statements are compiled in appendix B of this volume.

In 2019, the vision to expand the fellowship became a reality with the founding of Yachad BeYeshua. Since then, Yachad BeYeshua has gained traction as a membership organization, bringing together a remarkably diverse cross-section of Jewish followers of Jesus who all wrestle with how to bring together two key pieces of their religious selves—their Jewishness and their faith in Messiah.

Kinzer's dedication to this wider circle of Jewish followers of Jesus has raised additional questions regarding the notion of "bilateral ecclesiology," which stipulates that the global *ekklēsia* "must consist of two corporate subcommunities, each with its own formal or informal governmental and communal structures" and that "the Jewish branch of the twofold ekklesia must identify with the Jewish people as a whole and participate actively in its communal life."[13] The parameters of this vision seem to disallow for Jews *within* the gentile branch of the *ekklēsia*, which represent the vast majority of Jewish followers of Jesus worldwide and the primary engine behind Yachad BeYeshua's diverse membership.

In this way, Kinzer's work over the past decade has been characterized by a kind of sharpening and refining of his earlier theological framework, producing a more nuanced understanding of covenantal fidelity for Jewish followers of Jesus. This aspect of Kinzer's work is especially apparent in chapter 6 of this volume, where Kinzer offers a spectrum of what covenant fidelity might look like based upon the New Testament

---

13. Kinzer, *Postmissionary Messianic Judaism*, 152.

typology of Paul (whose work is intentionally focused on gentiles), James (who is firmly planted within the Jewish community in Jerusalem), and Peter (who seems to occupy a middle ground between Paul and James). The differing orientations of these New Testament figures provides a model of how Jewish followers of Jesus today might fulfill the calling to serve as a bridge between the gentile Christian community and the people of Israel in their diverse ecclesial contexts.[14]

On the question of Torah observance among Jewish followers of Jesus, appendix A in this volume offers another helpful window into this complex topic. The Messianic Jewish Rabbinical Council (MJRC) is an association of Messianic Jewish rabbis and leaders who are committed to a Messianic Judaism that takes seriously Jewish tradition and Jewish practice, and Kinzer has been among those who both envisioned and continue to lead the council. The MJRC has produced extensive "standards of observance," which aim to set forth the practical details of Jewish observance for followers of Jesus, and the MJRC's guiding vision for Messianic Judaism is reproduced in this appendix.

While this document sheds light on the perspective of one particular organization—which Kinzer has been instrumental in both founding and leading—key questions remain on how precisely Torah observance might translate for those outside an explicitly Messianic Jewish context. For example, the document states that "the MJRC views the participation of Jews in the Christian church as an exception to the normal vocation of Jewish disciples of Yeshua, which lies within the Jewish Yeshua-community." One might legitimately ask the question of whether, then, Messianic Jewish identity is somehow superior to or more desirable than Jewish existence within the Christian church. Though not always expressed explicitly, this is indeed a key question within the membership of Yachad BeYeshua. While the essays in this volume offer some measure of clarity on this question, it may also be the case that Kinzer's thought has yet to be entirely fleshed out in this regard.

---

14. When discussing Torah observance among Jewish followers of Jesus, the issue of rabbinic tradition becomes a central point of disagreement. On this, see Kinzer, *Israel's Messiah and the People of God*, ch. 3.

INTRODUCTION xxiii

## ESCHATOLOGICAL ORIENTATION AND LAND THEOLOGY

Classically, the three pillars of Judaism are God, Israel, and Torah. Kinzer's thought has offered sustained reflection on these central pillars, as was demonstrated quite clearly in *Israel's Messiah and the People of God*. Many claim that the land of Israel is a fourth pillar that carries just as much weight as the other three, and Kinzer's work over the past decade has reflected a deepening engagement with this fourth pillar—and particularly the role of the land in eschatological considerations. For Kinzer, Jesus's life, death, and resurrection are intimately paired with the destruction and rebuilding of Jerusalem, and the thread that ties together the Jewish people, the Torah, and the land is also tightly woven throughout the fabric of Jesus's prophetic message to the world. Such a claim has significant implications for both modern Zionism and the existence of Messianic Jews in our day, topics that for Kinzer are intricately connected.

Once again, we see *Israel's Messiah and the People of God* paving the way for Kinzer's later work, as chapters 5 and 6 in that volume address eschatology from a Messianic Jewish lens. The eschatological significance of the land is a main focus in *Jerusalem Crucified, Jerusalem Risen* and *Besorah*, and it is displayed clearly in chapters 11 and 12 of this volume. In Kinzer's geographical analysis of Luke-Acts, he critiques more prevalent readings and charts a different way to understand the text. For example, rather than concluding (as many scholars do) that the land of Israel loses theological significance on account of the book of Acts ending in Rome, Kinzer emphasizes the fact that the entire narrative of Luke-Acts is incomplete. Kinzer notes that the book of Acts reflects the gospel message's centrifugal movement outward, but it also reveals a repeated centripetal movement back to Jerusalem. Thus, the fact that the book of Acts ends in Rome means that a final return to Jerusalem is still to come. Here Kinzer's understanding of Acts 1:6–8 points in a strikingly different direction than the dominant thread of Christian interpretation.

In this regard, Kinzer's geographical analysis of the book of Acts parallels his soteriological conclusions. Rather than Paul's pronouncement in Acts 28:28 ("Therefore I want you to know that God's salvation has been sent to the gentiles, and they will listen!") representing the final word on Israel's salvation, Kinzer reads this verse intertextually with Acts 13:47 and Isaiah 49:6 ("I have made you a light for the gentiles, that you may bring salvation to the ends of the earth"), arguing that the salvation of the gentiles is a precursor to the final redemption of both the land and people of Israel. For Kinzer, geographical Israel and sociological Israel remain at the center of God's redemptive work and figure prominently in biblical eschatology.

To highlight the theological significance of the land of Israel (and the city of Jerusalem) forces one to wade into the complex waters of contemporary Zionism and the layered situation in the land of Israel today. Here Kinzer's thought is helpful in that he provides a theological framework that leaves room for a variety of different political perspectives. As he writes in *Jerusalem Crucified*, "within the broad framework of this ecclesial Zionism, there is ample room for vigorous debate and disagreement concerning the practical details of the Israeli-Palestinian conflict. I am attempting to provide a set of theological parameters within which advocates of the right, left, and center can all take their stand. In other words, the approach presented here does not dictate a particular political stance in dealing with the issues at hand."[15]

In one sense, Kinzer's sustained reflection on eschatology and land theology provides the frame for this book in its entirety. For Kinzer, the Christian church has been the guardian of the gospel message for centuries, though its preaching of this message has been consistently tainted by its own supersessionist orientation and enduring "Israel-forgetfulness."[16] While some have read the church's shortcomings in this regard as a fundamental critique of core Christian doctrine, Kinzer attempts to amend Christian doctrine in such a way as to reveal and correct this blind spot. According to Kinzer, the church holds within itself the resources to correct its supersessionism.[17] Kinzer perceives something significant taking place in our day, for we are beginning to see promptings toward a fundamental reorientation of Christian thought.

Hence, this book's three main sections. First, Christology must be reimagined as Messianology—how can we come to see the Christ of Christian theology as Israel's long-awaited Messiah, whose Jewish identity endures? Here we must wrestle with the oft-overlooked reality that Jesus is *still* Jewish; it is not just the case that Jesus *was* Jewish,

---

15. Kinzer, *Jerusalem Crucified*, 264.

16. See Soulen, *The God of Israel and Christian Theology*, 49–52.

17. In Kinzer's words, "the church faithfully preserved and carried within it the truths that would allow it eventually to reexamine its history and recognize supersessionism as an error demanding correction" (Kinzer, *Postmissionary Messianic Judaism*, 211).

but rather that Jesus *is* Jewish. Second, building upon the theological significance of the Jewish Jesus, ecclesiology must be reconstructed upon Israelology—how can Christian ecclesiology be increasingly formulated in light of the foundational reality of God's election of the people of Israel? In what ways do Jewish followers of Jesus (who have become corporately identifiable in our day) constitute an essential component of the body of Messiah, linking this body to the people of Israel? Finally, grounding an Israel-centric ecclesiology within historical teleology, eschatology must be regrounded within Zionology—how does the abiding centrality of the land of Israel inform our understanding of God's final redemption of Israel and the nations?

As this book makes clear, these three theological loci offer a foundation upon which a wholesale reappraisal of Christian theology can be built. To tackle Christology, ecclesiology, and eschatology from a Messianic Jewish and post-supersessionist lens is to point the way toward a Christian theological framework that takes seriously God's enduring covenant with the people of Israel in all its existential and theological density. If we can demonstrate Israel's enduring significance within the doctrines of Christ, the church, and the last things, perhaps we can begin to rewrite the way the gospel is understood and proclaimed.

We live in an era in which this kind of rethinking and reimagining of Christian doctrine has become widespread. Older paradigms of Judaism vs. Christianity, law vs. grace, faith vs. works, are increasingly being called into question. Dualism's supersessionist underpinnings are being evermore exposed. Within this unfolding conversation, Kinzer's voice has particular poignancy and it would seem that his voice is being heard more widely. One sign of Kinzer's growing influence can be seen through the Festschrift recently published in his honor and the remarkable group of scholars that it brought together.[18]

Here let me reference an excerpt from the introduction to *Israel's Messiah and the People of God*:

> Kinzer's method represents the cross-directional twin tasks of explaining the Jewish piece to Christians (who have historically perceived Judaism as either spiritually bankrupt because of its rejection of Yeshua or as a typologically significant precursor to Yeshua whose significance has since been superseded by the church) and the Christian piece to Jews (who have historically experienced and therefore justifiably perceived Christianity as

---

18. Kaplan, ed., *Covenant and the People of God*.

a threat to the very lifeblood of Jewish existence). In the implementation of this dual representation, Messianic Judaism emerges as the critical link, and Kinzer's theology offers a call to Jewish Yeshua-believers to embody the bridge-building role to which they have been existentially assigned.[19]

The aforementioned Festschrift seems to offer empirical evidence that Kinzer's attempts to challenge both the Jewish and Christian communities anew is in fact beginning to gain traction. Within the Festschrift, we see Christian thinkers appreciating rabbinic literature and Jewish thinkers reflecting on the problem of Christian supersessionism—in other words, we see the signs of a Jewish reappraisal of Christianity and a Christian reappraisal of Judaism.

Perhaps this volume will represent the next step in this ongoing cross-directional reassessment, and perhaps it will once again reveal the gift that Kinzer's voice continues to be in this ongoing conversation.

---

19. Kinzer, *Israel's Messiah and the People of God*, xi.

# PART I.

*Christology as Messianology:
The Jewish Jesus,
Yesterday, Today, and Forever*

CHAPTER 1

# Post-Supersessionist Messianology
## The Present and Future Jewish King

> *In this essay, Kinzer works to unpack the significance of the resurrected Jesus's enduring Jewish identity as well as his title as the King of the Jews. Kinzer posits a mutual dependence between King Jesus and his Jewish subjects, and a parallel dependence between Jews (the rightful subjects of Jesus's kingship) and gentiles (who must wrestle with the ontological otherness of their Messiah, the Jewish King). Ultimately, Kinzer argues, the eschatological unveiling of Jesus's currently hidden identity as the King of the Jews will chasten both the Jewish people (who have yet to recognize their King) and Christians (who have historically sought to worship the risen Lord while blotting out his role as the King of the Jews).*[1]

## JESUS'S ENDURING JEWISH IDENTITY

THE JEWISHNESS OF THE *historical* Jesus is now taken for granted. But the reality and significance of Jesus's *enduring* Jewish identity is only

---

1. An abbreviated version of this chapter was presented at an international symposium at the University of Vienna in July 2022. The focus of the symposium was "Jesus—Also the Messiah for Israel? The Messianic Jewish Movement and Christianity in Dialogue." The goal of the event was to foster theological engagement between European Christian scholars and leading Jewish disciples of Jesus, whether they self-identify as Messianic Jews, Jewish Christians, or Jewish Catholics. This article, along with the other papers from the symposium, is published in German (*Jesus der Messias Israels?*, ed. Kinzer et al.) and is to be published in English (*Jesus—the Messiah of Israel?*, ed. Kinzer et al.).

gradually becoming a subject of theological reflection. At the beginning of this century, Robert Jenson pointed to its significance:

> The risen Jesus is also flesh, in that he is risen bodily, for to be an embodied creature is to be flesh. Now, flesh is never an individual possession; that we are flesh means among other things that we have parents and ancestors, who—at least until we get to Adam—are not everyone's parents and ancestors. The Word who has come in the flesh belongs to the lineage of Abraham and Sarah, and this fact belongs to his identity, to what traditional Christology calls the "one hypostasis" of the Word who is Jesus.[2]

Jenson describes the resurrected Jesus as the bearer of Jewish flesh and suggests that this is an essential feature of his glorified identity. Moreover, he proposes that this identity implies an enduring association with those of the same lineage, namely, the Jewish people.

In the same year, Bruce Marshall offered a similar proposal, in even more explicit language:

> In the person of the Logos God makes his own the flesh of this particular Jew, Jesus of Nazareth. *God's ownership of this Jewish flesh is permanent.* In the end, when all flesh shall see the glory of the Lord, the vision of God will, so the traditional Christian teaching goes, be bound up ineluctably with the vision of this Jew seated at God's right hand. So in willing his own incarnation, it seems that God wills the permanence, indeed the eschatological permanence, of the distinction between Jews and Gentiles. *But Jesus cannot be a Jew, or be identified as such (as he will be even in the eschaton), all by himself, in isolation from his people.* He is a Jew, like any other, only in virtue of his descent from Abraham, and thus in virtue of his relationship to the Jewish people as a whole. And this suggests that in owning with unsurpassable intimacy the particular Jewish flesh of Jesus, God also owns the Jewish people as a whole, precisely in their distinction from us Gentiles; he cannot own the one without also owning the other.[3]

Marshall's formulation could not be clearer: "God's ownership of this Jewish flesh is permanent." And, since Jewish identity is inherently corporate, the resurrected Jesus retains a distinctive relationship with the

---

2. Jenson, "Toward a Christian Theology of Judaism." This essay appears in a volume that consists of papers delivered at a conference in 2001. Jenson's text was published earlier in *Pro Ecclesia* 9.1 (2000) 43–56.

3. Marshall, *Trinity and Truth*, 178 (emphasis added).

Jewish people as a whole. Marshall infers from this the striking claim that Jewish identity itself carries over into the eschaton.

Neither Jenson nor Marshall explore the wide-ranging ramifications of these bold assertions, and few other prominent theologians of this century have ventured further along the same path. But two recent publications—one by Kayko Driedger Hesslein and the other by Barbara Meyer—have begun to examine this new terrain.[4] Each reflects deeply on the Jewish identity of the resurrected Jesus. Barbara Meyer's *Jesus the Jew in Christian Memory* is of particular interest for the purposes of the present volume, since it devotes concentrated attention to the implications of Jesus's ongoing Jewish identity for the church's relationship to the Jewish people.

Like Jenson and Marshall, Meyer assumes the resurrection of Jesus and the Christology of the ecumenical councils, and she reflects on the Jewishness of Jesus in that context. In doing so, she acknowledges the novelty of such a project: "Jesus *was* a Jew, and it is correct for Christians to say that Jesus Christ *is* Jewish and *will always remain* Jewish. Yet historical Jesus research and [Chalcedonian] Christology remain at odds. . . . Hundreds of books have been written about the '*Historical* Jesus' and quite a few about Jesus the Jew *in history*. Christologies focusing on Jesus the Jew that use the *present* tense are fewer."[5] Like Jenson and Marshall, Meyer also perceives that the Jewishness of the resurrected Jesus implies his ongoing relationship with the Jewish people, and thus also with the shape-shifting historical reality of Jewish identity. "Speaking about Jesus in the *present* tense seems to belong to an exclusively Christian confessional language. But here we see that Christology is not just concerned with *historical* Judaism but also has a stake in *contemporary* Jewish self-understanding as well as everything that happened in between—from post-Second Temple Jewish history to the present."[6] Moreover, since the resurrected Jesus is also the Jesus of the world to come, one must add Christological assertions in the *future* tense, and reckon with the necessary implications concerning Jewish identity: "What does it mean that Jesus Christ *will be* Jewish? . . . We do not know how Jewishness will be expressed at the end of times. Jewishness was differently expressed in the

---

4. Hesslein, *Dual Citizenship*; Meyer, *Jesus the Jew in Christian Memory*.
5. Meyer, *Jesus the Jew*, 5, 11 (emphasis added).
6. Meyer, *Jesus the Jew*, 66 (emphasis added).

first and twenty-first centuries.... What we do know, however, is that this Jewish self-expression will not be disconnected from other Jewish lives."[7]

Meyer concludes the paragraph just cited by enunciating the central thesis of her entire volume: "This means that Jesus' otherness for Christian non-Jews will not be dissolved either."[8] As she states in her introduction, "my key argument is that the Jewishness of Jesus Christ engenders an otherness that opens up new intellectual, spiritual, and ethical horizons for the non-Jewish Christian."[9] She builds here on the philosophical exploration of otherness in the work of Levinas and those influenced by him. Since the overwhelming majority of "Christians" are non-Jews, the Jewish identity of Jesus creates a potentially fruitful distance between the master and those who in other respects are united to him by faith and baptism. And since his Jewish identity has content only in relation to the life of the Jewish people throughout history, it also establishes a potentially fruitful dependence of his disciples on the life and tradition of a community external to their own immediate sociocultural identity. Meyer employs the term "vulnerability" to describe this fruitful dependence: "Jesus' Jewishness is the most apparent signifier of Christianity's vulnerability. With Jesus the Jew at its heart, the Christian faith cannot succeed in isolation but holds an inbuilt connection to Judaism and Jews. After overcoming the aggression of rejecting this bond, Christians have the chance to experience the blessings of connectedness. Vulnerability is increased by attachment, but so is the vitality of the Christian community. I would go so far as to connect the vitality of Christ himself to the Christian attachment to the people of Israel."[10]

But what about *Jewish* disciples of Jesus? Meyer acknowledges our existence, and the fact that our relation to the Jewish Jesus differs from that of gentile Christians. After asserting that "the Jewish Jesus can never be in the Christian's domestic domain," she includes a qualifying footnote: "Except for people of Jewish family background and Christian belief, whether they understand themselves as Christian Jews or Jewish Christians."[11] But she never explicitly affirms the theological significance of that difference or details its meaning.

---

7. Meyer, *Jesus the Jew*, 103 (emphasis added).
8. Meyer, *Jesus the Jew*, 103.
9. Meyer, *Jesus the Jew*, 11.
10. Meyer, *Jesus the Jew*, 178–79.
11. Meyer, *Jesus the Jew*, 73n24.

Meyer has taken the discussion further than those who preceded her. But there is still further to go.

## BEARING WITNESS TO JESUS AS *KING* OF THE JEWS

Meyer teaches at the University of Tel Aviv. The Jewish/Christian conversation occupies a central place in her life, as well as in her theology. In the first words of her acknowledgments, the author identifies herself as "an anti-missionary Christian theologian."[12] While she discusses Jewish views of Jesus, her explicitly identified audience consists of "non-Jewish Christians," and her primary purpose consists in persuading that audience of its Christological dependence upon the Jewish people. Jesus is himself dependent upon the Jewish people for an essential aspect of his own identity, and as a result the followers of Jesus—who do not share his Jewish identity—need the Jews to be themselves so that their resurrected master can continue to be himself.

Meyer's anti-missionary stance, anti-supersessionist purpose, and gentile Christian audience cohere with her reluctance to consider a proposition that goes beyond Jesus's Jewish identity—namely, that he is and forever will be the *King* of the Jews, and thus also the *Lord* of Jewish identity. A messianology such as this also takes us beyond the preliminary Christological soundings of Jenson and Marshall. If Jesus is the *King* of the Jews, he is indeed dependent upon them, for the word king (like the word father) is intrinsically relational in meaning: a king without subjects is no king. But the subjects of this peculiar king (who uniquely is both human and divine) depend upon *him* even more than he depends upon *them*. The precise character of this dependence remains hidden, for the presence of the resurrected Jesus has gone largely unrecognized by the family over whom he reigns. But if in fact this particular Jew who was crucified as the King of the Jews has also been raised from the dead, and if in his resurrection he *remains* the King of the Jews, and if he is both human and divine, then over them he truly does reign.

Explicit (though fragmentary) witness to the resurrected Messiah has been maintained historically only in the life of the church, a community largely composed of those who are not his natural subjects. This establishes a hidden mutuality between the Jewish people and the church, a mutuality denied by Meyer, for whom Jesus is a Jew but not clearly the

12. Meyer, *Jesus the Jew*, ix.

*King* of the Jews, and for whom Christians are dependent upon Jews but Jews are not marked by the same relational vulnerability. Whenever Jesus is acknowledged by members of either community to be the King of the Jews, this hidden mutuality becomes manifest. Such people realize that they must look to and receive from members of another community and tradition in order fully to be themselves. Few on either side now confess Jesus to be the resurrected King of the Jews, or discern the communal mutuality this confession entails. Historical blinders (providentially permitted) still limit the epistemic capacities of these two intertwined communities, but their mutual dependence remains an ontological fact.

Speaking as one of those Jews referred to in Meyer's footnote and also as one who confesses Jesus to be the King of the Jews, I would propose that Jewish disciples of Jesus are called to embody and bear witness to this mutual dependence. As Meyer realizes, Jesus the Jew creates no distance for us in our relationship to him. His Jewish identity sustains our own Jewish identity. But the historical alienation of the two communities with which we identify opens up a different kind of *otherness* in our lives. Both our Jewish and Christian environments continually call into question the Jewish identity that Jesus has renewed and now sustains. Our uncanny controverted presence within these two worlds parallels that of the King of the Jews. This is because we represent the troubling communal mutuality his resurrected Jewishness entails. If we did not sense his intimate presence as our resurrected royal brother, we would quickly retreat into a less ambiguous Jewish or Christian self-identification.

## JESUS AS "KING OF THE JEWS" IN THE PASSION NARRATIVE

Those who first bore written witness to Jesus's messianic identity as King of the Jews were themselves Jews and not gentiles. Their witness is found in the passion narratives of all four canonical Gospels, where this title plays a prominent role. Nevertheless, as Wongi Park has shown, exegetes and theologians over the centuries have given little attention to the title's distinctive significance. They have generally treated the phrase as equivalent in meaning to "King of Israel." The effect, as Park shows, is that Jesus's kingship (i.e., his authority as *ho Basileus*, "the King") "obscures and overshadows his identity as *tōn Ioudaiōn*" ("of the Jews"). In other words, his "ethnoracial identity as an ethnic Judean is diminished and downplayed" by these interpreters.¹³ Given the post-supersessionist recovery of Jesus's Jewish identity, however, this matter deserves new scrutiny.¹⁴ Does this title, which all of the Gospels depict as inscribed upon the Roman instrument of Jesus's execution, tell us anything about Jesus's past and present relationship to those sharing his Jewish lineage?

Matthew, Mark, Luke, and John bear witness to Jesus as King of the Jews through the stories they tell. But within the narrative worlds they fashion, the phrase is employed only by non-Jews or by Jews in conversation with non-Jews (as in John 19:21). In contrast, when Jews in the Gospels refer to the royal identity of Jesus, they call him "the King of *Israel*" (Mark 15:32; John 1:49; 12:13). This distinction in usage makes sense in first-century terms, for Jews at that time—and in the pre-modern period in general—preferred the self-designation "Israel" when speaking or writing in-house.¹⁵ On the other hand, when speaking to or writing for gentiles, or when speaking or writing about situations in which Jews and gentiles interact, the name "Israel" tends to give way to the name "the Jews." Therefore, when the Gospels depict people referring to Israel's Messiah as "the King of the Jews," they are highlighting the gentile identity of those using the title.

The distinction between the titles "King of Israel" and "King of the Jews" has great theological import. In the post–New Testament Christian world, the term "Israel" has been used in a way that detaches it from its exclusive reference to the nation that traces its genealogical origins to Abraham, Isaac, and Jacob, Sarah, Rebecca, Rachel, and Leah. When Christians acclaim Jesus as "the King of Israel," they may readily equate Israel with the church and imply nothing more than the fact that Jesus rules over those who have been baptized in his name. While gentile Christians have claimed to be Israel, they have not claimed to be "Jews." That name in the New Testament is unambiguous in meaning and reference and it has remained unambiguous in the centuries that followed.

So, when Jesus is mocked by Pilate and the Roman soldiers as "King of the Jews," we have no doubt what the title means. He is honored and mocked as the rightful ruler of the Jewish people—a people to which the gentile speakers in the narrative do not belong, a people identified in relation to common ancestors, a common history, a common way of life,

13. Park, *The Politics of Race and Ethnicity*, 18.

14. For reflection on the term "post-supersessionist," see chapter 12 in the current volume.

15. Baker, *Jew*.

a common geographical center. Jesus is honored and mocked with a title that has indisputable national, political, and territorial connotations—a title that obstinately resists universalization and spiritualization.[16]

Moreover, from the perspective of Pilate and the Roman soldiers, the true object of mockery is not Jesus but the contemptible people he represents. As Park notes, "Jesus is made inferior as a Judean subject through a parody of what has been called 'the mocking of a king.' This ancient practice of miming conquered kings occurred in Alexandria.... Jesus is made to represent a conquered Judean king and the conquered territory of Judea and its inhabitants. In this way, *the message of Roman superiority and Judean inferiority* is dramatically enacted by the entire Roman garrison."[17] Park's analysis focuses on the Gospel of Matthew, but the theme is even more pronounced in the Gospel of John, which recounts the following tense interchange between Pilate and the Jewish chief priests.

> Pilate also had an inscription written and put on the cross. It read, "Jesus of Nazareth, the King of the Jews." Many of the Jews read this inscription, because the place where Jesus was crucified was near the city; and it was written in Hebrew, in Latin, and in Greek. Then the chief priests of the Jews said to Pilate, "Do not write, 'The King of the Jews,' but, 'This man said, I am King of the Jews.'" Pilate answered, "What I have written I have written." (John 19:19–22)

The chief priests do not object to the publication of the Roman charge that Jesus *claimed to be* the King of the Jews. On the other hand, they object vigorously to the wording of the charge that Pilate actually posted—for

---

16. In his dialogue with Pilate in the Gospel of John, Jesus states that his kingship is "not of this cosmos" (18:36). This has often been understood as a rejection of a "Jewish" conception of messiahship, in which the king has a special relation to a particular nation or territory and rules over an earthly (rather than a purely heavenly) domain. But this is not what John means by the phrase "this cosmos." For John, the phrase resembles the rabbinic term *olam hazeh* and refers to the current age and order of the world, which (for John) is subject to the power of dark forces. Jesus comes to save and give life to the world (John 3:16–17; 4:42; 12:47), but to do so he must deliver it from the power of the one who currently dominates its affairs (12:31). Jesus's kingship is not exercised according to the pattern on public display in the royal courts of the ancient world; nevertheless, he was crucified as the King of the Jews, and this title connects Jesus to a particular nation, territory, and political institution. There is no contradiction between these two assertions. In fact, as we will see, the first assertion explains the significance of the second. See Beasley-Murray, *John*, 331.

17. Park, *The Politics of Race and Ethnicity*, 124–25 (emphasis added).

that wording implies that Jesus not only *claimed* this title, but rightfully owned it. And that is why he was crucified. Pilate implies that when the Jews look at him, hanging naked on a cross, they are looking at their King, they are looking at themselves. And in forty years this metaphor would become a literal reality: the land will be littered with Jewish corpses amid the smoke rising from a smoldering Jerusalem.

This was Pilate's malicious intent according to the Gospels, whose readers all knew that Jerusalem herself had indeed been crucified in the likeness of her King. But the Jewish authors saw a deeper meaning in the title inscribed upon Jesus's cross. Pilate sought to contrast the glory and overwhelming force of Roman imperial rule with the lowly subservience of Judea and of Judea's King. The early followers of Jesus welcomed this contrast and made it central to their message, just as they eventually turned the brutal Roman mode of execution into a shocking symbol of their movement.

## JEWISH KINGSHIP AS SERVANT-KINGSHIP

If the resurrected Jesus is the same man who was nailed to the cross, albeit in an eschatologically transformed condition, then he remains today the King of the Jews. This establishes a relationship of interdependence between him and the Jewish people.

To assert such a mutual dependence would likely raise concerns for Meyer and other Christian theologians engaged in Jewish-Christian dialogue. And rightly so. There is a danger here of spiritualizing and Christianizing the gritty particularity of Jewish history, identity, and discourse. Under a philosemitic cloak could lurk a Christian imperialism asserting hegemony over the "partial truths" of a subordinate Jewish religious tradition.

I have already noted one source of protection against this danger, namely, the dependence of this sovereign on his subjects. While they are more dependent on him than he is on them—he is, after all, their ruler, and divine as well as human—he truly needs them in order to be himself, a Jewish King of the Jews. As Meyer stresses, this intimacy between Jesus and the Jewish people creates a salutary distance between Jesus and the church of the nations, and even establishes Christian dependence upon a religious community socially external to itself. The church's historical failure to acknowledge this dependence should chasten and humble her, and help to guard against the imperialist temptation.

Recovery of the title "King of the Jews" in its narrative context provides an additional source of protection against this temptation. As argued above, this title functions in the passion narrative as Roman imperial ridicule—not primarily directed at Jesus himself, but at the Jewish people. The Roman authorities treat Jesus as a stand-in, a living effigy, for this people whom they despise. They thereby signal their own power and superiority. But the Gospel tradition turns this ridicule upside down, transforming it into a judgment of Roman imperial authority and of the Jewish rulers whom the Romans have co-opted. Pilate sees Jesus as a nonentity, and sets him up as a fitting representative for the national nonentity to whom he belongs. The evangelists, on the other hand, see Jesus as the resurrected Lord and Messiah, who dies and rises to redeem and glorify his people. Through this crucifixion the Roman governor intends to humiliate the Jews. The evangelists imply that the event does the opposite.

The Synoptic story of the request of James and John anticipates and interprets the passion narrative in just this way.

> James and John, the sons of Zebedee, came forward to him and said to him, "Teacher, we want you to do for us whatever we ask of you." And he said to them, "What is it you want me to do for you?" And they said to him, "Appoint us to sit, one at your right hand and one at your left, in your glory." But Jesus said to them, "You do not know what you are asking. Are you able to drink the cup that I drink or be baptized with the baptism that I am baptized with?" They replied, "We are able." Then Jesus said to them, "The cup that I drink you will drink, and with the baptism with which I am baptized you will be baptized, but to sit at my right hand or at my left is not mine to appoint, but it is for those for whom it has been prepared." When the ten heard this, they began to be angry with James and John. So Jesus called them and said to them, "You know that among the gentiles those whom they recognize as their rulers lord it over them, and their great ones are tyrants over them. But it is not so among you; instead, whoever wishes to become great among you must be your servant, and whoever wishes to be first among you must be slave of all. For the Son of Man came not to be served but to serve and to give his life a ransom for many." (Mark 10:35–45; see Matt 20:20–28)

The story contrasts the character of true leadership in Israel with the manner in which the gentiles—and paradigmatically the Romans—exercise authority. James and John, thirsting for honor, wealth, and power, unwittingly imitate the imperial despots who lord it over the Jews, rather than the master on his way to Golgotha. Jesus is the rightful King of Israel, and that means governing not for his own benefit, but for the benefit of his subjects. It also means governing in a way that equips those governed to become responsible agents rather than disempowered slaves.

This interpretation of the passion narrative warns us against conceiving of the Jewish kingship of Jesus along the lines of those Roman authorities whose ways, according to that narrative, he condemned. The hidden rule of the resurrected Messiah over Israel can only be viewed as that of the servant-lord who washes the feet of his disciples. He is the King who empowers his subjects to share in his rule. Such a vision fits well with the audacious rabbinic conception of authority that asserts the independence of the sages, even from God (or at least from a *bat kol*, i.e., a heavenly voice), while at the same time including all of their ostensibly "independent" rulings within the divine revelation to Moses at Sinai (e.g., b. Bava Metzia 59b; Ex. Rab. 28:6; 47:1)! Like the government of the God depicted in rabbinic literature, the royal rule of the resurrected Messiah unleashes Jewish agency. If Jesus is the living King of the Jews who has ruled the Jewish people since his death and resurrection, his hidden messianic government has generated, or at least blessed, the emergence of that very tradition which has so boldly re-envisioned the relationship between divine sovereignty and responsible human action. The fact that his messianic government is veiled from those he governs only reinforces the servant character of his rule.

Once we grasp the meaning of the title "King of the Jews" in the context of the passion narrative, we will reject any triumphalist reading of Jewish history that assumes an established Christian image of Jesus and then superimposes it upon a simplified or spiritualized picture of the Jewish experience. Israel receives its name as the result of a wrestling match with God, and the Jewish people have never stopped wrestling. Israel's struggle with God is not a zero-sum competition, for the victory of each depends upon that of the other. This is how the God of Israel governs, and it is likewise the mode of authority exercised by his Anointed One.

## JESUS AS THE FUTURE KING OF THE JEWS

To confess Jesus as the past and present King of the Jews is to affirm a mysterious truth, a reality now veiled from sight. To confess Jesus as the future (i.e., eschatological) King of the Jews is to hope in the mystery unveiled.

The expectation that the Jews will "convert to Christianity" at the end of the age has long been a staple of Christian eschatological menus. It has also posed a stumbling block for post-supersessionist Christian theologians such as Barbara Meyer. Their resistance to this traditional motif is well justified. Triumphalist Christian thinking has pictured the revelation of Jesus to the Jews at the end of the age as a negation of the Jewish historical experience. In such a scheme the Jesus revealed to the Jews is the King of the gentiles, and the Jewish "conversion to Christianity" means the de-Judaization of the Jews.

If Jesus is the past, present, and future King of the Jews, then the eschatological unveiling of this mystery will challenge, chasten, refine, and consummate the historical experience of *both* the Jewish people and the church. It will reveal the mutual dependence that each has persistently contested. It will do so by manifesting to the church of the gentiles that their Lord is preeminently the King of the *Jews*, and by making known to the Jewish people that the name of their King has been, is, and forever shall be, Yeshua haNotzri, Jesus of Nazareth.[18]

In the context of such a King-of-the-Jews messianology, Jewish disciples of Jesus do more than witness to the mutual dependence of Israel and the church. Like John the Baptist, we bear witness to the Coming One, who as King of the Jews scandalizes both communities. Yet, as that very King, he is also the One who fulfills the truths guarded and treasured by each tradition and satisfies the longing of every heart.

---

18. For a fuller exposition of the eschatological "conversion of the Jews" and a post-supersessionist eschatology that takes into account Jesus's eternal identity as King of the Jews, see chapter 12 in the current volume.

CHAPTER 2

# Finding Our Way through Nicaea
## The Deity of Jesus, Bilateral Ecclesiology, and Redemptive Encounter with the Living God[1]

> *For many Messianic Jews, the Council of Nicaea and the creed that was born out of it are indelibly linked to Constantine's anti-Judaism and the theologically freighted decoupling of Passover and Easter. Viewed through this lens, the Nicene Creed is glaring in what it does not say or explicitly name about the God of Abraham, Isaac, and Jacob, and about Jesus, the Messiah of Israel. While acknowledging these dynamics and difficulties, Kinzer vindicates the Creed's content and key affirmations as a fundamental preservation of God's biblical nature and covenantal identity, drawing a striking parallel between Nicene Christianity and kabbalistic Judaism. In this way, Kinzer advocates a wholesale endorsement of the Creed's central theological assertions while recognizing its shortcomings and problematic omissions.*

---

1. This paper was originally presented in February 2010 at the Hashivenu Forum (an annual theological conference for leaders in the Messianic Jewish movement) in Los Angeles, California. The paper was published later the same year in *Kesher*, a Messianic Jewish theological journal (*Kesher* 24 [2010] 29–52). In 2012, the article was translated into Italian and appeared in the Jesuit theological journal *Rassegna Di Teologia* ("Nicea e la divinità di Yeshua," 601–24). Finally, it was published as appendix 4 in Kinzer, *Searching Her Own Mystery*.

## THE QUESTION AND ITS IMPORTANCE

A number of years ago a controversy erupted in the Israeli Messianic Jewish movement over the question, "Is Jesus God?" Some leaders had publicly answered the question with a definitive "No!" Their refusal to call Jesus "God" ignited a firestorm. In the eyes of many, these dissenting leaders had denied the basic tenet of Messianic Jewish faith.

Though common in Christian parlance, the wording of this question has problematic features, which we will examine later in this chapter. Nevertheless, the passionate responses evoked on both sides showed that the question touched on a matter of grave concern to all.

The main reasons for this concern are threefold. First, the message of the good news challenges all of its hearers to answer Jesus's own question to Peter, "Who do you say that I am?" (Mark 8:29). The mystery of Jesus's identity underlies the narrative of all four Gospels and constitutes the core proclamation of the apostles. The exalted character of Jesus is the central theme of the Johannine writings, which present him as the enfleshed divine Logos through whom all things were made, the bearer of the divine name who is one with the Father and who shared the Father's glory before the foundation of the world. While couched in a different idiom, this theme likewise permeates the Synoptic Gospels and the apostolic letters. "Who then is this, that even wind and sea obey him?" cry the stunned disciples after Jesus exercised authority over the elements (Mark 4:41). As the early Jesus movement grew, its basic confession of faith became the affirmation, "Jesus is Lord!" (Rom 10:9; 1 Cor 12:3; Phil 2:11). The good news itself makes the question of Jesus's transcendent identity a matter of fundamental importance.

Second, discussion of this question dominated the first four centuries of the Jesus movement and resulted in the creedal definitions that gave shape to the Christian theological consensus of the past sixteen centuries. For most of those who identify themselves as "Christians" and as members of the historical community known as the Christian church, the results of these councils define the substance of their faith, even if they have never heard of Nicaea or Chalcedon and even if they consider the Bible to be their only doctrinal authority. Affirmation of the deity of Jesus—and, for many, acknowledgment of the doctrine of the Trinity—constitutes both the center of their confession and the boundary that demarcates its unique character.

As Jewish disciples of Jesus, we may identify as members of the revived *ecclesia ex circumcisione* rather than "the Christian church"—which we see as the *ecclesia ex gentibus* (i.e., the church of the gentiles), legitimate but incomplete without its Jewish partner. Nevertheless, we cannot ignore the reality of the historical Christian community as the primary enduring witness to Jesus in the world. If we embrace bilateral ecclesiology,[2] then we must seek unity with the Christian church even as we maintain our own distinctive identity. Once again, the question of Jesus's transcendent identity—now embodied in explicit and official doctrinal formulations—becomes a matter of fundamental importance.

Third and finally, the denial of Jesus's deity has been almost as significant for classic forms of Judaism as its affirmation has been for the Christian faith. Until the Middle Ages, acknowledgment of Jesus's deity and worship of the trinitarian God were considered by Jewish authorities to be *avodah zara* (i.e., idolatry). Eventually this assessment changed in regard to gentile Christians, but not in regard to Jews who believe in Jesus. According to traditional Jewish sources, for a Jew to believe in Jesus as the divine Son of God—and not just as the human Messiah—is to violate the *Shema*, the central Jewish confession that undergirds all Jewish faith.

Jews and Christians have thus agreed on the central importance of the doctrine of Jesus's deity. The doctrine functioned for many centuries of Jews and Christians as a mutually accepted litmus test for distinguishing authentic Judaism from authentic Christianity. It provided a doctrinal correlate to the practical issue of Torah observance, drawing an unambiguous theological line between the two feuding religious communities, just as the Jewish observance (or Christian denigration) of circumcision, Shabbat, holidays, and Torah-based dietary laws established a clear boundary on the level of praxis. For the Jewish people, the chief community-defining positive commandment was "You shall observe the Torah" and the chief negative commandment was "You shall not believe that Jesus is the Son of God." For the Christian church, the chief community-defining positive commandment was "You shall believe that Jesus is the Son of God" and the chief negative commandment was "You shall not observe the Torah."

The classical Jewish view of the deity of Jesus becomes especially troubling for Jewish disciples of Jesus who are convinced of the truth of bilateral ecclesiology, and who consequently see themselves as members

---

2. For an explanation of this term, see p. 19 and Kinzer, *Postmissionary Messianic Judaism*, esp. ch. 4.

of the Jewish religious community and heirs of its tradition as well as partners with the Christian church within the twofold body of Messiah. Just as we are pressed from the Christian side to give up or dilute our conviction that Torah observance is incumbent on every Jew, so we are pressed from the Jewish side to give up or dilute our conviction that Jesus is more than a man. It would be far easier to deny bilateral ecclesiology and to live either as a Jewish Christian who affirms the deity of Jesus in classical Christian terms and treats Torah observance as a mere cultural option, or as a conventional Torah-observant Jew who respects Jesus as a rabbi, prophet, or even Messiah but refuses to honor him as divine or to seek any organic connection to the Christian church.

Thus, wherever we turn, we face this burning question, raised for us by the Jewish community in which we claim membership, by the Christian community with which we seek partnership, and by the good news itself, which has laid hold of our lives and claimed our unrestricted allegiance. As Jews steeped in *Tanakh*, formed by a religious tradition centered on confession of the unity of God and ever sensitive to the dangers of idolatry, how do we understand and articulate the transcendent identity of Jesus our Messiah, as presented to us in the good news? And how do we assess the Christian doctrinal tradition and its articulation of his identity?

## THE WAY OF APPROACH

We have now formulated our question. How shall we best proceed in addressing it? It would seem natural to begin by studying the relevant biblical teaching and then continue by examining and critiquing the classic Christian creedal formulas on the basis of that teaching. This approach appears logical and cogent since it reflects both the unique authority of Scripture within the tradition of the community of Jesus's disciples and the historical progression whereby later theological developments build upon earlier ones. It also conforms to the standard methodology of evangelical scholarship, which has shaped the theological education of most leaders in the Messianic Jewish world.

I will propose and model here a different approach to the question. Instead of beginning with Scripture, I will begin with the consensus confession of the Christian world, the Nicene Creed, and consider it alongside and in light of Scripture and within a Jewish frame of reference. I will not assume that the Nicene formulation is the best available or the most appropriate for us as Messianic Jews, but I will look for points of continuity between that formulation and the biblical teaching and will give it the benefit of the doubt when it is under scrutiny.

What is the value of such an approach?

First of all, it expresses an ecclesiological commitment that is controversial among Messianic Jews, but which I consider crucial. To grasp the nature of this commitment, we must ponder the meaning and implications of bilateral ecclesiology. This view perceives the *ekklēsia* to be a single yet twofold reality: the one community of the Messiah takes both Jewish and multi-national forms. The two forms are distinct, but inseparable. The Messianic Jewish community has its own distinct identity, but it also has an intimate partnership with the Christian church.

The history of the Christian church features an abundance of figures, events, practices, decisions, and ideas that trouble us as Messianic Jews. Fortunately, many of them also trouble our Christian friends. The Christian tradition, like the Jewish tradition, has proved itself to be dynamic, reflective, and self-correcting. We have witnessed remarkable self-correction in the past sixty years in the church's teaching regarding Judaism and the Jewish people, and the continuing nature of this process inspires hope for the church's future. It also opens the door to the bilateral partnership required by a common life in Messiah.

For some Messianic Jews, one of the troubling elements of Christian history is Nicene orthodoxy. However, unlike supersessionism, antinomianism, the Inquisition, and the blood-libel, it is inappropriate for us to ask our Christian partners to repent of the Nicene Creed. The Nicene consensus on Christology has endured over more than sixteen centuries and continues to define the basic contours of Christian faith. In those settings where commitment to Nicene orthodoxy wanes, the Christian church loses its grip on the good news as a whole and weakens in its faith and spiritual vitality.

The Christian church, which is our partner, is a Nicene church. Bilateral ecclesiology calls us to a corporate commitment to this church. If this is the case, we cannot dismiss the Nicene Creed in a cavalier fashion. We cannot treat it in a neutral way, as though it were one of many equally viable doctrinal proposals on the table. This creed summarizes the essential and enduring teaching of our ecclesiological partner and as a consequence we must take it seriously and treat it with respect. The Creed need not remain immune to all criticism, but it should always be given the benefit of the doubt. This is sufficient reason to begin our study with the Creed, viewed alongside Scripture and in light of Jewish thought.

A second reason for this approach is hermeneutical. Once Nicene orthodoxy prevailed, it became the lens through which all read the biblical text. Even those who oppose the Nicene consensus read Scripture looking for evidence to support their anti-Nicene position, demonstrating that they also fail to escape the new interpretative horizon established by the Creed.

There is value in historical scholarship that attempts to bracket off ways of reading the Bible that have pervaded Christian civilization for more than a millennium and a half. However, as soon as we move from historical reconstruction to theological analysis and assertion, we should reckon with our inability to abstract ourselves from the flow of history. We should not pretend that we can construct a normative theological system directly from Scripture, uninfluenced by the later theological consensus, and can then evaluate and critique that later consensus objectively on the basis of the system we have constructed. Of course, we can attempt to follow such an approach, and many do. But we should then be unsurprised if many of our readers fail to see a resemblance between the method we purport to follow and the process we actually practice.

I am far from suggesting that a later theological consensus should automatically determine how we read the biblical text. That would be an untenable position for a Messianic Jewish theologian who must continually challenge conventional Christian and Jewish assumptions. I am only arguing that we need to keep both the later Christian theological consensus and the biblical material in sight and seek to read each in light of the other—and also in light of additional relevant factors, such as the Jewish theological tradition. Scripture has logical and theological but not methodological priority.

In effect, I am proposing a theological and hermeneutical approach in which we as Messianic Jews take our place as part of the Jewish community with its tradition of interpretation and as a partner to the Christian community with its tradition of interpretation, and from that place listen and respond to the Bible's witness to the God of Israel and the Messiah of Israel. From this place of communal connection, we learn to hear what Jews and Christians have heard before. However, because we are connected to *both* communities and traditions, we also hear new things that these communities' mutual and unnatural isolation prevent them from hearing.

We can describe this as a hermeneutic of *dialectical ecclesial continuity*. In this context, I am using the term "ecclesial" to refer to both the Jewish and Christian communities as historical realities. When we read as those covenantally bound to both of these communities, we read and listen expecting to discover continuity between the message of Scripture and the consensus interpretations it has received in the communal tradition. This expectation may not always be realized, but it nevertheless directs our reading and listening.

Of course, these two communities have disagreed with one another on fundamental matters. This is why our hermeneutic must be *dialectical* as well as *ecclesial*. We view these two communal traditions as one ruptured whole, the broken fragments of a schism that should never have occurred. To read and hear dialectically is to seek to gather up the fragments, to perform a *tikkun*—a repair of what has been broken. We expect each tradition to offer correction and healing to the other.

With our question defined and our approach to it explained, we are now ready to plunge into the deep theological waters that lie before us.

## THE NICENE PROBLEMS

### The Problem with the Council

The Council of Nicaea, which was convened in 325 CE, gave its name to a creed that is still sung as part of the weekly liturgy in many Christian churches. As such, the name carries a positive resonance in the ears of most Christians.

This is not so for Messianic Jews. At best, our visceral reaction to Nicaea is ambivalent—and for understandable reasons. First among them is the role played by the Emperor Constantine. The emperor initiated the council and influenced its results. He desired a united church to promote a united empire. Thus began the long history of church-state entanglement that has had such dire consequences for the Jewish people.

A second concern arises from the lack of representation at Nicaea of the *ecclesia ex circumcisione*. Granted, at this time the community of Jewish disciples of Jesus who continued to identify and live as Jews was small and marginalized. But it did still exist, as Epiphanius and Jerome later attest. We do not know whether Nazarene bishops were deliberately excluded from the council, or whether they chose to stay away, or whether they were so marginalized that the question of attendance never arose on either side. In any case, it is difficult for Messianic Jews to view Nicaea as a truly "ecumenical" council since it was unilateral rather than bilateral in composition. It was a council of the *ecclesia ex gentibus*, the church of the nations.

The most serious problem with Nicaea from a Messianic Jewish perspective is the explicitly anti-Jewish tenor of its conclusions regarding the celebration of Easter. An official synodal letter from the council rejected any reckoning of the date of Easter in relation to the Jewish calendar:

> We further proclaim to you the good news of the agreement concerning the holy Easter . . . that all our brethren in the East who formerly *followed the custom of the Jews* are henceforth to celebrate the most sacred feast of Easter at the same time with the Romans and yourselves and all those who have observed Easter from the beginning.[3]

The concern of the Nicene Council was to end a situation where Christians followed "the custom of the Jews." The bishops rejected any sign that the church was dependent on the Jewish people for its faith or way of life. This intent becomes even clearer in the letter of the Emperor Constantine announcing the results of the council:

> It was declared to be particularly unworthy for this, the holiest of all festivals, to follow the custom [the calculation] of the Jews, who had soiled their hands with the most fearful of crimes, and whose minds were blinded. . . . We ought not, therefore, to have anything in common with the Jews . . . and consequently, in unanimously adopting this mode, we desire, dearest brethren, to separate ourselves from the detestable company of the Jews, for it is truly shameful for us to hear them boast that without their direction we could not keep the feast.[4]

Nicaea thus represents a definitive moment in the history of Christian supersessionism when the Christian church in alliance with the Roman Emperor formally renounced its bilateral constitution.

As a result of these three factors, Nicaea evokes a different visceral response from Messianic Jews than it does from most Christians. The council as a whole symbolizes for us the church's conscious and decisive *turning away* from the Jewish people and *turning to* the Roman Empire. We must acknowledge this inner reaction and learn how to explain it to

---

3. Schaff and Wace, *Seven Ecumenical Councils*, 54 (emphasis added).

4. Schaff and Wace, *Seven Ecumenical Councils*, 54.

our Christian friends. But it need not determine our judgment of the Nicene Creed.

When Christians honor the Council of Nicaea, they are not paying homage to a Constantinian synthesis of church and state that most no longer see as valid and that even the Catholic Church now finds lacking. They are not denying a vision of a bilateral church of Jews and gentiles, which most have never even conceived of as a possibility. They are not making the supersessionist claim that the Christian church lacks any organic connection to or dependence upon Judaism and the Jewish people; in fact, it is theologians loyal to Nicene orthodoxy who have taken the lead over the last forty years in combating supersessionism. When Christians honor the Council of Nicaea, they are doing one thing and one thing only: they are paying homage to Jesus and glorifying him as the divine Son who is "the reflection of God's glory and the exact imprint of God's very being" (Heb 1:3).

The Nicene Creed is thus analogous to the church's celebration of Christmas, which is the Creed's ritual correlate. The latter traces its origins to a pagan festival. The former derives from a political process influenced at times by unsavory motives and interests. Neither the holiday nor the Creed should be judged by the purity of its sources or the circumstances of its adoption, but instead by the way it has been understood and practiced by Christians through the centuries.

## The Problem with the Creed

These preliminary considerations concerning the Nicene Council clear the way for us to examine the Nicene Creed and to assess it on its own terms. Before we look at what it says, however, we must raise a significant problem that Messianic Jews have with the Creed itself. The problem we see is not with what the Creed says, but with what it fails to say.

I refer to what Kendall Soulen calls structural supersessionism. Unlike punitive and economic forms of supersessionism, structural supersessionism involves a sin of omission rather than commission.[5] It sum-

---

5. For definitions of these terms, see Soulen, *The God of Israel and Christian Theology*, 29–31. Soulen now prefers the term "Israel-forgetfulness" to describe the reality he formerly designated as "structural supersessionism" (see Soulen, *Irrevocable*, 178n10). This shift in terminology results from Soulen's advocacy for a more precise definition of "supersessionism" in which the term refers to a theological error involving the contradiction of an authoritative doctrinal affirmation, namely, God's irrevocable election

marizes the basic narrative of God's dealings with the world in a manner that ignores the central role played by the Jewish people. It tells the story in a way that moves directly from the creation and fall of human beings to the incarnation, death, and resurrection of the Son of God. The people of Israel appear solely as background to the main plot. This supersessionist Christian narrative takes an authoritative form in the Nicene Creed. Like all major Christian confessional statements before and after, the Nicene Creed omits any reference to the people of Israel and its crucial role in the story of God's dealings with the world.[6]

Structural supersessionism constitutes both the most difficult form of supersessionism to overcome, and the easiest. It is most difficult because the church must do more than merely reassess particular doctrinal positions, such as the enduring validity of Israel's election; the church must reconstruct its entire theological framework in a manner that gives Israel its proper place in addressing every theological topic. But it is also the easiest form of supersessionism to address because it does not require the repudiation of any authoritative doctrinal positions from the church's theological tradition. Instead, it calls for a doctrinal development that *adds to*, rather than subtracts from, the church's confession of faith. To overcome structural supersessionism, the church must only recontextualize its historically transmitted deposit of faith within the framework of God's dealings with Israel and the nations.

Thus, the structural supersessionism of the Nicene Creed need pose no problem for us here. We are not evaluating the adequacy of the Creed as an embodiment of the ecclesial canonical narrative. If we did, we would certainly find it lacking. It requires the addition of material dealing with the people of Israel, material that would provide the necessary context for the affirmations it makes about the person of Jesus. However, our purpose here is only to assess those affirmations. We are concerned with what the Creed says, not with what it fails to say.

Having examined the problems with Nicaea from a Messianic Jewish perspective, we are now ready to examine what the Creed teaches about Jesus.

---

of the Jewish people (ibid., 5–6, 175–77n2). I find Soulen's recent argument convincing. Nevertheless, for our purposes in this chapter, either term will do. The critical issue here is not the term but the reality it designates.

6. "This omission is reflected in virtually every historic confession of Christian faith from the Creeds of Nicaea and Constantinople to the Augsburg Confession and beyond" (Soulen, *The God of Israel*, 32).

## THE NICENE CREED

### What the Creed Denies

To know what to expect from the Nicene Creed and the right questions to ask concerning it, we must understand the nature of explicit and official doctrine in the history of the Christian church. George Lindbeck provides a helpful introduction.

> Controversy is the normal means whereby implicit doctrines become explicit, and operational ones official. For the most part, only when disputes arise about what it is permissible to teach or practice does a community make up its collective mind and formally make a doctrinal decision. . . . In any case, insofar as official doctrines are the products of conflict . . . they must be understood in terms of what they oppose (it is usually much easier to specify what they deny than what they affirm).[7]

This runs counter to our usual assumptions about official doctrine. We normally conceive of church doctrine as though it were analogous to scientific theory, offering propositional affirmations about reality formulated in technical terms coined for their clarity and precision. Church doctrine does involve affirmations about reality, but they are rarely unambiguous in nature, as demonstrated by the debates concerning their interpretation that invariably follow the establishment of explicit and official doctrine. As Lindbeck points out, what is affirmed may be ambiguous, but what is denied must be clear.

In light of this perspective, let us begin our study of the Nicene Creed by looking at the doctrinal positions that the original creed of Nicaea anathematized:

> But as for those who say, There was when He was not, and, Before being born He was not, and that He came into existence out of nothing, or who assert that the Son of God is from a different (*ex heteras*) hypostasis or substance (*ousia*) [from the Father], or is created, or subject to alteration or change—these the Catholic Church anathematizes.[8]

Nicene orthodoxy arises as a response to and rejection of Arianism. The Arians believed that the Son of God was a creature. They accepted the biblical teaching that he existed before becoming incarnate and that the

---

7. Lindbeck, *The Nature of Doctrine*, 75.
8. Kelly, *Early Christian Doctrines*, 232. Bracketed material added.

world was made through him, but they held that "there was [a time] when He [i.e., the Son of God] was not." If all reality may be classified as either eternal and uncreated or temporal (i.e., with a beginning in time) and created, the Arians place the pre-incarnate Son of God in the "temporal and created" category. He is the first created entity, the highest of the angels, the most exalted being in all creation. But he is not eternal, and he is not truly divine.

The Arian position reflected the Hellenistic philosophical assumptions dominant in the period. According to those assumptions, the eternal realm of divinity was absolutely transcendent and could have no direct point of contact with the temporal and material world. Such a system of thought excluded divine incarnation in principle. But its implications went far beyond the exclusion of incarnation. In effect, it suggested that the transcendent God was ultimately unknowable and could not be truly present within the created order. *Such a system of thought excluded in principle the living God of Scripture, the self-revealing one who enters into an intimate covenantal relationship with the people of Israel.* In rejecting Arianism, the Nicene Creed took a stand *against* the common philosophical notions of the day, and *for* the biblical portrayal of the God of Israel.

## What the Creed Affirms

Now that we have a clear idea of what the Nicene Council sought to deny with its creed, we are ready to consider what it affirmed.[9] For our purposes, it will be sufficient to look at the opening section of the Creed.

> We believe in one God, the Father Almighty,
> maker of heaven and earth and of all things visible and invisible.
> And in one Lord, Jesus Christ,
> the only begotten (*monogenē*) Son of God,
> begotten (*gennēthenta*) of his Father before all worlds,
> Light from (*ek*) Light, true God from (*ek*) true God,
> begotten (*gennēthenta*), not made,
> having the same *ousia* (*homoousion*) as the Father,
> through (*dia*) whom all things were made.

The basic framework of this confession of faith derives from Paul's teaching in 1 Corinthians 8:5–6:

---

9. We will be examining the form of the Nicene Creed adopted at the Council of Constantinople in 381 CE, which has become its standard version. This creed does not differ in Christological teaching from the one adopted at Nicaea.

> Indeed, even though there may be so-called gods in heaven and on earth—as in fact there are many gods and many lords—yet for us there is one God (*Theos*), the Father, from (*ek*) whom are all things and for whom we exist, and one Lord (*Kyrios*), Jesus Christ, through (*dia*) whom are all things and through (*dia*) whom we exist.

Paul likely uses the term *Kyrios* here as a Greek substitute for both the tetragrammaton (i.e., the "four-letters" which spell the proper name of God in Hebrew) and the Hebrew word *Adonai* ("My lord"), which in Jewish practice acts as a surrogate for the tetragrammaton. In this way Paul builds upon the most fundamental biblical confession of faith, the *Shema*, highlighting the two primary divine names (*Theos/Elohim* and *Kyrios/Adonai*) and the word "one."[10] Paul thus expands the *Shema* to include Jesus within a differentiated but singular deity.[11] The Nicene Creed adopts Paul's language ("one God, the Father, . . . one Lord, Jesus Christ"), and thereby affirms its own continuity with the *Shema*. Paul's short confession is a messianic interpretation of the *Shema*, and the Nicene Creed is an expanded interpretation of Paul's confession.

Drawing upon Second Temple Jewish traditions that see the creation of the world as occurring through the mediation of a hypostatic wisdom or spoken word, Paul presents "God" as the one "*from (ek) whom* are all things," and the "Lord" as the one "*through (dia) whom* are all things." The Nicene Creed likewise draws upon Paul's terminology here, describing God the Father as "the maker of heaven and earth and of all things" and Jesus the Lord as the one "*through (dia)* whom all things were made" (i.e., by God the Father). It thereby preserves both (1) the Pauline *distinction* between God the Father and the Lord Jesus by designating each of them with a different divine name (*Theos* and *Kyrios*) and by employing the characteristic Pauline preposition *dia* for the role of Jesus in the work of creation; and (2) the Pauline *identification* of God and Jesus through ascription to them of the two primary biblical names for Israel's singular deity, through reference to their joint activity as the source of all created things, and through reiteration of the word "one." Once again, Paul offers a messianic interpretation of existing Jewish tradition in light of the incarnation, and the Nicene Creed offers an expanded interpretation of Paul's teaching.

---

10. See Hurtado, *Lord Jesus Christ*, 114.

11. As the context makes clear, Paul's expanded messianic *Shema* is aimed, like its traditional Jewish model, at the rejection of pagan idolatry and polytheism.

The Nicene Creed elaborates on this Pauline (and Jewish) framework by adding explanatory language drawn from elsewhere in Scripture. The one Lord, Jesus the Messiah, is also "the only-begotten (*monogenous*) Son of God" (John 1:14, 18; 3:16, 18; 1 John 4:9). In John this word may or may not carry the connotation of "begetting"—it may simply mean "only (Son)."[12] The Nicene Creed, however, exploits the word's range of verbal associations by adding two references to the Son's "begetting": "begotten (*gennēthenta*) of his Father before all worlds," and "begotten, not made." The Creed thus brings together the Johannine *monogenēs* with Psalm 2:7 ("You are my Son, today I have begotten you"; see Acts 13:33; Heb 1:5) and interprets John's *monogenēs* in light of Psalm 2 as "only-begotten Son."

But the Creed also interprets Psalm 2 in light of John. What is the meaning of the "today" in which the Son of Psalm 2 is begotten? Is this a reference to Miriam's conception of Jesus? To Jesus's birth? To his immersion in the Jordan at the hands of John?[13] To his resurrection from the dead?[14] For John the evangelist, the existence of the Son of God antedates all these events in the earthly life of Jesus and precedes even the creation of the world (John 1:1–5, 18; 6:46; 17:5). Therefore the "today" of Psalm 2:7 must be eternal, rather than temporal. The Creed's exegetical juxtaposition of John and Psalm 2 thus yields the completely appropriate phrase, "begotten of his Father before all worlds."[15]

The Creed draws two conclusions from its fundamental proposition that the Son is "begotten of his Father before all worlds." These two conclusions are conveyed in the phrases "Light from (*ek*) Light, true God from (*ek*) true God."[16] First of all, the Son draws his being from (*ek*) the Father. Their relationship has a *taxis*, a structure or form, in which the Father is the ultimate source of the Son's existence and nature. That structure is eternal rather than temporal; as a star never exists without emitting light, so the Father never exists without the Son. Secondly, the Son shares the Father's nature. As the Father is "Light," so the Son is "Light";

---

12. Arndt and Gingrich, *A Greek-English Lexicon*, 527.

13. As implied by variant readings of Luke 3:22.

14. As implied by Acts 13:33.

15. Oskar Skarsaune argues that this phrase also "is an encapsulated version of Proverbs 8:22–31" and thus reflects the Wisdom Christology that is a central motif of the Nicene Creed. See Skarsaune, *Shadow of the Temple*, 333.

16. The phrase "Light from Light" alludes to Wis 7:26 and Heb 1:3, again expressing Wisdom Christology (Skarsaune, *Shadow of the Temple*, 333).

as the Father is "true God," so the Son is "true God." Though the Son is ordered after and in relationship to the Father, he is not a demigod, a secondary divinity at a lower level of being from the Father.

These two affirmations about the Father and the Son always belong together. They produce the ambiguity that has always characterized discussion of the Son's "subordination" to the Father. The Son is subordinate to the Father in the sense that he derives his existence from the Father and serves the Father in the fulfillment of the Father's purposes. But the Son is not subordinate to the Father in the sense of possessing a secondary level of divinity, as though occupying a lower rung in a Neoplatonic hierarchy of being.

The Son is "begotten, not made." This contrast between begetting and making is crucial for the teaching of the Creed. The Son is not like a painting or a sculpture that springs from the genius of an artist but remains fundamentally different in kind from the person of the artist. Just as offspring in the temporal created order are of the same kind as those who generate them, so in the eternal uncreated order the Son is as much divine as is the Father from whom he derives his being.

The contrast between "begetting" and "making" helps explain the most famous phrase of the Creed, "having the same *ousia* (*homoousion*) as the Father." In this context *ousia* appears to mean the kind of entity that something is.[17] Thus, the *homoousion* does not add anything new to what has already been presented in the Creed. It does not provide an explanation or theory for how this could all be so. Instead, it expresses through one technical Greek term what the Creed states elsewhere in more allusive biblical language.

The Nicene Creed thus offers a highly plausible rendering of the apostolic teaching on the divinity of Jesus in light of controversies that had emerged in the early centuries of the Jesus movement. Though it spoke in the language of its own time and place, it did not conform to the philosophical theories that were currently in fashion. Instead, the

---

17. For this view of the *homoousion*, see Skarsaune, *Shadow of the Temple*, 333–35. J. N. D. Kelly likewise thinks that the original intent of this term at Nicaea was to mean "of the same nature" (Kelly, *Early Christian Doctrines*, 234–37). Over time the term took on the additional meaning of "numerical identity," i.e., that the Father and Son (and Spirit) are together one being (Kelly, *Early Christian Doctrines*, 245–47), while the related term *hypostasis* expressed the distinct identities of the Father, Son, and Spirit. (As the creedal anathemas demonstrate, at Nicaea *hypostasis* and *ousia* are treated as synonyms.) Nevertheless, no true theological consensus emerged on the precise meaning of the terms *ousia* and *hypostasis*. All agreed only that the former expressed the unity of Father, Son, and Spirit, and the latter expressed their distinction.

Creed upheld a commitment to an authentic encounter with the living God who acts in a revelatory and redemptive manner within the world. It maintained the Jewish and biblical witness to the qualitative difference between the transcendent creator and that which is created, the particular personal character of the creator as the God of Israel, and the reality of this God's activity within the created order. It affirmed that God can be known and encountered in the person of Jesus the Messiah.

The Nicene Creed does this as an expansion of a Pauline confession of faith, which was itself an expansion of the *Shema*. In this way, it implicitly points us back to the basics of Jewish monotheism and presents Jesus as the one who realizes in this world the revelatory and redemptive purposes of *Adonai*, God of Israel and creator of all.

## MEDIEVAL JEWISH PARALLELS TO THE ARIAN CONTROVERSY

Jewish history provides us with a surprising parallel to the Arian controversy and the Nicene response. The similarity supports our contention that what is at stake at Nicaea is not merely an orthodox Christology, but the authenticity of human encounter with the redemptively self-revealing God of Israel.

Rabbinic texts treat the biblical accounts of God's self-revealing presence in a realistic fashion. The sages are not embarrassed by biblical anthropomorphism. They assume that the figure who appeared to Moses, Isaiah, Ezekiel, and Daniel, and to all of Israel at the sea and at Sinai, was none other than *Adonai*, the God of Israel. In fact, rabbinic tradition sometimes makes the anthropomorphism of the biblical theophanies look restrained. God is there portrayed as wearing *tefillin* (i.e., phylacteries), praying, and arguing about the Torah with the angels. In recent decades, scholars have even employed the language of incarnation to describe this dimension of the rabbinic imagination.[18]

The ninth-century Karaites, influenced by Greek philosophical currents absorbed into Islamic thought, attacked the anthropomorphism of the rabbinic texts. To ward off these attacks, Saadia Gaon drew upon the same philosophy that guided the Karaites. He reinterpreted rabbinic thought in a way that eliminated all anthropomorphism, even from the

---

18. For example, see Neusner, *The Incarnation of God*.

biblical theophanies. His formulation had tremendous consequences for later Jewish thought, and is worth citing at length:

> Peradventure however, someone, attacking our view, will ask: "But how is it possible to put such constructions on these anthropomorphic expressions and on what is related to them, when Scripture itself explicitly mentions a form like that of human beings that was seen by the prophets and spoke to them . . . let alone the description by it of God's being seated on a throne, and His being borne by the angels on top of a firmament (Ezekiel 1:26)." . . . Our answer to this objection is that this form was something [specially] created. . . . It is a form nobler even than [that of] the angels, magnificent in character, resplendent with light, which is called *the glory of the Lord*. It is this form, too, that one of the prophets described as follows: *I beheld till thrones were placed, and one that was ancient of days did sit* (Daniel 7:9), and that the sages characterized as *Shekhinah*. Sometimes, however, this specially created being consists of light without the form of a person. It was, therefore, an honor that God had conferred on His prophet by allowing him to hear the oracle from the mouth of a majestic form created out of fire that was called *the glory of the Lord*, as we have explained.[19]

On the one hand, Saadia treats realistically the biblical theophanies. He does not doubt that Ezekiel, Isaiah, and Daniel truly saw an enthroned human figure, referred to in the text as *Adonai*. He also does not doubt that such a figure possessed objective existence beyond the imagination of the prophet. On the other hand, his philosophical commitment to absolute divine transcendence—which he understands as a necessary corollary of the divine unity—excludes the possibility that this enthroned human figure can in fact be the eternal uncreated One. Therefore, he concludes that the form seen by the prophets—the *Kavod* (Glory) or *Shekhinah*—must be a created entity, more exalted than the angels, but not divine.

As Gershom Scholem notes, Saadia's interpretation became "a basic tenet of the [Jewish] philosophical exegesis of the Bible." We find it in such classic writers as Yehudah Halevi and Maimonides. Scholem also points out its radical novelty.

> These respected authors could hardly have ignored the fact that this conception of the *Shekhinah* as a being completely separate

---

19. Saadia Gaon, *Book of Beliefs and Opinions*, II:10, 121.

from God was entirely alien to the talmudic texts, and could only be made compatible with them by means of extremely forced interpretation of these texts. Nevertheless, these philosophers preferred "cutting the Gordian knot" in this way rather than endanger the purity of monotheistic belief by recognizing an uncreated hypostasis.[20]

The parallel here to the Arian interpretation of the Logos should be evident. The underlying concerns are identical: a desire to guard the purity of divine transcendence and unity understood in terms of Greek philosophical conceptions. The problems encountered as a result of this concern are likewise identical: the realistic biblical presentation of God's self-revelation to Israel. Finally, the strategies adopted to overcome the problems are the same: the thesis that the one who is called by the divine name and who apparently manifests the divine presence is a created entity, distinct from God and at a lower level in the hierarchy of being.

Just as the Jewish philosophical reinterpretation of the *Kavod/Shekhinah* parallels the Arian reinterpretation of the Logos, so the kabbalistic response to the Jewish philosophers parallels the Nicene response to the Arians. Like the Nicene fathers, those who championed the tradition of the *Zohar* agreed with their opponents on the ineffable and transcendent nature of God. These Jewish mystics employed the term *Eyn Sof* (i.e., the Infinite One) to refer to this aspect of the divine reality. However, also like the Nicene fathers, the kabbalists viewed the self-revelation of God (the biblical *Kavod*, whom they referred to as the *sefirot*) as *both* distinct from *and* one with *Eyn Sof*. The infinite and transcendent nature of God required the distinction, but the objective reality and truthfulness of divine revelation required the unity. If the *Kavod* revealed to Israel is not truly and fully divine, then God remains unknown to the world and Israel's claim to a covenant with a redemptively self-revealing God is rendered fraudulent.

Even the language used by the kabbalists to express the relationship between the *sefirot* and *Eyn Sof* resembles the language employed within the stream of Nicene orthodoxy. "The kabbalists insisted that Ein Sof and the sefirot formed a unity 'like a flame joined to a coal.' 'It is they and they are It.'"[21] This language distinguishes both *kabbalah* and Nicene orthodoxy from Neoplatonic thought, in which each stage of emanation involves a gradation in the hierarchy of being and in which

20. Scholem, *On the Mystical Shape of the Godhead*, 154–55.
21. Matt, *Zohar*, 33.

everything below the ineffable "One" occupies a lower ontological status in that hierarchy. "The hidden God in the aspect of *Ein-Sof* and the God manifested in the emanation of *Sefirot* are one and the same, viewed from two different angles. There is therefore a clear distinction between the stages of emanation in the neoplatonic systems, which are not conceived as processes within the Godhead, and the kabbalistic approach."[22] Thus, while kabbalistic thought in some ways resembles Neoplatonism and was influenced by it, on this fundamental point the two systems diverge. *Kabbalah* here has more in common with Basil of Caesarea than with Plotinus.

This commonality derives less from direct influence than from similar issues and concerns. For both the Christian and the Jewish traditions, Greek philosophy challenged the biblical presentation of the God of Israel and the living faith of the communities who worshipped that God. Nicene orthodoxy and Jewish mysticism responded by drawing insights and terminology from the challenging philosophical systems and employing them within a new framework provided by Scripture and the tradition of the worshipping community. The philosophical terminology of *ousia* and emanation now served faithful testimony to the infinite transcendent God who acts within the world to establish a covenant relationship with a people, a relationship in which this God is genuinely and redemptively known.

## POST-NICENE CHRISTOLOGY IN MESSIANIC JEWISH PERSPECTIVE

We have examined the teaching of the Nicene Creed concerning the deity of Jesus in light of Scripture and Jewish tradition, employing the hermeneutic of *dialectical ecclesial continuity*. This examination has exposed nothing objectionable in the teaching of the Creed, but instead has confirmed it as a faithful witness to Israel's God and Messiah by the church of the nations in the particular circumstances of the fourth-century Greco-Roman world.

However, affirmation of the Nicene Creed need not imply uncritical reception of the normative Christian piety and theological expression that it generated. Here, we must stress the *dialectical* component in our

---

22. Scholem, *Kabbalah*, 98.

hermeneutic. At this point our Jewish sensibility comes to the forefront and raises pressing questions.

First, many Messianic Jews question whether Christian thought and practice have dealt adequately with the differentiation of the Father and the Son. As noted above, the Creed rules out any inequality of ontological status between the Father and Son while recognizing that the Son derives his being from the Father and is thus ordered after and toward the Father. It rules out one type of "subordination" while implying the other.

However, in the history of Christian spirituality this delicate balance became increasingly precarious as the equal divinity of the Son was stressed at the expense of the distinction between the Father and the Son. Especially in the Western church, this exaltation of the Son threatened the unique position of the Father as the source and goal of all things. Consequently, many Christians have a diminished sense of the inner order and differentiation within the divine life, an order that was expressed in the early Jesus community by its normal mode of worshipping the Father, through the Son, in the Spirit.[23]

Though the Messianic Jewish movement possesses few universal characteristics, a reasonable candidate for this designation is the custom

---

23. Many Christian theologians of the twentieth and twenty-first centuries have recognized the need to recapture the structure or *taxis* of differentiation between the Father and the Son. For example, John Zizioulas writes: "In making the Father the 'ground' of God's being—or the ultimate reason for existence—theology accepted a kind of subordination of the Son to the Father without being obliged to downgrade the *Logos* into something created. But this was possible only because the Son's otherness was founded on the *same substance*" (Zizioulas, *Being as Communion*, 89). Similarly, Colin Gunton: "There is, in the biblical representation of the way in which the acts of God take shape in time, some support for Zizioulas' giving of priority to the Father. It is often said that when the New Testament writers use the word 'God' *simpliciter*, they are referring to God the Father, so that Irenaeus is true to Scripture in speaking of the Son and Spirit as the two hands of God, the two agencies by which the work of God the Father is done in the world. . . . Such talk of the divine economy has indeed implications for what we may say about the being of God eternally, and would seem to suggest a subordination of *taxis*—of ordering within the divine life—but not one of deity or regard. . . . The Spirit is the giver of faith, not in himself, nor even, strictly speaking, in Christ, but in the Father through Christ. In that respect, we return to the theme that God *simpliciter* is God the Father, the fount and goal of our being. But we neither receive our being in the first place apart from Christ, the mediator of creation and salvation, nor are directed to our goal apart from the Spirit, the perfecting cause" (Gunton, *The Promise of Trinitarian Theology*, 197, 199). Finally, from Thomas F. Torrance: "All the revealing and saving acts of God come to us from the Father, through the Son and in the Holy Spirit, and all our corresponding relations to God in faith, love and knowledge are effected in the Spirit through the Son and to the Father" (Torrance, *The Christian Doctrine of God*, 147).

of addressing formal congregational worship to God the Father rather than to Jesus the Son. This almost instinctive pattern of Messianic Jewish prayer arises, I suggest, as a result of a Jewish sensibility that sees Jesus as the one who brings us to the Father, who mediates a relationship with the Father by revealing rather than replacing the Father. He can only do this because he is fully divine. But he must do this because the Father is the source and goal of his own existence.[24]

Secondly, the continuation of the second article of the Nicene Creed affirms unambiguously the historical humanity of Jesus, who was born of Mary and suffered under Pontius Pilate. Nevertheless, the challenge posed by Arianism led the Christian church to stress Jesus's divine rather than human nature. Just as the delicate balance between the equality and differentiation of the Father and the Son was threatened, so also was the balance between Jesus's divinity and humanity. Christians found it increasingly difficult to accept at face value the biblical texts that point to Jesus's ignorance of future happenings, growth in knowledge, need for companionship, fear of death, and learning of obedience amid temptation.

The Creed's lack of reference to Israel rendered it vulnerable to this imbalance. If the person and work of Jesus had been properly situated in relation to his own people, it would have been more difficult to swallow up his humanity in his divinity. If the Creed had mentioned not only his birth but also his circumcision, it would have buttressed its affirmation of his concrete and particular human identity. Instead, the reverse happened: the accentuation of Jesus's divinity at the expense of his humanity made it more difficult for the Christian church to grasp the significance of Israel or to recognize the implications of the fact that it had been incorporated into the body of a resurrected Jew.

Once again, a concern about this historical imbalance tends to characterize the Messianic Jewish movement as a whole. Our Jewish sensibility attunes us to the importance of bodily realities. Our convictions about the enduring significance of our own Jewish identity are connected to our confession of the enduring significance of Jesus's Jewish identity—for us, but also for the nations of the world, and for all creation.

These two reservations about the outworking of Nicene Christology in the life of the Christian church reveal the problematic nature of the

---

24. A concern about the role of God the Father as the primary addressee of prayer appears in the two most seminal texts of the early Messianic Jewish movement: Juster, *Jewish Roots*, 241, and Stern, *Messianic Jewish Manifesto*, 94.

question with which we began our paper: "Is Jesus God?"[25] This three-word question seems simple and straightforward, yet it contains at least two ambiguities that render any answer similarly ambiguous. These two ambiguities correspond to our two reservations stated above. First, the question could mean, "Is Jesus the fullness of divinity, so that there is no Father distinct from the Son, from whom the Son receives his existence and to whom that existence is eternally oriented?" The answer to that question, according to Nicaea, is a resounding "no." Secondly, the question could mean, "Is the flesh and blood of the man Jesus divine, so that it is uncreated, eternal, and thus unlike our own flesh and blood that is created and comes into being at a particular time?" Once again, the answer to that question, according to Nicaea, is a resounding "no."

One might say, "Nobody who asks this question means it in either of these ways!" This may be the case. However, in light of the two historical imbalances in Christian spirituality and thought described above, we have good grounds for assuming that many of those who ask the question fail to consider with sufficient care exactly what they do mean when they ask it. Moreover, as Messianic Jews we must also consider what our fellow Jews understand when they hear such a question, and when they hear it answered in the affirmative. What they hear and understand is usually as far beyond the limits of normative Christian faith as it is of Jewish orthodoxy.

Our hermeneutic of *dialectical ecclesial continuity* thus enables us to receive appreciatively from our Christian ecclesial partner but also to offer proposals for rebalancing and repair that derive from our participation in the ongoing stream of Jewish ecclesial tradition. We can affirm the Nicene Creed and then add our voice to the continuing argument as to how it should best be interpreted and practiced.

---

25. Referring to Jesus as "God" is rare in the New Testament, but becomes extremely common in the early centuries of the Christian church. It is a reflection of a Christian linguistic convention known as the sharing of attributes (*communicatio idiomatum*), in which verbal expressions specifically appropriate to Jesus's divine or human nature are applied also to his integrated divine-human person (see Kelly, *Early Christian Doctrines*, 143; 296–301). This ancient practice is not illegitimate, as it is also attested (albeit infrequently) in Scripture (e.g., John 20:28). However, our Jewish sensibility alerts us to its potential for misunderstanding and abuse.

## CONCLUSION

The primary contention of this chapter finds expression in the parallel discovered between Arius and Saadia, Nicaea and *kabbalah*. In accordance with the clear teaching of Scripture, we see Jesus not only as the Messiah but also as *Chochmah* (Wisdom), the Logos, and the *Kavod*, the mediator of all God's work in creation, revelation, and redemption. Obviously, mainstream *kabbalah* does not accept this view, but it does affirm a distinct hypostatic reality, represented by the *sefirot*, which fulfills an analogous role. Both Nicene orthodoxy and *kabbalah* accept the philosophical acknowledgment of God as infinite, transcendent, invisible, and incomprehensible. But they also reject philosophical interpretations that negate the reality of God's involvement with and in the world and which so separate God from creation as to render God utterly unknowable. They both accomplish this correction of the philosophical currents in their own religious traditions by distinguishing between God the Father and God the Son, or between *Eyn Sof* and the *sefirot*, while simultaneously asserting their inseparable unity.

Thus, what is at stake here is not an articulation of doctrinal truth that lacks any direct bearing on our lives. We are not debating the number of angels that can dance on the head of a pin. Instead, we are seeking to bear verbal witness to the reality of a redemptive encounter with the living God in a way that does justice to the authenticity of that encounter and which effectively invites others to share in it. This is what it means for us to confess the deity of Jesus.

A promising answer to an important question always raises several new questions. Our answer to the question of Jesus's deity immediately provokes a host of new queries, three of which deserve note and comment as we conclude this initial stage of the journey.

First, affirmation of the deity of Jesus leads inevitably to the question of the hypostatic identity of the Spirit and from there into discussion of the triunity of God. Thus, the Council of Nicaea (325 CE), which addressed the issue of Jesus's deity, was followed by the Council of Constantinople (381 CE), which addressed the deity and distinct identity of the Holy Spirit. We cannot adequately appreciate the significance of the deity of Jesus for our life until we have taken this further stage of the journey. According to Scripture, the Spirit joins us to Jesus, who brings us to God the Father. Not only are we encountering God in Jesus; in union with him, we are being ushered into God's mysterious inner life. Once again, *kabbalah* offers suggestive parallels. But that is a discussion for another day.

Second, affirmation of the deity of Jesus leads to the question of how this truth should function in the definition of our identity as a Messianic Jewish community. As noted earlier, the Christian church has treated this doctrine both as its theological center and as its external line of demarcation. In many contexts denial of the deity of Jesus places one outside the church's communal boundary. While we might question whether this should be so, we can also appreciate the rationale for such an exclusionary practice. For gentiles, union with Jesus opens up for the first time participation in the covenant that God made with the patriarchs and matriarchs. Rejection of Jesus's role as divine mediator of God's creative, revelatory, and redemptive purposes puts the covenant status of these gentiles in jeopardy.

However, the Messianic Jewish community finds itself in a different situation. Our position in the bilateral *ekklēsia* involves partnership with the Christian church and also membership in the Jewish people. Messianic Jews are born into the covenant with the patriarchs and matriarchs, and then discover its full meaning and power in Jesus. When someone in our community rejects the deity of Jesus, they are putting in jeopardy the full realization of their covenantal identity, but *not* their covenantal identity itself. They are usually motivated, at least in part, by pressures exerted from the wider Jewish community. In effect, they are choosing a closer social connection to the covenant community of Israel at the expense of a connection to the church. They are accepting the negative doctrinal boundary marker asserted by the wider Jewish community.

As part of the bilateral *ekklēsia*, we refuse to accept the Jewish community's negative doctrinal boundary marker, just as we refuse to accept the Christian community's negative boundary marker dealing with our covenantal practice of the Torah. (Once again, we realize the significance of our hermeneutic of *dialectical* ecclesial continuity.) But should we exclude from our midst those Messianic Jews who adhere to these negative boundary markers, i.e., who deny the deity of Jesus, or who deny the covenantal obligation of Torah? I am not convinced that we should. Affirmation of the deity of Jesus and affirmation of the covenantal obligation of Torah observance for Jews are the two central principles of our communal existence, and we can rightly require that our leaders uphold them. They are our center, but they need not constitute our outer boundary.

Third, as we have just seen, affirmation of the deity of Jesus brings us into conflict with the wider Jewish community that we call our own. Is it viable on a long-term basis for us to identify so wholeheartedly with a community that has erected a social and cultural boundary that consists of a denial of what we so centrally affirm? I would answer: probably not. In the same way, bilateral ecclesiology lacks long-term viability if the Christian church maintains its negative boundary concerning the covenantal obligation of Torah.[26] These two negative boundary definitions provided the church and the Jewish community with a comfortable, unambiguous, mutually accepted border, fenced and well patrolled. They also supported the illusion that these two social bodies represented two religions, each of which made total sense apart from the other. Our existence as a corporate Messianic Jewish presence bears witness to the arbitrary and unsustainable nature of this border and of the religious illusion it perpetuates.

We exist as a movement in part to protest this negative border. Such a protest constitutes a crucial element in our prophetic calling. Moreover, our long-term viability depends on the success of that protest. We already see significant changes in the church's attitude toward its negative boundary. While the Messianic Jewish view on the Torah has not yet carried the day, the contrary view is no longer a universal presupposition. We can and should hope and pray for the same changes in the Jewish community's attitude toward its negative boundary.

But this will never happen if we surrender our affirmation of the deity of Jesus, lose sight of its true significance, or yield to pressure and hide it from public view. It will also never happen if this affirmation becomes for us an abstract proposition, prominently displayed as a mark of doctrinal orthodoxy but divorced from the revelatory and redemptive power to which it is meant to bear witness. It is my hope that future generations of Messianic Jews will exalt the Torah as the covenantal constitution of the Jewish people while joyfully confessing the deity of Jesus, light for revelation to the gentiles and the glory of his people Israel.

26. Of course, our movement does recognize a sense in which full-orbed observance of the Torah should function as a boundary—not between the *ekklēsia* and the Jewish people, but between the *ecclesia ex circumcisione* and the *ecclesia ex gentibus*. This boundary distinguishes but does not divide—it is not a fortified border between two feuding countries but a line marking out the territory of two provinces within the same nation. And it is not a negative boundary (except in the limited sense that it does not bind Christians), for the Christian church should honor the Torah and endorse its full-orbed observance by all Jews.

CHAPTER 3

# Judaism and the Divine-Human Jesus

*Here Kinzer addresses the claim commonly made by Jewish thinkers that a Jewish affirmation of Jesus's divinity is a contradiction in terms. Drawing upon key voices in contemporary Jewish scholarship (whose expertise spans the spectrum from biblical studies to Chasidism), Kinzer demonstrates the way in which an embodied God has consistently figured prominently in Jewish thought. He shows that incarnation cannot be categorically excluded from the divine will, even if the majority of the Jewish world rejects that God became incarnate in the person of Jesus. In this light, enduring Jewish rejection of Jesus's divine-human identity must be made on* a posteriori *grounds (based upon the historical trajectory of Judaism and Christianity) rather than on philosophical or theological* a priori *grounds.*[1]

## "ABSOLUTE MONOTHEISM" AND JUDAISM

THE TWENTY-FIRST CENTURY HAS seen no shortage of books dealing with the historical Jesus and Judaism. Zev Garber and Kenneth Hanson's recent addition to this library, *Judaism and Jesus*,[2] has at least one feature that distinguishes it from the rest: though the authors identify as Orthodox Jews, they take seriously the work of Messianic Jews and they value

---

1. This essay was first presented as part of an online panel reviewing the book *Judaism and Jesus* by Zev Garber and Kenneth L. Hanson in December 2020 at the annual North American Meeting of SBL-AAR. It was then published in *Upholding God's Word*, ed. Jim Melnick et al., 281–89.

2. Garber and Hanson, *Judaism and Jesus*.

our contribution to the discussion of Judaism and Jesus in the twenty-first century.

Nevertheless, their respect for our unique perspective on Jesus does not imply acceptance of our Jewish legitimacy. In fact, Garber and Hanson unequivocally deny that legitimacy, at least for Messianic Jews who affirm Jesus's dual divine-human identity. Chapter 6 of the book is devoted to this denial. The chapter is written by Hanson but echoes themes stated by Garber elsewhere in the volume. Hanson here interacts repeatedly with my writings. While respecting my scholarship, he deems my efforts futile: from his perspective, any attempt to elaborate a *Jewish* affirmation of Jesus's divinity amounts to a contradiction in terms.

I will not here defend the writings that Hanson critiques. Instead, I will examine the single proposition underlying his argument and contend that this proposition is unsupported by texts central to the Jewish tradition.

Hanson states the proposition clearly and succinctly: "However Kinzer and others may try to finesse the point, the incarnation has always been and will always remain incompatible with the traditional Jewish understanding of *the 'oneness of God'*—encapsulated in the *Shema*."[3] As seen here, Hanson's case rests on a particular interpretation of the divine *echad* (i.e., the Hebrew word normally translated as "one") confessed in the *Shema*, an interpretation alleged to be universal among faithful Jews throughout history. The same point is reiterated by Garber, who on three occasions uses the phrase "absolute monotheism" as shorthand for an understanding of the *Shema* which excludes divine *differentiation* or *incarnation*.[4] In a move common to nineteenth- and twentieth-century Judaism, Garber and Hanson interpret the *Shema* in Maimonidean terms as an ontological statement concerning the meaning and implications of divine simplicity and transcendence. As Hanson states, "the 'otherness' of Israel's deity . . . became the very essence of ethical monotheism."[5] From this perspective, denying that the Logos was incarnate in Jesus of Nazareth is not an *a posteriori* historical judgment but an *a priori* metaphysical assumption. As Louis Jacobs argued in the last century, "Jews have held that God, being God, *cannot* assume human flesh."[6] The God of Israel is, by definition, *disembodied*.

---

3. Garber and Hanson, *Judaism and Jesus*, 83 (emphasis added).
4. Garber and Hanson, *Judaism and Jesus*, 24, 50, 66.
5. Garber and Hanson, *Judaism and Jesus*, 89.
6. Jacobs, "Belief in a Personal God," 103. Jacobs penned these words in response to

Garber and Hanson either ignore or minimize evidence of traditional Jewish views contrary to this "absolute monotheism." From the outset, their Maimonidean interpretation of the *Shema* is presented as the uniform teaching of the "traditional Israelite religion" of the Hebrew Bible.[7] Moving on to Second Temple Judaism, they acknowledge that the Logos theology of Philo shares some common elements with New Testament incarnationalism, but dismiss Philo as representing a compromised "Hellenistic Judaism" which "presents its own set of problems with respect to traditional Jewish notions of deity."[8] The high Christology of John is not viewed against the backdrop of Enochian or Qumran texts, but is instead treated as "more an expression of gnosticism than Judaism."[9] According to Garber and Hanson, rabbinic Judaism emerges as the legitimate heir to the "absolute monotheism" of the Bible and initiates a purifying process in which these "Hellenistic" and "gnostic" influences are eliminated: "any texts from Jewish antiquity that advanced the notion of multiplicity within the 'Godhead' . . . were systematically excluded from the Jewish canon and afforded no authority or place in Jewish faith traditions."[10]

But what about esoteric descriptions of the divine body in the *heikhalot* texts, or of the *sefirot* in *kabbalah*? Garber and Hanson do not attempt to reconcile these core Jewish traditions with the "absolute monotheism" that allegedly "has always been and will always remain" an essential feature of Jewish belief, but they categorically deny that such traditions provide any support for Messianic Jewish claims: "In the Judaism that has evolved down to the present it is hardly acceptable for anyone to hide behind the rubric of 'Jewish mysticism' as a defense of 'binitarianism' or 'Trinitarianism.'"[11] As for the orthodox Jewish mystics of our own day, Hanson acknowledges that some Chabadniks have gone too far in their veneration of the last Lubavitcher Rebbe, but he presents their incarnational theology as an aberration that is utterly discontinuous with the "absolute monotheism" that presumably characterized earlier Chabad Chasidism and the Chasidic movement as a whole.[12]

---

Orthodox Jewish theologian Michael Wyschogrod, who, as we shall see, claimed the opposite.

7. Garber and Hanson, *Judaism and Jesus*, 7.

8. Garber and Hanson, *Judaism and Jesus*, 88–89.

9. Garber and Hanson, *Judaism and Jesus*, 92.

10. Garber and Hanson, *Judaism and Jesus*, 94.

11. Garber and Hanson, *Judaism and Jesus*, 95.

12. Garber and Hanson, *Judaism and Jesus*, 100.

## "ABSOLUTE MONOTHEISM" IN RECENT JEWISH SCHOLARSHIP

This picture of an "absolute monotheism" held universally by faithful Jews through the centuries might have been credible to informed Jewish readers a century ago. A brief summary of relevant Jewish scholarship of the past two or three decades shows that it is no longer so.

We begin with Jewish biblical studies. In *The Bodies of God and the World of Ancient Israel*, Benjamin Sommer demolishes the Maimonidean reading of the Pentateuch, arguing that all streams of the biblical tradition concur in the belief that Israel's God has a body; the source traditions disagree only on where that body is located and whether it is fixed in a singular location (heaven for Deuteronomy, the Tabernacle/Temple for the Priestly writings) or fluidly present in various places at the same time (as in J and E traditions).[13] Sommer concludes the volume by pointing to rabbinic, kabbalistic, and Christian theological constructs that emerge as natural extensions of this biblical view of God.[14]

Daniel Boyarin and Moshe Idel carry the counter-Maimonidean narrative forward in their studies of Second Temple Judaism, undercutting any reading of the period that marginalizes binitarian Logos theology.[15] The many varieties of this theological perspective were not Platonic, stoic, or gnostic accretions distorting the pure "absolute monotheism" of the Bible, but central components of multiple streams of Second Temple Judaism, including the proto-rabbinic movement itself.

Alon Goshen-Gottstein and Jacob Neusner continue the story by describing the embodied deity of the rabbinic tradition. In the words of the former, "one of the central issues that sets rabbinic theology apart from later medieval developments is the attribution of body or form to the godhead."[16] On the other hand, the emerging rabbinic establishment did attempt to suppress views of divine differentiation, such as the binitarianism common in the Second Temple period. As Boyarin and Idel note, it is all the more remarkable that such suppressed currents re-emerged in the Jewish mystical tradition, a phenomenon that Idel calls "the great

---

13. Sommer, *The Bodies of God*.
14. Sommer, *The Bodies of God*, 126–37.
15. Boyarin, *Border Lines* and *The Jewish Gospels*; Idel, *Ben*.
16. Goshen-Gottstein, "The Body as Image of God," 171. See also Neusner, *The Incarnation of God*.

by-pass."[17] This re-emergence is evident in the *heikhalot* literature with its depiction of Metatron as the name-bearing angel of Exodus 23 (referred to as "the little YHVH") and also with its exotic *Shiur Komah* texts, which detail the measurements of the divine body. The latter tradition may even have left its mark on the *Alaynu* prayer found in the Rosh Hashanah and daily liturgy. Boyarin and Joseph Dan suggest that this prayer was originally binitarian, addressing both "the Master of all" (*Adon ha-kol*) and the "Creator of the beginning" (*Yotzer bereshit*).[18]

Idel's "great by-pass" reaches its canonical telos in medieval *kabbalah*. The kabbalistic distinction between *Eyn Sof* and the *sefirot* undermines any assertion that the Maimonidean doctrine of divine simplicity functioned as a normative Jewish conviction before the modern era. David Novak has even argued that widespread Jewish acceptance of the kabbalistic vision of a differentiated deity led medieval Jewish authorities to alter their halakhic assessment of the Christian doctrine of the Trinity.[19] In contrast to the Maimonidean view of divine transcendence, Elliot Wolfson highlights the incarnational impulse operative in kabbalistic tradition. He shows how *kabbalah* treats the *sefirot* as equivalent to the divine body on the one hand and the divine Name and heavenly Torah on the other. God's body is a text, perceived through an informed study of its earthly inscription and activated through observance of the commandments contained therein. The *mitzvot* of the Torah enable Israel to become an agent of divine enfleshment.[20]

The kabbalistic tradition permeated popular Jewish spirituality via the eighteenth-century Chasidic movement, which also carried it into our own century. Shaul Magid has studied the incarnational thrust of that movement, demonstrating both its divergence from Maimonidean theism and its many similarities to Christian thought. He argues that Chasidic incarnationalism developed as a natural expression of *kabbalah*

---

17. "The cultural move that I called the 'great by-pass' of the rabbinic literatures ... brought back some theological elements that existed in Jewish sources in late antiquity, were relegated to the margin by ... rabbinic literature, but made their way back in one way or another, and were accepted by many of the main representatives of rabbinic Judaism" (Idel, *Ben*, 162); "Much of the later rabbinic tradition rejected the rejection of binitarian theology that the Rabbis attempted to enforce" (Boyarin, *Border Lines*, 292n55).

18. Boyarin, *Border Lines*, 120, 124, 292n57; Dan, *The Ancient Jewish Mysticism*, 71–72.

19. Novak, *Jewish-Christian Dialogue*, 48–51.

20. Wolfson, "Judaism and Incarnation," 239–54.

in an insular Jewish setting unaffected by the presence of Christian on-lookers.[21] Elliot Wolfson, in turn, focuses upon the theology of Chabad Chasidism. He shows how the panentheistic orientation of Chabad links the last Lubavitcher Rebbe to his six predecessors. In so doing, Wolfson also makes intelligible the incarnationalism of the radical Chabadniks who hail the last Rebbe as "divinity in physical garb" (*elohut bilevush gashmi*).[22]

## "ABSOLUTE MONOTHEISM" AND THE *SHEMA*

With this brief overview of relevant twenty-first-century scholarship in mind, let us look specifically at Jewish readings of the *Shema*, since that single verse from Deuteronomy plays such an important role in Garber and Hanson's treatment of Messianic Judaism. Everett Fox is in step with much of contemporary Jewish biblical scholarship in seeing the *echad* of the *Shema* as a summons "to worship YHWH alone."[23] This coheres with the Jewish liturgical tradition which views Israel's recitation of the *Shema* as "taking on the yoke of *malkhut shamayim*," that is, as acknowledging YHWH's sovereignty (m. Berachot 2:2). It also fits the Jewish exegetical tradition of Deuteronomy 6:4, summarized by Rashi: "'YHWH,' who is '*our* God' now, but *not* the God of the other nations, He is destined to be the '*One* God,' as it says . . . , 'On that day YHWH shall be one and his name one' (Zechariah 14:9)."[24] Rashi thus reads the *Shema* in light of Zechariah 14, which makes YHWH's oneness an eschatological hope rather than a timeless metaphysical truth. This amounts to a dynamic relational understanding of *echad* in contrast to the static ontological view proposed by Garber and Hanson.

The Jewish mystical tradition blazes a more daring path. The Zohar sees the three divine names contained in the *Shema* (*YHWH*; *Elohaynu*; *YHWH*) as referring to three of the *sefirot* (*Chesed*; *Gevurah*; *Tiferet*). In the liturgical recitation of the *Shema* a Jew unifies the three.[25] Similarly, the Zohar understands "*YHVH*" in Zechariah 14:9 as a reference to *Tiferet*, and "his Name" as *Shekhinah*. The verse thus speaks of the messianic

---

21. Magid, *Hasidism Incarnate*.
22. Wolfson, *Open Secret*.
23. Fox, *The Five Books of Moses*, 880.
24. Rashi, *Commentary on the Torah*, 5:70.
25. Matt, *Zohar*, 21–22.

future when *Tiferet* and *Shekhinah* are one.²⁶ The liturgical unification of the *sefirot* accomplished in Israel's recitation of the *Shema* thus anticipates and facilitates their eschatological unification.

The Chasidic stream of Jewish mysticism, as exemplified by Chabad, reads the *Shema* less in terms of inner divine differentiation and more in terms of incarnation. As Wolfson states, "in Habad symbolism, *YHWH* names the essence that is above nature and Elohim its appearance in nature. . . . The conjunction of *YHWH* and Elohim bespeaks the mystery of incarnation (*hitgashshemut*). . . . In professing [in the *Shema*] that '*YHVH* is *Elohaynu*,' the worshipper gives verbal assent to and thereby participates in the puzzle of incarnation, the commingling of the metaphysical and physical. . . . By proclaiming the oneness of God, worshippers theurgically 'draw down the disclosure of the light of the Infinite that is above the aspect of place, so that it will be revealed in the aspect of place and the place will be annihilated . . . and this is 'the Lord is one.'"²⁷

None of these exegetical and liturgical traditions conform to the "absolute monotheism" that Maimonides championed and that Garber and Hanson treat as axiomatic. With that axiom eliminated, the argument in chapter 6 of *Judaism and Jesus* lacks cogency.

## HEARING AN OLD STORY IN A NEW WAY

Admittedly, the dethroning of Maimonidean monotheism does not in itself entail acceptance of Messianic Jewish incarnationalism as a legitimate expression of Jewish faith. While Jewish tradition as a whole does not regard divine differentiation and incarnation as *a priori* impossibilities, it has universally denied that God has taken human form in Jesus of Nazareth. Michael Wyschogrod describes the situation well, depicting it as a divergence in the stories that Jews and Christians hear from the Word of divine revelation:

> At a certain point, the Jewish story diverges from the Christian. I am convinced that it is necessary to formulate the matter in these terms, to speak of stories that diverge, because too often rationalistically minded Jewish theologians have made it appear that Judaism resists incarnation on some *a priori* grounds as if the Jewish philosopher can somehow determine ahead of time

26. Matt, *The Zohar, Pritzker Edition*, 4:40n175.
27. Wolfson, *Open Secret*, 82, 84, 89–90.

just what God does or does not allow. The truth is, of course, that it would be difficult to imagine anything further removed from authentic Jewish faith which does not prescribe for God from some alien frame of reference but listens obediently to God's free decisions, none of which can be prescribed or even anticipated by humanity. If Judaism cannot accept incarnation [that is, divine incarnation in Jesus] it is because it does not hear this story, because the Word of God as it hears it does not tell it and because Jewish faith does not testify to it. And if the Church does accept incarnation, it is not because it somehow discovered that such an event had to occur given the nature of God, or of being, reality, or anything else, but because it hears that this was God's free and gracious decision, a decision not predictable by humankind.[28]

Similar positions have been articulated by Hershel Matt and Pinchas Lapide.[29] Wyschogrod, Lapide, and Matt all reject a Maimonidean "absolute monotheism" that would rule out Jesus's divine-human identity on *a priori* philosophical or theological grounds. They agree with Garber and Hanson that an incarnationalist view of Jesus is incompatible with Jewish faith—but they adopt this position as an *a posteriori* judgment confirmed by the historical witness and corporate consciousness of the Jewish people.

Of course, the witness of the Jewish people—before the historical rupture initiated by the Enlightenment and "emancipation"—also ruled out deistic, naturalistic, and atheistic versions of Judaism. That fact did not prevent forms of Judaism that espouse such views from arising in the past century and attaining widespread acceptance as legitimate expressions of the Jewish religious consciousness. Only Jews who affirm the divine-human identity of Jesus are now excluded from the Jewish conversation—even when we are otherwise living traditional Jewish lives, and holding (in other respects) traditional Jewish theological opinions.

Given the attitudes toward Messianic Jews that remain dominant among Jewish communal leaders, Zev Garber and Kenneth Hanson have shown courage in engaging publicly with us. They have not excluded us from the conversation. Garber and Hanson believe that all Jews should take brother Jesus seriously, and they respect us for hearing in his message a summons to Jewish covenantal fidelity. Nevertheless, they disagree

---

28. Wyschogrod, *Abraham's Promise*, 215–16.

29. Matt, *Walking Humbly with God*, 207–8. For relevant citations from Lapide, see Jocz, *The Jewish People and Jesus Christ*, 184–85.

profoundly with our incarnationalist perspective on his identity. I have here called into question the cogency of their argument. For Jews such as myself, taking brother Jesus seriously means encountering in him the unique and unsurpassable revelation of the God of Israel.

I am convinced that eventually the Jewish people as a whole will make a place for us among its tents. Acknowledging that Maimonidean "absolute monotheism" is only one possible reading of the *Shema* and seeing that our views of God cohere with those espoused by other Jews through the centuries, they will make room for Jesus, the God-filled apocalyptic prophet and messianic-claimant, as well as for his Jewish disciples. And, in the fullness of time, they will do far more than this.

Certainly not today. Probably not tomorrow. But perhaps the day after tomorrow.

# PART II.

*Ecclesiology as Israelology:
Jewish Disciples of Jesus
and the Twofold People of God*

CHAPTER 4

# Israel Within
Jewish Ecclesial Communities
as Prophetic Sign and Theological Challenge

> *Kinzer reflects on the notion of revelation as a reinterpretation of tradition in light of significant events in history. He points to the way in which this process shapes key framing moments and concepts in the biblical narrative and argues that a similar approach must be taken in our day, particularly regarding the historically and theologically significant re-emergence of an identifiable Jewish presence within the ekklēsia. For Kinzer, this historical development (which, notably, has coincided with the rebirth of the Jewish state) requires theological interpretation and poses poignant questions to fundamental aspects of the church's identity and self-understanding. If taken seriously, these questions require a reassessment of Christian thought ranging from doctrinal particulars to biblical hermeneutics.*[1]

## THEOLOGY AND HISTORY

IN PAST WRITINGS I have argued that a theological reading of Scripture requires consideration of historical developments in the post-biblical world—in particular, those developments associated with realities central

---

1. This chapter originated as an oral presentation for a Reformed theological conference in the Netherlands in 2018 addressing the theme "Israel as Hermeneutical Challenge." This chapter also appears in a forthcoming volume entitled *Israel as a Hermeneutical Challenge*, ed. Michael Mulder et al.

to the biblical text.² In *Jerusalem Crucified, Jerusalem Risen* I underlined two such historical developments from the last century: the re-establishment of a Jewish national home in the land promised to Abraham and the birth of Messianic Judaism.³ I focused on the former but also noted the uncanny links between this seismic world-historical phenomenon and the latter—a marginal spiritual movement, ostensibly no more than a tiny ripple in a vast ecclesial ocean.

Jewish Jerusalem perished in 70 and 135 CE, only to rise from the ashes in the modern era. The history of Jewish ecclesial communities followed a similar arc. These communities were centered in Jerusalem, and the catastrophes of 70 and 135 CE turned them into isolated island villages threatened by elevated gentile waters on one side and a wall situated on higher ground erected against them by their fellow Jews on the other. In subsequent centuries, they eventually disappeared from the historical record.⁴ Then, in a surprising twist of history, the twentieth century witnessed their rebirth. If the resurrection of Jewish Jerusalem as a geopolitical reality has hermeneutical implications for ecclesial theology, might this also be the case for the resurrection of the Jewish communal expression of faith in Jesus?

In the present essay I propose that the re-emergence of Jewish ecclesial communities in the modern era should be viewed as a prophetic sign and theological challenge, akin to the rebirth of Jewish Jerusalem. They are twin historical developments with equally profound theological implications. I will point to two examples of such implications, each of which involves a warning to distinguish the part from the whole.

## "A PEOPLE FOR HIS NAME FROM AMONG THE GENTILES"

Analyzing the human side of the revelatory process, Paul van Buren defined revelation as Israel's reinterpretation of its tradition in response to

---

2. Kinzer, *Postmissionary Messianic Judaism*, 38–46, and *Jerusalem Crucified*, 7–10.

3. Kinzer, *Jerusalem Crucified*, 240–70.

4. The past two decades have seen a flowering of new studies of what has traditionally been called "Jewish Christianity." See, for example, Skarsaune and Hvalvik, *Jewish Believers in Jesus*; Jackson-McCabe, *Jewish Christianity Reconsidered*; Jones, *The Rediscovery of Jewish Christianity*; Jones, *Pseudoclementina Elchasaiticaque*; Burns, *The Christian Schism*; Jackson-McCabe, *Jewish Christianity*; Reed, *Jewish-Christianity*.

significant events in its history.[5] The Mosaic revelation involved interpretation of the Abrahamic tradition in light of the exodus from Egypt. Most of the prophetic books of Scripture arose as a response within the Mosaic tradition to the Babylonian exile and the return to Jerusalem under Persian rule. The apostolic revelation reinterpreted the biblical tradition as a whole in response to the events of Jesus's crucifixion and resurrection. In each case, God acted in the history of the people of God, and that action was understood in light of the people's corporate memory of previous revelation. At the same time, the interpretation of the latest divine intervention in history resulted in a new perspective on the tradition.

In the apostolic community, this revelatory process continued as new events unfolded in its midst. The most significant of these concerned gentiles who were turning to the God of Israel. Acts 10 describes visions given to Cornelius and Peter, the first directing Cornelius to send for Peter (vv. 1-6), the second commanding Peter to accept the invitation of the centurion (vv. 9-20). These heavenly communications set the story on its course, but they are not the decisive moments in determining its outcome. The divine intervention upon which the story hinges occurred as Peter addressed the household of Cornelius, recounting the life, death, and resurrection of Jesus (vv. 34-48). Peter later describes what then transpired: "And as I began to speak, the Holy Spirit fell upon them just as it had upon us at the beginning. And I remembered the word of the Lord, how he had said, 'John baptized with water, but you will be baptized with the Holy Spirit.' If then God gave them the same gift that he gave us when we believed in the Lord Jesus Christ, who was I that I could hinder God?" (Acts 11:15-17).

The descent of the Spirit upon these gentiles was objectively attested through the same visible manifestations that accompanied the experience of the apostles on Pentecost (Acts 10:46; 2:4, 11). Observing these manifestations, Peter recalled the words of the resurrected Jesus (Acts 11:16; see 1:5), which themselves alluded to the earlier words of John the Baptist (Luke 3:16).[6] Peter thus interpreted the event at hand in light of the tradition and experience of the apostolic community, and the newly interpreted event enabled him to understand the wider significance of

---

5. Van Buren, *A Theology of the Jewish-Christian Reality*, Part 1, 37-40. Van Buren calls this the "creaturely shape of revelation." He acknowledges that "revelation . . . comes from God" (37), but gives little attention to the divine side of the revelatory process. His analysis is helpful as far as it goes, but it does not go far enough.

6. Witherington, *The Acts of the Apostles*, 364.

the words transmitted by that tradition. Acting on the basis of this revelatory process, Peter baptized Cornelius and his household without further ado.[7]

This incident proved crucial for resolving the broader question of gentile participation in the new movement, but the resolution itself came only at the Jerusalem Council (Acts 15:1–21). Adhering to the principle displayed in the Cornelius episode, the Antioch *ekklēsia* welcomed a large number of gentiles into its ranks (Acts 11:19–21). This community then commissioned Paul and Barnabas to travel to Asia Minor, establishing new ecclesial bodies among the gentiles (Acts 13:1–3). Hearing of these successful initiatives deriving from Antioch, some concerned Jewish disciples of Jesus traveled to Antioch from Jerusalem and complained that matters were getting out of hand (Acts 15:1). Evidently, they were willing to accept a few uncircumcised adherents (such as Cornelius and his household) as an exception to a general rule, but at this point it appeared to them that the exception had *become* the rule. In response to their protest, the Antioch community sent Paul and Barnabas to Jerusalem to bring the question to the "apostles and elders." The *ekklēsia* now required an authoritative decision regarding gentile involvement in the Jesus community.

The dynamic of the Jerusalem Council resembles that seen in the Cornelius incident. After debating the pros and cons of the question—perhaps on the level of biblical interpretation or prudential consideration of likely consequences (Acts 15:7a)—the discussion shifted to reflection on recent events. Peter told of his experience with the household of Cornelius, portraying it as a divine intervention constituting a policy-setting precedent. "And God, who knows the human heart, testified to them by

---

7. Robert Tannehill treats Acts 10–11 and 15 as a case study in how Peter and the early *ekklēsia* discerned the will of God in important matters (Tannehill, *The Narrative Unity of Luke-Acts*, 128–45, 183–93). He notes that it is not Peter's vision alone that is revelatory, but the conjunction of the vision with the appearance of the messengers from Cornelius (128–29). Even then Peter does not commit himself to a particular interpretation of his vision until he has met Cornelius and heard his story firsthand (130). When Cornelius and his household receive the Holy Spirit and begin speaking in tongues, Peter and his colleagues connect what they are seeing to what they themselves experienced at Pentecost (129): "The descent of the Holy Spirit on the Gentiles is depicted as a repetition of Pentecost" (142). The corporate process of discerning God's will does not end here, however, for "the new insight" gained by Peter and the new "relationship" established between Jews and gentiles "must be justified publicly before the church (11:1–18), and its implications must be worked out in public debate with contrary understandings of God's will (15:1–29)" (132).

giving them the Holy Spirit, just as he did to us; and in cleansing their hearts by faith he has made no distinction between them and us" (Acts 15:8–9). Peter here interprets what he witnessed in Caesarea in light of the words of John the Baptist and the resurrected Jesus, the experience of Pentecost, and the vision he received in Jaffa. Apart from that surprising encounter in the home of a gentile, the earlier teachings of Jesus and John and Peter's experience in the upper room and in the house of Simon the Tanner would not have led him to the place he is now. But given that encounter, he cannot understand those teachings and experiences in any other way.

The recounting of significant recent events continued as Barnabas and Paul "told of all the signs and wonders that God had done through them among the gentiles" (Acts 15:12). These new dramatic manifestations of the divine purpose served to confirm Peter's testimony, demonstrating that what had happened to Cornelius and his household was not an exception to a rule but a new norm. Taking full account of these real-life incidents, James now offers (vv. 13–21) his experience-informed reading of Amos 9:11–12 (and, in his halakhic decree [vv. 19–20], also of Leviticus 17–18).[8] "The Lord returns to rebuild the fallen tent of David, *so that* (*hopōs*) all other peoples may seek the Lord. In other words, the eschatological restoration of God's people was always intended to attract Gentiles to seek God."[9] James interpreted events in the light of Scripture, and Scripture in the light of those events. The final result was an authoritative ecclesial decision regarding the inclusion of gentiles in the Jesus community.

James began his speech with these words: "Simeon has related how God first looked favorably on the gentiles, to take from among them a people for his name" (v. 14). The phrase "a people for his name" is unusual in that it describes these gentiles as a corporate reality resembling Israel, yet distinct from Israel and even in some sense distinct (but not separate)

---

8. For detailed arguments supporting the thesis that the halakhic decree of James draws upon Leviticus 17–18, see Zellentin, *Law beyond Israel*; Oliver, *Torah Praxis*, 365–98; and the following articles on this subject by Richard Bauckham: "James and the Jerusalem Church," 452–75; "James and the Gentiles (Acts 15.13–21)," 154–84; "James, Peter, and the Gentiles," 91–142; "James and the Jerusalem Council Decision," 178–86. While these detailed arguments are new, the importance of Leviticus 17–18 for Acts 15 has long been noted. See, for example, Jervell, *Luke and the People of God*, 144; Juel, *Luke-Acts*, 90, 106–7, and Loader, *Jesus' Attitude*, 374–75, 378. Some scholars, however, remain unconvinced that Leviticus 17–18 lies behind the halakhic decree of James (e.g., Witherington, *The Acts of the Apostles*, 460–65; Wilson, *Luke and the Law*, 84–94).

9. Witherington, *The Acts of the Apostles*, 459.

from the Jewish members of the *ekklēsia* who are a subset of Israel. Jacob Jervell notes this strange phrase and draws an inference regarding Luke's ecclesiology: "With the admission of Gentiles to the people of God, there are now two groups within this people."[10] God has acted in dramatic fashion, and something new has arisen as a consequence; but the new reality has neither replaced nor utterly transformed the old (i.e., Israel), but instead has extended it into previously uncharted territory.

## THE DEATH AND RESURRECTION OF JEWISH ECCLESIAL COMMUNITIES

Jervell's reading of Acts 15:14 flies in the face of ecclesiological assumptions unquestioned over two millennia of church history. According to those premises, the Jerusalem Council demolished all barriers to Jewish-gentile ecclesial interaction, with the long-term intention of eliminating entirely the Jew-gentile distinction in the life of the Jesus community. The halakhic decree issued by James and confirmed by "the apostles and elders" (Acts 15:20, 28–29; 21:25; see also 16:4) has been viewed as a pastoral "recommendation" aimed at facilitating communal "harmony" between gentiles and Jews in a transitional period.[11] Gentile believers in Jesus were being asked to bear in love with their overly scrupulous Jewish brothers and sisters with the expectation that those Jewish members of the *ekklēsia* would eventually abandon their antiquated way of life.

The problem with this reading of Acts 15 is that it conflicts with the rest of the book of Acts. The entirety of the Lukan corpus treats the Torah as Israel's sacred trust, whose authority is upheld by Jesus and the apostles.[12] Jervell's interpretation of the Jerusalem Council takes full account of its literary context and enables us to see the coherence of the Lukan perspective on Israel and ecclesiology.

> This division of the church into two groups is the presupposition for the apostolic decree.... The entire argument is carried by the difference between the two groups. It is presupposed that Jewish Christians keep the law; this point of view harmonizes with the account in Acts as a whole. On the other hand, Gentile

---

10. Jervell, *Luke and the People of God*, 190. For a more recent treatment of Acts 15:14 which reinforces Jervell's conclusion, see Oliver, "The First 'Paul within Judaism' Perspective?" See also Tannehill, *The Narrative Unity*, 186–87.

11. Marshall, *The Acts of the Apostles*, 253, 255.

12. See Kinzer, *Jerusalem Crucified*, 160–224.

Christians need not keep the law in its entirety. James supports this by appealing to Moses as a witness for his decision (v. 21). The apostolic decree is nothing but Mosaic law [i.e., Leviticus 17–18], which is applied to Gentiles living together with Israel. Actually, Luke at this point has two authorities for the decree: Moses and James.[13]

It is unfortunate that Jervell uses the word "division" to characterize Jew-gentile differentiation in Acts of the Apostles, since one of the purposes of the apostolic decree is to open the way for intimate *communion* in the Messiah between Jews and gentiles. The "two groups" are part of the one "people of God." But Jervell correctly perceives the assumptions governing the narrative. All of the participants in the Jerusalem Council were Jews who believed that the resurrection of Israel's Messiah was a divine intervention in history aimed at renewing the Jewish people and leading it into its promised inheritance. The outpouring of the Holy Spirit on gentiles motivated these Jews to reinterpret some aspects of their belief, but it did not entail that belief's wholesale rejection. The gentile believers in Jesus had now become "a people for his name," but Israel was already such a people and remained such, and Jews within the *ekklēsia* remained part of that Israel. The one people of God was now a twofold reality.[14]

None of the apostles or Jerusalem elders could have conceived of a future in which the *ekklēsia* of the Messiah consisted exclusively of gentiles, or in which the Jews who entered its ranks ceased to express visibly their corporate identity as members of the Jewish people. The challenge they faced involved the inclusion of gentiles within the people of God *as gentiles*. They would have been astonished at the notion that Jews could only be part of that people if they ceased to live *as Jews*. Yet, within a century such an astonishing notion had become thinkable and within three centuries it had become an accepted ecclesial norm.

The decisive turning point was the destruction of Jerusalem in 70 CE, reinforced sixty-five years later by the failure of the Bar Kokhba revolt and the prohibition of Jewish habitation in the devastated city. Here again the interplay of historical events and biblical tradition produced theological developments in both the *ekklēsia* and the wider Jewish world.

---

13. Jervell, *Luke*, 190 (emphasis added).

14. In *Postmissionary Messianic Judaism* I coined the term "bilateral ecclesiology" to refer to the twofold character of the one people of God. See Kinzer, *Postmissionary Messianic Judaism*, 151–79.

However, the growing rift between the two communities was reflected in the contradictory conclusions reached in this process of theological development. For the Jewish world, these events were a catastrophic recapitulation of the Babylonian exile which pointed forward to a future restoration—a restoration whose glory had been anticipated by the exilic prophets but was never realized in the return to the land under the Persian Empire. For the *ekklēsia*—now mainly gentile in leadership and composition—these events were viewed as a vindication of the prophetic words of Jesus (Mark 13:2) and as a definitive final judgment on the Jewish people which terminated its priestly role in the world and displayed the folly of its hope for an earthly kingdom.[15]

The dominant ecclesial assessment of the events of 70 and 135 CE resulted in the suppression of Jewish corporate life within the Jesus community.[16] This development was facilitated by the loss of Jerusalem as a Jewish ecclesial center and the dispersion of its community of Jewish disciples of Jesus. Thus, the destruction of Jerusalem fostered the gentilization of the *ekklēsia* in two ways: as an external event in Jewish history demanding theological interpretation and as an internal sociological earthquake that altered the communal configuration of the worldwide *ekklēsia*. No longer could the community of Jesus's disciples send their material gifts to their Jewish brothers and sisters in Jerusalem as an expression of gratitude for the spiritual riches bestowed on the gentiles (Rom 15:25–27). No longer could gentile believers in Jesus pray for the "saints" in Jerusalem who represented the olive tree into which they as gentiles had been grafted (Rom 11:16–24). The destruction of Jerusalem thus eventuated in the death of a visible corporate Jewish presence in the body of the Messiah.

In the nineteenth century, many Jews began to contemplate and prepare for the restoration of a Jewish commonwealth in the land of their ancestors. In the same period, national self-consciousness awoke among Jewish disciples of Jesus for the first time in fifteen centuries.[17] In 1813,

---

15. On the divergent responses to the destruction of Jerusalem by ecclesial gentiles and Jews outside the Jesus movement, see Kinzer, *Jerusalem Crucified*, 23–27. Martin Luther is a classic example of a church leader who saw the millennial exile of the Jews from their land as proof that God is finished with them (Harvey, *Luther and the Jews*, 73–85).

16. For discussion of the literary sources that document this suppression, see Kinzer, *Postmissionary Messianic Judaism*, 181–212.

17. For a thorough presentation of the connection between Zionism and the rebirth of Jewish ecclesial communities, see Kinzer, *Jerusalem Crucified*, 240–70. For more

forty-one Jewish believers in Jesus formed the *Beney Avraham* in London. In 1866, the Hebrew-Christian Alliance was established, again in Britain. (This was a mere four years after Moses Hess wrote his groundbreaking Zionist tract, *Rome and Jerusalem*.) The first exponent of an indigenous Jewish ecclesial community, Joseph Rabinowitz, came to faith in Jesus while on a mission to Palestine in 1882 investigating settlement possibilities for Jewish communities who were then enduring pogroms in Eastern Europe.[18] The modern Messianic Jewish movement arose in the wake of the Israeli victory in the Six Day War (1967). Just as the death of Jewish national life in Jerusalem and its environs was followed by the destruction of Jewish ecclesial life, so the hope and realization of a resurrected Jewish commonwealth is closely correlated with the renewed corporate identity of many Jewish disciples of Jesus.

For those paying attention to such historical developments, the story of the emergence of Messianic Judaism is well known. Most who identify as Messianic Jews have inherited theological and cultural paradigms from evangelical Protestantism and maintain close ties with sympathetic evangelical supporters.[19] Less well-known are parallel phenomena among Jews in Catholic and Russian Orthodox communities. In 1955, the Association of Saint James was founded as a Catholic body seeking to develop Hebrew-speaking Catholic communities in the young state of Israel. (In 1990 this association became an official Vicariate administering the Hebrew-speaking parishes in the land.)[20] In this Israeli context Fr. Elias Friedman, a Jewish Carmelite monk, first proposed in 1965 the establishment of a distinct Jewish Catholic community.[21] In 1979 (the same year as the formation of the first congregational association in the Messianic Jewish movement), Fr. Friedman founded the Association of Hebrew Catholics.[22] While this organization has spread mainly in the English-speaking world, a similar movement has emerged among Jewish Catholics in France, inspired by the example and teaching of the late

---

detail on the history of Messianic Judaism, see Kinzer, *Postmissionary Messianic Judaism*, 263–302.

18. Kjaer-Hansen, *Joseph Rabinowitz and the Messianic Movement*.

19. On the emergence of Messianic Judaism in the 1970s and its roots in evangelical Protestantism, see Ariel, *Evangelizing the Chosen People*, 220–51.

20. For more on the Association and Vicariate of St. James, see its website: http://www.catholic.co.il.

21. Fr. Friedman later expressed his vision for Jewish Catholicism in *Jewish Identity*.

22. See www.hebrewcatholic.net/.

Jewish archbishop of Paris, Cardinal Jean-Marie Lustiger. Like Messianic Jews and like Fr. Friedman, Cardinal Lustiger identified publicly with the life and destiny of the Jewish people.[23]

Even less well-known in the West is the rise of the corporate self-consciousness of Jews in the Russian Orthodox Church.[24] A central figure in this story was the priest, scholar, evangelist, and martyr, Fr. Alexander Men.[25] He was born in 1935 to two Jewish parents. His mother was drawn to the Orthodox Church before Alexander was born and he was baptized as a child and raised as an Orthodox Christian. His father, on the other hand, was never baptized, but lived as an active member of the Russian Jewish community. In this way Alexander grew up identifying with both communities and traditions. After being ordained a priest, Fr. Alexander wrote numerous books that influenced thousands of Russians. Among those thousands were many Jews, and ironically their entry into the Russian Orthodox Church tended to strengthen their identity as Jews.

One of the Jewish disciples of Fr. Men tells the story of how Alexander first decided to become a priest.

> Alik Men' was thirteen years old, a bar mitzvah boy, when Israel came into existence, and he told me: "I was terribly concerned with how I could contribute to the cause of Jewish survival. So I decided something very strange. Okay, I decided, I'll become a priest." And that very day he went to enter Moscow Theological Seminary. Obviously, he was not accepted; he was only thirteen years old. A boy.... So it is interesting that he connected the two things this way.[26]

According to this account, Alexander's priestly vocation drew inspiration from Israel's birth as a modern nation-state. The flowering of his priestly ministry among Russian Jews similarly coincided with the aftermath of the Six Day War. We thus see a movement of Jews entering the Orthodox Church—and strengthening their own awareness of their Jewish identity—at the same time as the emergence of the Messianic Jewish and Hebrew Catholic movements.[27]

---

23. See Lustiger, *The Promise*, and Duchesne, *Jean-Marie Lustiger*.

24. For an academic study of this phenomenon by a Jewish scholar, see Kornblatt, *Doubly Chosen*.

25. Hamant, *Alexander Men*. See also Kornblatt, *Doubly Chosen*, 69–83.

26. Kornblatt, *Doubly Chosen*, 72.

27. It is noteworthy that Cardinal Lustiger met Fr. Alexander in 1989, one year before the latter was brutally murdered. The cardinal wrote in moving terms of this meeting in

Thus, as Jewish Jerusalem was being reborn, a nascent Jewish corporate presence began to take shape in diverse sectors of the *ekklēsia*. For decades this phenomenon received little theological attention, but the situation appears to be changing. Some Christian leaders are recognizing that the emergence of Jewish ecclesial movements and communities poses a challenge to the *ecclesia ex gentibus* analogous to that raised for the *ecclesia ex circumcisione* in the first century by the outpouring of the Holy Spirit on gentiles.[28] Is this new ecclesial phenomenon likewise a significant work of the Holy Spirit with important theological implications, or is it a heresy, a sect, or a passing fad of little consequence? Or does it perhaps contain diverse elements worthy of all these varied assessments?

The latter is most likely. There are multiple swirling currents in our era claiming to renew the Jewish character of the *ekklēsia* and its theological heritage, and aberrations abound. But amid all this, a core truth stands out: the simultaneous rise of ecclesial movements among Jewish evangelical, Catholic, and Russian Orthodox followers of Jesus is a historical development of theological significance.[29] While there have always been Jewish believers in Jesus, not since the early centuries of the Jesus movement have there been such who (1) publicly identify as Jews and not just as Christians; (2) claim to be fully part of the Jewish people as well as the *ekklēsia*; and (3) associate with one another to form Jewish corporate entities within the *ekklēsia*. The emergence of such Jews, beginning in the early nineteenth century, is a unique historical development that demands our attention.

I propose that these Jewish ecclesial movements manifest a work of the Holy Spirit crying out for theological interpretation. This assessment gains strength when viewed against the backdrop of the Jerusalem Council's decree affirming God's act of taking from the gentiles "a people for

---

the introduction to the French edition of Yves Hamant's biography of Fr. Alexander. For the English translation of Lustiger's introduction, see Hamant, *Alexander Men*, 209-12.

28. In the year 2000 Pope John Paul II initiated an informal dialogue with a set of Messianic Jewish leaders through the agency of the Theologian of the Papal Household, then Fr. (later Cardinal) Georges Cottier. The history of that dialogue, and my own theological contributions to its progress, are found in Kinzer, *Searching Her Own Mystery*. For discussion of the terms *ecclesia ex circumcisione* and *ecclesia ex gentibus*, see *Searching Her Own Mystery*, 17-20.

29. This fact is accentuated by an even less documented phenomenon, namely, the growing number of Jesus-believing Jews who live as part of traditional Jewish communities. Since many of these people are discreet in speaking of their faith in Jesus, it is not possible to determine their exact numbers or assess trend lines. But I know the phenomenon well from numerous personal contacts.

his name," and the decree's negative photographic image in the post 135 CE ecclesial suppression of internal Jewish corporate life. God is once again establishing a witness to the resurrected Messiah in the midst of those who are the original—and still enduring—"people for his name." Has the crucified Jerusalem been raised from the dead? To take the question seriously is the first step in arriving at an answer that is faithful to the biblical tradition while also being open to the revelatory work of the Holy Spirit in history.

## THEOLOGICAL CHALLENGES POSED BY THE REBIRTH OF THE JEWISH *EKKLĒSIA*

The theological challenge faced by the *ekklēsia* when it encounters the living reality of Israel raises questions for every branch and doctrine of Christian theology.[30] However, most Christian responses to the living reality of Israel involve far less radical theological introspection. This is understandable because the reality under consideration (i.e., the Jewish people) is often perceived to be external to the life of the *ekklēsia*. Even when Christian response to this reality rises to the point of considering the Jewish people to be *closely related* to the *ekklēsia*, the two are still treated as related but *separate* entities.

This is not the case when the living reality of Israel in question consists of a Jewish corporate presence in the midst of the *ekklēsia* itself. Once this *internal* reality is taken seriously, the challenge posed to long-established ecclesial canons of faith and order is inescapable. Moreover, the enduring bond tying these Jewish ecclesial communities to the wider Jewish world raises troubling questions about the self-sufficiency of the *ekklēsia* in relation to the living reality of Israel, which is ostensibly "external" to ecclesial existence and identity.[31]

As a Messianic Jewish practitioner as well as a theoretician, virtually everything I have written in the past twenty-plus years could be

---

30. Already in 1985, Johannes Cardinal Willebrands, president of the Vatican Commission for Religious Relations with the Jews, recognized the extent of this challenge: "Our task is to face adequately . . . the questions that a renewed vision of Judaism poses to many aspects of Catholic theology, from Christology to ecclesiology, from the liturgy to the sacraments, from eschatology to the relation with the world and the witness we are called to offer in it and to it" (Willebrands, *Church and Jewish People*, 28).

31. The issue of Israel's "external" and "internal" relation to the *ekklēsia* is the major concern of my book *Searching Her Own Mystery*, as is evident from the title itself.

considered an extended reflection on the theological challenges posed to the *ekklēsia* (and the Jewish people) by the living reality of Jewish ecclesial communities.[32] I focused initially on ecclesiology.[33] My lengthy engagement with Catholicism then led to reflection on Christological and sacramental themes.[34] More recently, my attention has turned to eschatology and the content of the gospel message.[35] I have argued throughout that the reality of Jewish ecclesial communities demands from Christians a rethinking of every sphere of theology. "Israelology" is not merely a particular topic in theology, at a comfortable remove from the core of the ecclesial deposit of faith.[36] Instead, it resides near the heart of the network of truths that compose that deposit, and, like Christology, affects every other theological sphere.[37]

There are two additional theological challenges that relate to the wholeness or catholicity of the people of God. The first is hermeneutical in nature. The second concerns the historical continuity and discontinuity of the life of the *ekklēsia*. In both, the issue at hand is the tendency to mistake the part for the whole.

The first of these theological challenges posed by living Jewish ecclesial communities concerns the unique authority traditionally ascribed to the Pauline writings. Especially in the Western church, Paul has been viewed as the apostle par excellence. His battle to carve out a distinct niche for gentile believers in Jesus has been understood as a wholesale repudiation of "the works of Torah," understood as the distinctive religious practices that constitute what is now known as Judaism. This interpretation treats Paul as the exponent of a universal message that transcends and replaces the narrow confines of Jewish practice. The classic Catholic form of this reading speaks of a *fulfillment* of the Jewish law by Christ which renders its literal ceremonial and judicial commandments dead

---

32. For an introduction to my thinking that covers a spectrum of issues and expresses my views at different points in time, see Kinzer, *Israel's Messiah and the People of God*.

33. Kinzer, *Postmissionary Messianic Judaism*.

34. Kinzer, *Searching Her Own Mystery*.

35. Kinzer, *Jerusalem Crucified, Jerusalem Risen*.

36. "Comparative dogmatics . . . should start with ecclesiology and, included in that, with what might be called 'Israel-ology.' The two cannot be separated in a scriptural narrative approach: Israel and the Church are one elect people, and rethinking their relation is fundamental to ecumenism. This rethinking must be theological" (Lindbeck, *The Church in a Postliberal Age*, 200).

37. On the connection between Christology and Israelology in the overall structure of Christian doctrine, see Marshall, *Trinity and Truth*, 169–79.

and their practice deadly.[38] While literal observance of the Jewish law (i.e., the "old" law) is now forbidden, it has been replaced by a Christian law (i.e., the "new" law), which includes a sacramental system that effects a union with Jesus in his fulfillment of the old law.[39] The typical Protestant version agreed that the "old" law was dead and deadly, but saw its replacement not in a "new" law embodied in an ecclesial sacramental order but instead in the faith of the individual believer.[40] In either case, a supposed Pauline gospel that repudiated Jewish "works of Torah" took its place at the heart of the biblical canon, operating hermeneutically as the implicit guide to all biblical interpretation.[41] Jewish Scripture (i.e., the Christian Old Testament) was read through this lens, as were the Gospels, the Acts of the Apostles, the General Epistles, and the Apocalypse of John.[42]

These interpretations of Paul and the preeminence they assign to his teaching assume the providential demise of the *ecclesia ex circumcisione*. The *ecclesia ex gentibus* was now the *ecclesia simpliciter*. The significance

---

38. See Tapie, *Aquinas on Israel and the Church*. The use of the terms "dead" and "deadly" in reference to the Jewish law derives from Aquinas and is found in the context of his summary of the views of Jerome and Augustine. See Kinzer, *Postmissionary Messianic Judaism*, 201–9.

39. See Levering, *Christ's Fulfillment of Torah and Temple*.

40. Edmund Schlink summarizes the Lutheran position, rooted in its reading of Paul, as follows: "Apart from faith in the Gospel, man will lose his way in the Bible. . . . The necessary result . . . is only Roman legalism, which still teaches Old Testament ceremonies as divine law and uses them exegetically as a basis for the priesthood, for masses, etc." (Schlink, *Theology of the Lutheran Confessions*, 71). The Reformed tradition adopted a more positive view of the "old" law, particularly its moral and civil ordinances; but Reformed theologians continued to treat the ceremonial law, now fulfilled in Christ, as dead and deadly in its literal observance.

41. This is especially evident in the work of Luther, who, while interpreting the Pauline doctrine of justification by faith, stated that "on this article rests all that we teach and practice against the pope, the devil, and the world" (*Smalcald Articles*, Part II, Article I, cited in Tappert, *The Book of Concord*, 292). But it is equally true of the entire Western tradition (other than the radical reformation), as demonstrated by the unrivalled theological influence exercised through the ages by commentaries on Romans and Galatians.

42. While drawing extensively from the Pauline theological heritage, the Eastern Christian tradition ascribed more weight to the Johannine writings. This supplied a hermeneutical lens that was more Christological and less ecclesiological than that prevalent in the Western tradition. Nevertheless, the Johannine polemics against *hoi Ioudaioi* established a Jesus vs. Judaism model in the East, which ultimately differed little from the Christianity vs. Judaism or faith vs. works (i.e., Judaism) models prevalent in the West. In addition, the book of Acts and the Synoptic Gospels exercised no more direct influence in the East than in the West. They were read through the dual lens of John and Paul, and their witness to the *ecclesia ex circumcisione* was thereby muted.

of the opening twelve chapters of the book of Acts, which focus on Peter and the Jerusalem community, was now limited to displaying the historical link between the Old and New Testament people of God. The manifestly Jewish ecclesial reality of Acts 1–12 provided no model that could or should be imitated. On the other hand, the remaining chapters of the book of Acts, which describe Paul and his missionary exploits, provided a permanent paradigm for the ongoing life of the Jesus community. They portrayed Paul as the apostle entrusted with the gospel for the gentiles—that is, the one and only universal gospel which brought into being the one and only people of God. In this way Acts prepared readers of the biblical canon to receive the Pauline letters that followed as foundational teaching. Peter may technically have retained his status as the chief of the apostles, but even the church of Rome viewed itself as the church of Peter *and* Paul, and the *de facto* impact of a universalized Pauline theology far outweighed that of Peter.

The resurrection of a corporate Jewish ecclesial presence in the modern era challenges this Western hermeneutical consensus. Is Paul really combatting the distinctive practices of Judaism and undermining the enduring positive theological significance of genealogical Israel in order to establish a universal ecclesial order in which there is no visible distinction between Jew and gentile? Is he not rather fighting to create an equal place for gentiles *as gentiles* (i.e., as those from the nations who are no longer idolaters) in the one people of God?[43] Consequently, should we not take more seriously the limited scope of Paul's apostolic sphere, which he acknowledges when he states that he had been called "to bring about the obedience of faith *among all the gentiles*" (Rom 1:5; see also Rom 15:16; Gal 1:15–16; 2:7–10)? If a distinct Jewish corporate space is essential for the *ekklēsia* to be fully itself, then the Pauline writings cannot function as the universally appropriate hermeneutical lens for interpreting the biblical message as a whole.[44]

---

43. Many recent Pauline studies, operating according to historical (rather than theological) methodology, have reinterpreted the Pauline letters in just this way. See, for example, Nanos and Zetterholm, *Paul within Judaism*; Boccaccini and Segovia, *Paul the Jew*; Thiessen, *Paul and the Gentile Problem* and *A Jewish Paul*; Fredriksen, *Paul: The Pagans' Apostle*; Nanos, *Reading Paul within Judaism* and *Reading Corinthians and Philippians within Judaism*; Tucker, *Reading Romans after Supersessionism*; and Campbell, *Romans: A Social Identity Commentary*.

44. Spurred by engagement with Messianic Jews, Douglas Harink has recently argued that the insights of "bilateral ecclesiology" lead naturally to the acknowledgment of a "bilateral New Testament." In his words, "as a hermeneutical principle, we must see that Paul's message is only secondarily *for* Jews, and only *about* Jews in the context of

At the same time, the reemergence of a corporate Jewish ecclesial presence elevates the hermeneutical significance of the book of Acts and sheds light on the paradigmatic character of the Jerusalem community it depicts (the first twelve chapters of Acts may no longer be casually dismissed as the record of a transitional phase of ecclesial history). The hermeneutical centrality of Acts coheres with twenty-first-century studies of the New Testament canon that suggest that the book of Acts is the hinge on which the entire canon turns, with the Jerusalem Council serving as the key to its canonical message.[45] The antecedent Marcionite canon centered on the Pauline letters was recontextualized by ordering those letters *after* the Gospels, and by positioning Acts as the hermeneutical lens for understanding Paul. In this way Paul's role was subordinated to that of Peter, the Twelve, and even James, who together represented the Jerusalem center of the *ekklēsia*. This sheds light on Luke's account of Paul's visits to Jerusalem after each of his missionary journeys (15:2; 18:22; 21:15)—the first and the last of which conclude with authoritative directives from James which Paul readily obeys (15:13–21; 21:18–26). Just as the *ecclesia ex gentibus* is only a part and not the whole of the people of God, so her preeminent apostle is only a part and not the whole.

The second challenge posed by the resurrection of Jewish ecclesial communities concerns the historical continuity of the people of God. Here the challenge differs for Protestants (on one side) and Catholics and Orthodox Christians (on the other). From their inception, the churches of the Reformation based their legitimacy on the claim that the church of Rome had fallen into apostasy and was now corporately equivalent to the harlot of Revelation 17–18, with its bishop taking the role of the Antichrist.[46] The Reformers differed in their assessment of when this fall had occurred and, as centuries passed and new Protestant movements were born, the tendency was to push the "great apostasy" further and further back in time. Regardless of when the rupture was alleged to have taken place, the necessity for visible and institutional continuity was denied as a matter of principle. As the Scots Confession of 1560 put it, "the notes, signs, and assured tokens whereby the spotless bride of Christ is known

---

the specific mission to the nations" (Harink, "Accountabilities, Tensions, Transformations," 60).

45. See Trobisch, *The First Edition of the New Testament*, 80–82; Miller, *How the Bible Came to Be*, 78–80.

46. See Schlink, *Theology of the Lutheran Confessions*, 279–83, for a summary of the sixteenth-century Lutheran teaching on the Antichrist and his kingdom.

from the horrible harlot, the false Kirk, we state, are neither antiquity, usurped title, lineal succession, appointed place, nor the numbers of men approving an error."[47] If visible continuity were essential, the churches of the Reformation had no leg on which to stand.

Judaism is itself a diverse and complex tradition, but all expressions of Jewish religious life share one thing in common: commitment to the historical continuity of the Jewish people. Jewish identity is fundamentally about genealogical descent from Abraham, Isaac, and Jacob, Sarah, Rebecca, Rachel, and Leah, and continuing their covenant relationship with God until the coming of the messianic age. As Franz Rosenzweig noted, the paradigmatic Jewish relationship is cross-generational.[48] It is this relationship that ensures the continuity of the family and that symbolizes the diachronic drive at the heart of Jewish life.

Jewish ecclesial communities bring this diachronic momentum to their corporate expression of faith in Jesus. Their witness raises a question for Protestants: have we adequately reflected on what it means to be the visible people of God, a community of faith extended through time, and not merely a collection of redeemed individuals? Have we borne sufficient witness to the transforming grace of the good news embodied in a people transmitting across generations not only texts and truths but also a renewed corporate life? Protestants are accustomed to defending themselves against the historical claims of the Catholics and the Orthodox, but the challenge raised by resurrected Jewish ecclesial communities cannot be dealt with by arguments concerning governmental structure or sacramental theology. The questions here are more basic: who, what, and where is Israel? What is the relationship between biblical Israel, the apostolic *ekklēsia*, the Jewish people, the historical church(es), and my own Protestant congregation?[49]

---

47. Presbyterian Church (USA), *Constitution of the Presbyterian Church*, 3.18.

48. "It is the alliance between grandson and grandfather; through this alliance the people becomes the eternal people; for when grandson and grandfather behold one another, they behold in each other at the same moment the last grandson and the first grandfather. So the grandson and the grandfather, both of them, and both together are for the one who stands between them the true embodiment of the eternal people.... In old men and in children we experience our Judaism immediately" (Rosenzweig, *The Star of Redemption*, 367).

49. It is striking that the Scots Confession cited above describes the church of Rome as Satan's "pestilent synagogue," and in denying the need for visible ecclesial continuity cites the example of Jerusalem: "For... Jerusalem had precedence above all other parts of the earth, for in it were priests lineally descended from Aaron, and greater numbers followed the scribes, pharisees, and priests, than unfeignedly believed and followed

A final question for Protestants arises from the Jewish practice of national solidarity. Jewish communities around the world differ in their theological beliefs and religious practices, yet they all recognize one another as part of the same people. The diachronic continuity of Jewish life translates into a synchronic awareness of kinship across doctrinal and geographical borders. When a Jewish community in Europe or Latin America suffers physical attack, Jewish communities of all stripes rally together to offer a common response. When commemorating the Shoah, entire Jewish communities gather, regardless of denominational difference—Chabad, Orthodox, Conservative, Reform, Reconstructionist, Humanist. With all the passionate disagreement that exists among Jews, the sense of being part of one people remains strong. Can the same be said for Christians, especially Protestants? When Coptic churches are burned in Egypt and Coptic Christians are murdered, do Baptists feel as though their own flesh and blood has been assaulted? When Assyrian Christians in Iraq are expelled from their homes, do nondenominational Protestants feel the pain as their own? For many Protestants, the assumption of radical discontinuity on the diachronic level translates into acceptance of radical division on the synchronic level. The living reality of Jewish ecclesial communities calls this acceptance into question.

The treasures carried by the *ekklēsia*—the gift of the Holy Spirit, the presence of the resurrected Jesus, the truths of the good news—are not accessible apart from the earthen vessels that contain them in this world. In the language of Augustine, the *totus Christus* includes his entire earthly body, his people.⁵⁰ That is why the risen Jesus could ask of Saul, "why do you persecute *me*?" (Acts 9:4). Protestants are too often tempted to separate the treasure from the humble container. When succumbing to this temptation, they mistake the part for the whole. Jewish ecclesial communities challenge Protestants to unite body and mind, flesh and spirit, matter and form.

Jewish ecclesial communities offer a different kind of challenge to Catholic and Orthodox Christians. The vision that these Christians share makes continuity of office, teaching, and spiritual life an essential mark

---

Christ Jesus and his doctrine . . . and yet no man of judgment, we suppose, will hold than any of the forenamed were the Kirk of God" (3.18).

50. For the recent attempt of Protestant theologians to recapture this Augustinian theme, see the articles of J. David Moser, Kevin J. Vanhoozer, Michael Horton, and Michael Allen in a *Pro Ecclesia* symposium on Totus Christus (*Pro Ecclesia* 29.1 [2020] 3–67).

of the one, holy, catholic, and apostolic *ekklēsia*. They proudly claim to be the rightful heirs of an unbroken tradition. Protestants question this claim but do so only on the basis of rival doctrinal affirmations abstracted from the biblical text. Resurrected Jewish ecclesial communities, on the other hand, challenge Catholic and Orthodox appeals to continuity on the basis of a more ancient genealogical connection. They bear in their own bodies a Jewish flesh that they share with Mary, the Twelve, James, the early Jerusalem community, and Jesus himself. A renewed Jewish ecclesial reality asks of Catholics and Orthodox this difficult question: in the absence of a Jewish corporate expression in your midst, may you truly claim unbroken continuity with the apostles? Cardinal Lustiger argued that the word "catholic"—which means "according to the whole"—originally referred to the *ekklēsia*'s character as a body of Jews and gentiles.[51] Is a church without a corporate expression of Jewish life fully catholic? Moreover, does not such a Jewish corporate expression need to take its place at the heart rather than the periphery of the catholic *ekklēsia*?

This challenge becomes all the more potent when it is recalled that the Catholic and Orthodox churches lack such Jewish corporate environments because authorities within their traditions deliberately and forcefully eliminated them.[52] These church bodies bear responsibility for the deficit that is now revealed by the resurrection of Jewish ecclesial communities. It is not an accident of history but a choice made by the most respected voices of the historical gentile *ekklēsia*.

Catholic and Orthodox Christians rightly value the continuity of the people of God and they have preserved treasures for which all believers in Jesus should be grateful. When encountering Protestant churches, they justifiably consider them as younger siblings. When encountering groups

---

51. Lustiger, *Promise*, 6, 125; *On Christians and Jews*, 15.

52. The outlawing of distinctive Jewish practice in the Catholic and Orthodox traditions was formalized in Canon 8 of the decisions of the Second Council of Nicaea in 787 (see Kinzer, *Postmissionary Messianic Judaism*, 209). This canon was implemented through imposition upon Jewish candidates for baptism of a vow by which they solemnly renounced Jewish practice (see Parkes, *The Conflict of the Church and the Synagogue*, 394–400). The canon also took its place as part of the standard moral teaching of the church, as seen by this formulation of Thomas Aquinas: "Just as it would be a mortal sin now for anyone, in making a profession of faith, to say that Christ is yet to be born, which the fathers of old said devoutly and truthfully; so to it would be a mortal sin now to observe those ceremonies which the fathers of old fulfilled with devotion and fidelity" (*Summa Theologica of St. Thomas Aquinas*, 2:1086). During the dark days of the Spanish Inquisition, many Jewish believers in Jesus suffered death for violating this prohibition.

of Jewish disciples of Jesus, on the other hand, the tables are turned. As Pope John Paul II recognized, the Jewish people are the older sibling.[53] Jewish disciples of Jesus represent the older brother, now entering with the Father into the banquet hall.[54] Might the entry of the Jewish brother not only serve to chasten Catholic, Orthodox, and Protestant, but also encourage these scattered gentile siblings to move away from the corners of the room and meet in the center as fellow members of one body?

Once again, the challenge posed by Jewish ecclesial communities consists of the call to a greater catholicity. For too long, Christians—whether Protestant, Catholic, or Orthodox—have been tempted to mistake the part for the whole. That "whole" includes not only a remnant of Jews, but the Jewish people as a corporate body. As the apostle Paul recognized, the Jewish remnant who become disciples of Jesus represent their kinsmen who have not yet entered the banquet hall (Rom 11:16). Ultimately, the "partial hardening" will come to an end and at that time "all Israel" will rejoice in the feast (Rom 11:25–26). Only then will the catholicity of the *ekklēsia* be expressed in eschatological fullness.

## CONCLUSION

Just as Peter the Jew was compelled to reconsider what Jesus and Scripture taught about gentiles in light of what he experienced in Jaffa and Caesarea, so gentile Christians today are summoned to rethink what Jesus and Scripture teach about Jews in light of the new realities they are encountering. The regathering of Jewish people to their ancestral land and the rebirth of Jewish ecclesial communities are historical phenomena that demand a theological response. Israel *outside* the borders of the *ekklēsia* challenges Christians to rethink their view of Israel's enduring covenant and the role of the Jewish people in history. Israel *within* the *ekklēsia* challenges Christians to rethink Christian identity itself. Both realities call Christians to a humble recognition that they are a part and not the whole.

Might that humble response prepare the way for Israel outside to *become* Israel within—or, from another angle, for the *ekklēsia* of the

---

53. Pope John Paul II, *Spiritual Pilgrimage*, 63.

54. On the theological significance of the parable of the prodigal son (and his older brother) in the context of Luke and Acts, and in the historical context of the twenty-first century, see Kinzer, *Jerusalem Crucified*, 154–55; Kinzer, *Postmissionary Messianic Judaism*, 121–22.

nations to take its place as Israel's partner at the eschatological banquet? That we do not know for sure. But we do know that we are summoned to live worthily of the One who called us, Jews and gentiles, to be a twofold people for his name.

CHAPTER 5

# Recovering the Jewish Character of the *Ekklēsia*

Jewish Disciples of Jesus and the Jewish-Christian Schism

> *A great deal of scholarship exists on the path and process that led to Judaism and Christianity becoming two distinct and mutually exclusive religious traditions. Kinzer examines this historical development from a theological lens, assessing its alignment with the divine will and its long-enduring consequences. For Kinzer, the presence and significance of Jewish followers of Jesus in the early centuries CE offers the frame by which we ought to understand the remarkable re-emergence of a visible Jewish wing of the ekklēsia in our own day, and what this might mean for our understanding of "catholic Christianity."*[1]

---

1. An abbreviated version of this chapter was presented in 2019 at a conference on "The Jewish Roots of Christianity" at Beeson Divinity School in Birmingham, Alabama, organized as an initiative of The Institute of Anglican Studies at Beeson. The current chapter was published alongside the other conference papers in McDermott, *Understanding the Jewish Roots of Christianity*, 184–200.

## JEWISH ROOTS AND JEWISH CHARACTER

FOR MANY CHRISTIANS TODAY, there is an intense interest in the Jewish roots of their faith.[2] It demonstrates the perennial appeal of studies that aim to shine light on the *ekklēsia* in its earliest phases. But the current interest is novel in focus, for in previous centuries most Christians thought of Judaism as a legalistic and arid religion that paled in comparison to Christianity. Many Christians now admire Judaism and are eager to trace their own tradition back to such a respected source.

While the study of ancient origins has its own intrinsic attraction for scholars and those of a romantic disposition, contemporary Christian fascination with the Jewish roots of Christianity derives less from interest in the past and more from concern for the present and the future. The recovery of Jewish *roots* offers the promise of recovering the *ekklēsia*'s Jewish *character*. The desire for such a recovery arises especially among certain evangelicals who find their own ecclesial traditions lacking in spiritual depth, liturgical substance, and communally formative praxis. But it also emerges among Christians devoted to their traditions who seek missing puzzle pieces for a divided and spiritually lethargic *ekklēsia*.

My concern in the present chapter is the recovery of the Jewish character of the *ekklēsia* in the present and the future. The primary thesis is simple: this recovery requires the visible corporate presence of Jewish disciples of Jesus within the *ekklēsia*. To be Jewish, the *ekklēsia* needs Jews and it needs them to live in a way that accentuates rather than hides their identity as Jews. The secondary thesis is also simple: to create an environment where the difficult task of restoring a distinct Jewish expression of ecclesial life is possible, Christians must conduct a ruthless historical self-assessment of actions, beliefs, attitudes, and practices that contributed to the mutually exclusive identity-formation of the Christian and Jewish traditions. Here attention is given to historical roots, but the roots in question are those that produced enmity and separation rather than those that yielded a hidden continuity.

Since the latter thesis is a condition for the realization of the former, I will begin there. But my concern throughout is theological and

---

2. While evangelical writings on this theme are voluminous and widely recognized, similarly motivated Catholic works are also appearing and gaining a large audience. A noteworthy example of this are the popular books by Catholic biblical scholar Brant Pitre, *Jesus and the Jewish Roots of the Eucharist* and *Jesus and the Jewish Roots of Mary*.

prescriptive (i.e., present- and future-oriented), rather than historical and descriptive.

## DID SOMETHING GO WRONG?

For Christians who esteem the Jewish tradition, it is self-evident that at a certain point or points in her history the *ekklēsia* took a wrong turn. Her proper consciousness of her own election expanded to include an improper judgment concerning genealogical Israel's rejection. But this wrong turn can be understood in two different ways. The first accepts the distinguishing of the two communities as a necessary, providential, and irreversible historical development. That was not the wrong turn. Instead, the error consisted in the church's denial of the enduring covenantal status of genealogical Israel, and of the partnership that God intended for these two distinct communities. Such a perspective on the separation is commonly held by Christians engaged in Jewish-Christian dialogue, since it poses no threat to the current identities of each dialogue partner.

Philip Cunningham, a leading Catholic authority on Jewish-Christian relations, articulates the position clearly:

> I think most Christians and Jews unthinkingly assume that "something went wrong" with the parting of the ways—the origins of Christianity and rabbinic Judaism as separate communities. This separation is thought to have been contrary to God's will. . . . I suggest an alternative presupposition to "something went wrong" in retelling the Christian story today. Why can we not suppose that the origins of our two traditions unfolded *according* to God's will?[3]

Thus, God wills that the *ekklēsia* be "a Gentile assembly rooted in Israel's story."[4] On one side stands the genealogical descendants of the biblical patriarchs and matriarchs; on the other side stands a community of gentiles who share in the Jewish spiritual inheritance. This was the divine purpose all along.

The main problem with this construal is Christological: it suggests that Jesus has no significance for the Jewish people apart from the creation of a new "Gentile assembly rooted in Israel's story." This is a strange way of construing a message concerning one who died with the words

---

3. Cunningham, *Seeking Shalom*, 199–200.
4. Cunningham, *Seeking Shalom*, 215.

"King of the Jews"[5] inscribed above his head, and whose name became forever linked to Israel's royal title "Christos/Messiah."[6] But this Christological problem also has ecclesiological consequences: if the story of Jesus has no significance for Jews, then the resurrected Jesus has no ongoing point of contact with his own kin and so also has no such point of contact to offer the "Gentile assembly" gathered in his name.

The second approach to the wrong turn challenges the necessity of the separation itself. Christians who take this approach view the parting as a tragic schism rather than a providential differentiation. As Hans Urs von Balthasar put it, "what providence intended was the unity of the two peoples, not the rift between them, the schism. . . . [T]he divorce which uprooted the young Church from its mother-soil not only caused immeasurable harm to the Israel that remained behind, but involved a serious danger for the Church."[7] In similar fashion, Thomas Torrance describes the split as "a disastrous schism," a "rift in the one people of God from which neither Jews nor Christians have yet recovered."[8]

In a collection of essays entitled *The Jewish-Christian Schism Revisited*, John Howard Yoder depicts the "standard account" of the rupture as a narrative that assumes its historical inevitability:

> The historical development of the first three centuries of our era ended with the presence, in many of the same places, of two separate, mutually exclusive systems (intellectual, cultural, social) called "Jews" and "Christians." Therefore the standard account claims that this mutual exclusiveness must be assumed to have been inevitable, i.e. logically imperative, even when and where the actors in the story which led to that outcome did not know that yet.[9]

Yoder then challenges this assumption: "If God's purpose might have been to offer a different future from the one which actually came to be, then we do not do total justice to God's intent in the story by reading it as

---

5. For more on the significance of this title, see chapter 1 in this volume.

6. On the significance of this word attached to the name "Jesus" in the New Testament, see Novenson, *The Grammar of Messianism*.

7. Balthasar, *Martin Buber and Christianity*, 99. Writing as a Catholic before Vatican II, Balthasar places the onus of this schism on the shoulders of the Jewish people rather than the *ekklēsia*, but he refuses to accept the rupture as a divinely willed historical event that had beneficial effects.

8. Torrance, *Theology in Reconciliation*, 27.

9. Yoder, *The Jewish-Christian Schism*, 31.

if the outcome he did not want, but which did happen, had to happen."[10] Daniel Boyarin offers a related historiographical critique, focusing less on divine intent and more on the decisions and actions of authorities on both sides: "Rather than a natural-sounding 'parting of the ways,' such as we usually hear about with respect to these two 'religions,' I will suggest an imposed *partitioning* of what was once a territory without border lines."[11]

As articulated by Cunningham, the first perspective on the split accepts the *gentile* character of the *ekklēsia*, while nevertheless asserting that she is "rooted in Israel's story." The *ekklēsia* thus has a relationship to Israel through a partially shared narrative, but she does not reside in the midst of Israel, nor does Israel reside in her midst. The second perspective, on the other hand, presumes that such a mutual indwelling was divinely willed, and only rebellious human actions severed the visible bond. It is this second way of defining the wrong turn of the *ekklēsia* that befits Christians seeking not only a better relationship with Jews, but also the recovery of the Jewish character of their own faith and life.

## MUTUALLY EXCLUSIVE IDENTITY-FORMATION

In this chapter, I am focusing on the character of the *ekklēsia* and her role in the "Jewish-Christian schism." However, as we reflect on the wrong turn taken by the *ekklēsia* in relation to the Jewish people, we must acknowledge that both sides tacitly conspired to produce the schism. They did so by constructing negative boundaries that denied the affirmative core at the heart of their partner's identity.

Jewish corporate identity in the early centuries of the Common Era was founded on the conviction that genealogical Israel was beloved, chosen, and set apart by the creator of the universe for a particular priestly task in the world. That conviction received its definitive grounding and formulation in the Torah, which also provided the concrete practices ordering Israel's priestly life. Jews disagreed in their interpretation of the story told by the Torah and the manner in which its commandments were to be lived out. But a broad consensus existed in the belief that God had chosen Israel to be a priestly people and that Israel's priestly life involved (among other things) observing Sabbath and festivals, circumcising sons

10. Yoder, *Jewish-Christian Schism*, 47.
11. Boyarin, *Border Lines*, 1.

on the eighth day after birth, avoiding certain foods, and looking in hope and longing for the restoration of Jerusalem.[12]

At the heart of ecclesial identity from this community's earliest days was the conviction that Jesus was the Messiah of Israel and the Lord of the universe. Her members were baptized into union with the crucified and risen Lord. Ecclesial faith in Jesus eventually assumed a creedal form recited by the baptized to demonstrate their loyalty to the one who had redeemed them. The Creed spoke not only of the divine Son but also of the Father and the Holy Spirit, but the trinitarian confession derived from the revelation imparted through the incarnation of the eternal Logos in Jesus of Nazareth.

After a sustained period of mutual struggle, the Jewish people and the *ekklēsia* translated their core affirmations into reciprocal boundary-marker negations. As Daniel Boyarin has shown, the diverse and flexible Jewish monotheism of the first century narrowed in the following era to exclude veneration of the one regarded by some Jews as the incarnate Logos.[13] In parallel fashion, the Jesus movement of Torah-observant Jews and allied gentiles described in Acts of the Apostles narrowed in the following era to become a community of gentiles excluding Jewish identity and practice.[14] In this way, the *ekklēsia* rejected not only the Jewish people but also her own Jewish roots and character. She, like the Jewish people, had constructed a negative boundary consisting of the denial of the other's core affirmation.

To a later era, these historical developments appear logical and inevitable. But that is an optical illusion created by casting a backward gaze on the flow of history. In the present we assume that we are responsible agents making choices that have consequences. Future outcomes are contingent on those choices. Those outcomes are not the necessary products of inexorable forces. There is no good reason to hoard this perspective for the present and the future, and deny it to the past.

Jewish and ecclesial core affirmations did not inevitably morph into mutual boundary-setting negations. Our ancestors were responsible agents and their corporate decisions resulted in "the partitioning of Judaeo-Christianity." We must live with the historical consequences of

---

12. See Burns, *The Christian Schism in Jewish History*, 61–99.

13. Boyarin, *Border Lines*, 89–147.

14. On Acts of the Apostles, see Kinzer, *Jerusalem Crucified*, 160–224. On developments in the post-apostolic view of Torah and the Jewish people, see Kinzer, *Postmissionary Messianic Judaism*, 181–212.

those decisions, but we are not doomed to sanctify their choices or repeat their mistakes. We also are responsible agents, and our responsibility includes the obligation to assess their actions in light of the possibilities that have opened up in our own day.

## THREE PARTIES IN CONFLICT RATHER THAN TWO

The denial of one another's core affirmations resulted eventually in mutually exclusive communal identities. The "Gentile assembly" of Christians could now relate to the Jewish people only as a reality alien to its own corporate self. But what about those who embraced *both* core affirmations and did so as genealogical descendants of the patriarchs and matriarchs?

The imagery of separation, rupture, or schism suggests two parties who once shared a common social space and then at some point (or points) ceased to do so. Missing from such a construal of Jewish and Christian history is a feature of the early Jesus movement that was a bone of contention from the start: namely, its essential twofold constitution as a community of gentiles *and* Jews. The Jesus-believing gentiles had been initiated into a Jewish social and cultural environment that demanded that they renounce worship of their ancestral gods. They had joined a community centered in Jerusalem and led by Jews. But these gentiles did not thereby become Jews. As the New Testament demonstrates, the tension introduced by this awkward arrangement was the source of many disputes within the young *ekklēsia*. It was also the source of conflict with the rest of the Jewish world.

When signs of acute stress surfaced in the second century, *three* corporate characters appear in the drama rather than merely two: (1) the wider Jewish community, (2) the Jewish members of the *ekklēsia*, and (3) the emerging gentile Christian church. Viewing the schism from the Christian side, James Dunn noted this thirty-plus years ago: "The parting of the ways was more between mainstream Christianity and Jewish Christianity than simply between Christianity as a single whole and rabbinic Judaism."[15] More recently, Anders Runesson has made the same point: "It seems clear that the real parting of the ways, the process that created what is now the Christian church, took place between Jewish

---

15. Dunn, *The Partings of the Ways*, 239.

believers in Jesus and non-Jewish believers in Jesus, *not* more generally between 'Jews' on the one hand and 'Christians' on the other."[16]

While Dunn makes this observation in the context of a book devoted to historical description of the "partings of the ways," he proceeds to cautiously raise the normative question addressed by Balthasar and Yoder: "Whether Jewish Christianity could or should have been retained within the spectrum of catholic Christianity is an important question which it may now be impossible to answer."[17] Despite such caution, Dunn believes that developments in our own day call us to attempt the impossible: "But it is a question which we need to address now with renewed seriousness in the light of the current phenomena of messianic Jews."[18]

As Dunn notes with British understatement, "Jewish Christianity" was not "retained within the spectrum of catholic Christianity." To be blunt, it was forcibly suppressed. As Jerome famously stated at the turn of the fourth century, "insofar as they want to be both Jews and Christians, they are neither Jews nor Christians."[19] For this church father, and for the Christian tradition that followed after, the separation between Jew and Christian was an irreversible and divinely ordained fact, not a tragic schism. In suppressing Jewish life within, "catholic Christianity" denied its own Jewish character. Subterranean Jewish roots continued to provide essential nutrition, but the visible expression of Jewish life had been purged from the *ekklēsia*.

Almost a century ago, James Parkes depicted the difficult circumstances endured by these early Jewish disciples of Jesus:

> There is no more tragic group in Christian history than these unhappy people. They, who might have been a bridge between the Jewish and the Gentile world, must have suffered intensely at the developments on both sides which they were powerless to arrest. Rejected, first by the Church, in spite of their genuine belief in Jesus as the Messiah, and then by the Jews in spite of their loyalty to the Law, they ceased to be a factor of any importance in the development of either Christianity or Judaism. . . . And they on their side might well say . . . that the Gentile Church by its attitude made the acceptance of the Messianic claims of

---

16. Runesson, "Who Parted from Whom?," 70.

17. Dunn, *Partings*, 239.

18. Dunn, *Partings*, 240.

19. Jerome's statement occurs in the context of a letter exchange with Augustine. It is found in Letter 40 of *The Works of St. Augustine*.

Jesus impossible to the Jew; and that the perpetual statement of the Gentile leaders that the Jews continued to reject Christ was fundamentally untrue, because they were being offered Him only upon conditions which were false and impossible for a loyal Jew to accept—in other words, an attitude to the whole of Jewish history and to the Law which was based upon Gentile ignorance and misunderstanding, and was quite unsupported by the conduct of Jesus Himself.[20]

As Dunn recognized more than thirty years ago, the modern Messianic Jewish movement poses a challenge to modern "catholic Christianity." That challenge calls for historical reflection and assessment, but even more it summons the *ekklēsia* to responsible decision-making in the present which will shape the ecclesial future. A third actor in the ongoing drama has once again entered the stage, and the *ekklēsia* from among the nations must decide anew whether to embrace her, reject her, or pretend she does not exist.

## JEWISH DISCIPLES OF JESUS IN THE MODERN ERA

Writing in 1991, James Dunn referred to the "current phenomena of messianic Jews." He was taking account of a movement that at that time was only two decades old. It was one particular expression of the Jesus movement of those days and it displayed the marks of the evangelical Protestant environment in which it was born.

Dunn's focus on this new movement was understandable. Messianic Jewish congregations had been established. Through them many Christian leaders encountered a Jewish ecclesial reality for the first time. But the Messianic Jewish movement did not spring into being *ex nihilo*. It already had a long history, albeit under a different name. Moreover, similar Jewish stirrings were occurring in the context of ecclesial traditions remote from the evangelical scene. To adequately assess the significance of the "current phenomena," as Dunn calls it, we must place it in a broader context.

The Messianic Jewish movement of the 1970s was a mutation of the Hebrew Christian movement which had begun a century and a half before.[21] The birth of Hebrew Christianity in the early nineteenth century

20. Parkes, *The Conflict of the Church and the Synagogue*, 92–93.
21. On the history of Messianic Judaism and its pre-history in Hebrew Christianity, see Kinzer, *Postmissionary*, 263–302; Rudolph, "Messianic Judaism in Antiquity and in

constituted a radical shift in Christian sensibility. For the first time in more than a thousand years, Jewish followers of Jesus viewed their membership in the Jewish people in a positive light and claimed that their faith in Jesus was compatible with their Jewish identity. Furthermore, they banded together and formed organizations aimed at mutual support. The first such entity was the *Beney Avraham* (Children of Abraham), established in England in 1813. More enduring was the Hebrew Christian Alliance founded in 1866, likewise in England. All the participants in these new organizations were Jewish Protestants, loyal members of various Protestant denominations. But they were now also proudly proclaiming their identification with the Jewish people.

In the 1880s, Joseph Rabinowitz worked to establish the first Hebrew Christian congregation in Kishinev, Bessarabia (Moldova).[22] His efforts gained worldwide attention and led to the formation of other Hebrew Christian congregations in various locations. In part as a response to Rabinowitz, the idea of an international Hebrew Christian church captured the imagination of many Anglicans. The respected scholar G. H. Box promoted the project aggressively as did Paul Levertoff, a Jewish Anglican priest and one of the world's leading authorities on Jewish mysticism.[23] While these initiatives were unsuccessful, they reveal how drastically Christian attitudes toward the Jewish-Christian schism had changed.

The influence of Rabinowitz extended beyond Protestant and Anglican spheres. One of the most renowned Russian religious philosophers of the late nineteenth century, Vladimir Solovyov, wrote an article about Rabinowitz in 1885.[24] Solovyov argued that Russians should not view the Kishinev experiment as a Protestant or sectarian phenomenon, but instead as a renewal of the Jewish expression of the church. Solovyov, in turn, was the hero of Fr. Alexander Men (1935-90), a Jewish priest and martyr of the Russian Orthodox Church.[25] Thousands entered the Orthodox Church through the ministry of Fr. Alexander and many of them

---

the Modern Era," 21-36; Cohn-Sherbok, *Messianic Judaism*; Rausch, *Messianic Judaism*; Jocz, *The Jewish People and Jesus Christ*, 201-61.

22. See Kjaer-Hansen, *Joseph Rabinowitz and the Messianic Movement*.

23. See Jocz, *Jewish People and Jesus Christ*, 238-39. On Levertoff, see the biographical sketch provided by his translator, Brian Reed, in Levertoff, *The Religious Thought of the Chasidim*, 205-56.

24. Solovyov, *The Burning Bush*, 330-45.

25. See Hamant, *Alexander Men*. Fr. Alexander kept a picture of Solovyov on the wall of his study.

were Jews. Fr. Alexander continued to identify as a Jew and encouraged his Jewish followers to do the same.[26] It is striking that the evangelistic work of Fr. Alexander prospered among Jews in Russia in the 1970s and 1980s, the very decades that gave birth to the Messianic Jewish mutation of Hebrew Christianity.

Independent of both the Hebrew Christian/Messianic Jewish movement and the parallel phenomenon in the Russian Orthodox Church, a similar impulse took hold in the Catholic world. In 1955, the Association of Saint James was founded as a Catholic body seeking to develop Hebrew-speaking Catholic communities in the young State of Israel.[27] In this Israeli context, Fr. Elias Friedman, a Jewish Carmelite monk, first proposed in 1965 the establishment of a distinct Jewish Catholic community.[28] In 1979 (the same year as the formation of the first congregational association in the Messianic Jewish movement), Fr. Friedman founded the Association of Hebrew Catholics.[29] While this organization has spread mainly in the English-speaking world, a similar movement has emerged among Jewish Catholics in France, inspired by the example and teaching of the late Jewish archbishop of Paris, Cardinal Jean-Marie Lustiger. Like Joseph Rabinowitz, Fr. Alexander Men, and Fr. Elias Friedman, Cardinal Lustiger identified publicly with the life and destiny of the Jewish people.[30]

Few Christians are aware of these remarkable figures and fewer still have noticed the connections that link each to the others. Once the developments have been identified and viewed synoptically, the volume of the question raised by the Messianic Jewish movement is amplified tenfold. Did the *ekklēsia* indeed take a wrong turn when it suppressed

26. On this movement of Jews who became Orthodox Christians, see Kornblatt, *Doubly Chosen*.

27. For a historical novel about one of the important Israeli Jewish Catholic figures of this era, Fr. Daniel Rufheisen, see Ulitskaya, *Daniel Stein*. The author is a Russian Jewish Orthodox Christian.

28. Fr. Friedman later expressed his vision for Jewish Catholicism in *Jewish Identity*.

29. See www.hebrewcatholic.net/.

30. See Lustiger, *The Promise* and Duchesne, *Jean-Marie Lustiger*. It is noteworthy that Cardinal Lustiger wrote an introduction to Yves Hamant's biography of Fr. Alexander Men, in which he described his one meeting with the Russian priest. The introduction begins in this way: "When I found myself face to face with Fr. Alexander Men, I felt I had known him all my life. He seemed like a brother, a friend who would always be close to me, despite the fact that we only spoke for perhaps ten minutes" (Hamant, *Alexander Men*, 209).

Jewish life in its midst? Did she thereby tear asunder the people of God, deny her Jewish roots, and disfigure her Jewish character? Do these varied contemporary movements provide a new opportunity to reverse this disastrous course?

## DEVELOPMENTS IN CATHOLIC THOUGHT

While few Christians have noted the reemergence of Jewish Jesus communities in the modern era or have deemed them worthy of attention, the Roman Catholic Church constitutes a prominent exception to this generalization. In *Searching Her Own Mystery*, I tell the story of the Roman Catholic–Messianic Jewish Dialogue Group, which began in 2000 and continued until 2016.[31] The formation of this group was not an official act of the Vatican (nor of the Messianic Jewish community), but a private initiative of some influential leaders on both sides. On the Catholic side, the "influential leaders" who supported the project included Cardinal Lustiger, Pope John Paul II, Pope Benedict XVI, and (in its final phase) Pope Francis. Catholic participants in the Dialogue Group included the late Cardinal George Cottier, theologian of the Papal Household, and Cardinal Christoph Schönborn, archbishop of Vienna.[32]

It is remarkable that the leadership of the Catholic Church, which has been at the forefront of engagement with the Jewish community since the Second Vatican Council, has taken notice of the Messianic Jewish movement. But that fact coheres with the consistent witness of Cardinal Lustiger, who was a key advisor to Pope John Paul II on Jewish affairs.[33] The pope's appointment of Lustiger as archbishop of Paris in 1980 was controversial, in large part because of Lustiger's Jewish background and commitments. In the 1970s, he had been studying Hebrew and preparing to immigrate to Israel.[34] When he was named bishop of Orléans in 1979, Lustiger wrote to the pope, "reminding him who I was and who my parents were." That first episcopal appointment was difficult enough for French Catholics to swallow. Would they now accept a Jewish archbishop

---

31. Kinzer, *Searching Her Own Mystery*, 35–37.

32. Cardinal Schönborn wrote the foreword to *Searching Her Own Mystery*, xi–xiii.

33. The story of Cardinal Lustiger's relationship with Pope John Paul II and their joint concern for Jewish maters is told in Ilan Duran Cohen's 2014 movie, *The Jewish Cardinal*.

34. Connelly, *From Enemy to Brother*, 283.

of Paris? Adding fuel to the fire, the Jewish community also was concerned "with the elevation of a convert who had always said that he still considered himself a son of the Jewish people."[35] Lustiger's claim to a post-baptismal Jewish identity had challenged the mutually exclusive definitions of "Jew" and "Christian" regnant in both communities. Undeterred, the Polish pope elevated Lustiger, who soon became his close friend.

In his writings, Cardinal Lustiger refers to a fifth-century mosaic in the Roman church of Saint Sabina, which depicts two female figures, one representing the *ecclesia ex circumcisione* (the church from the circumcision), the other representing the *ecclesia ex gentibus* (the church from the gentiles).[36] He refuses to treat the loss of the *ecclesia ex circumcisione* as a natural and inevitable historical development, but instead describes it as "both a sin and tragedy."[37]

Moreover, he sees the "rebirth of the State of Israel" as creating a situation in which "an *Ecclesia ex circumcisione* . . . once again becomes conceivable."[38] Cardinal Lustiger's thinking on this topic takes a radical turn when he discusses the original (and still valid) meaning of the term "catholic" (i.e., "according to the whole") as referring to the church's twofold character as the *ecclesia ex circumcisione* and the *ecclesia ex gentibus*.[39] In other words, the *ekklēsia* is "'according to the whole' because she is composed of both Jews and pagans."[40] For Lustiger, true catholicity requires a visible Jewish presence in the *ekklēsia*.

Official Catholic teaching appears to be inching in the direction first explored by Cardinal Lustiger. That became evident in the 2015 Vatican document *The Gifts and Calling of God Are Irrevocable*, produced by the Commission for Religious Relations with the Jews in commemoration of the fiftieth anniversary of *Nostra Aetate*. The new document contains seven sections. The second section is entitled "The special theological status of the Jewish-Catholic dialogue." Portraying the unique nature of

---

35. Weigel, *Witness to Hope*, 390.

36. Lustiger, *On Christians and Jews*, 131. In a 1985 document entitled "Notes on the Correct Way to Present the Jews and Judaism in Preaching and Catechesis in the Catholic Church," the Vatican Commission for Religious Relations with the Jews also refers to the *ecclesia ex circumcisione* and the *ecclesia ex gentibus* (section III, paragraph 23).

37. Lustiger, *On Christians and Jews*, 70.

38. Lustiger, *The Promise*, 126.

39. Lustiger, *The Promise*, 125.

40. Lustiger, *The Promise*, 6. See also Lustiger, *On Christians and Jews*, 15.

the Jewish-Christian relationship, paragraph 15 of that section recounts the early history of the Jesus community:

> The first Christians were Jews; as a matter of course they gathered as part of the community in the Synagogue, they observed the dietary laws, the Sabbath and the requirement of circumcision, while at the same time confessing Jesus as the Christ, the Messiah sent by God for the salvation of Israel and the entire human race.... In the early years of the Church, therefore, there were the so-called Jewish Christians and the Gentile Christians, the *ecclesia ex circumcisione and the ecclesia ex gentibus*, one Church originating from Judaism, the other from the Gentiles, who however together constituted the one and only Church of Jesus Christ.

The language favored by Cardinal Lustiger is here employed in a Vatican document, but only in reference to the early centuries of the *ekklēsia*. Does this twofold constitution of the *ekklēsia* still have meaning today? Is catholicity still related in some way to the *ekklēsia*'s character as a community that unites gentiles with Jews? The document appears to address this question affirmatively in its sixth section, entitled "The Church's mandate to evangelize in relation to Judaism." That section drew much media attention because of the statement in paragraph 40 that "the Catholic Church neither conducts nor supports any specific institutional mission work directed towards Jews." The ensuing media frenzy led most commentators to miss the crucial opening sentence of paragraph 43: "It is and remains a qualitative definition of the Church of the New Covenant that it consists of Jews and Gentiles, even if the quantitative proportions of Jewish and Gentile Christians may initially give a different impression." Echoing Cardinal Lustiger's definition of catholicity, this statement suggests that the rebirth of a visible *ecclesia ex circumcisione* hoped for by the Cardinal would be welcomed by Rome.

Such an interpretation of paragraph 43 draws support from the structure of the document as a whole. As noted, *The Gifts and the Calling of God Are Irrevocable* consists of seven sections. Close analysis of the arrangement of those sections suggests that the document is ordered in a chiastic pattern, with the first section corresponding to the seventh, the second to the sixth, the third to the fifth, and the fourth (entitled "The relationship between the Old and New Testament and the Old and New

Covenant") standing as the document's centerpiece.[41] If this is correct, then the statement in paragraph 43 (in the sixth section) corresponds to the material concerning the *ecclesia ex circumcisione* and the *ecclesia ex gentibus* in paragraph 15 (in the second section). Thus, the "qualitative definition of the Church" as a community consisting of "Jews and Gentiles" reflects the permanent ecclesial constitution that in the early *ekklēsia* took a twofold corporate form, and that could take such a form once again.

Leaders in the Catholic Church appear to be seeing something that many other Christians are missing. Just as they pioneered a new way forward in relation to the Jewish people at the Second Vatican Council—a way that other churches then followed—so they once again may comprise the vanguard in recovering the Jewish character of the *ekklēsia* through restoring its twofold constitution.

## WHAT IS AT STAKE?

The Messianic Jewish movement, the Hebrew Catholic movement, and Jewish streams in the Russian Orthodox Church are miniscule phenomena in a global context. They are easy to ignore in the face of the massive environmental, demographic, political, economic, and social crises that command worldwide attention. But the *ekklēsia* will do so at her own peril.

These modern spiritual currents cannot be disentangled from the wrong turn that produced the Jewish-Christian schism. And that rupture was, as Balthasar saw, the

---

41. Here are the section titles of the document, with the chiastic pattern elaborated:
   1) A brief history of the impact of "Nostra aetate" (*Where Jewish-Catholic dialogue has been*)
      2) The special theological status of Jewish-Catholic dialogue (*A sui generis relationship from the beginning*)
         3) Revelation in history as "Word of God" in Judaism and Christianity (*Christ & Torah*)
            4) The relationship between the Old and New Testament and the Old and New Covenant
         5) The universality of salvation in Jesus Christ and God's unrevoked covenant with Israel (*Christ & Israel*)
      6) The Church's mandate to evangelize in relation to Judaism (*Still a sui generis relationship today*)
   7) The goals of dialogue with Judaism (*Where Jewish-Catholic dialogue is going*)

primary schism, of which . . . all the subsequent schisms within the Church are but reproductions. . . . No attempt to bridge the later breaches in the unity of the Church can be usefully pursued or seen in the light of a promising conclusion except with reference to the original schism from which they all follow. Nor is the matter between Israel and the Church one which can be studied as though it were a subsidiary ecumenical question; it needs to be treated in a quite different way, and far more radically than divisions among Christians.[42]

Balthasar's friend, Karl Barth, was of the same opinion. In the year following the conclusion of the Second Vatican Council, Barth offered these words of counsel to the members of the Vatican's Secretariat for Christian Unity: "The ecumenical movement is clearly driven by the Spirit of the Lord. But we should not forget that there is finally only one genuinely great ecumenical question: our relations with the Jewish people."[43]

The *ekklēsia* now has the opportunity to rediscover her Jewish roots *and* to recapture her Jewish character. In so doing, she may experience unanticipated fruit in spheres that seem distant from the matter at hand. More is at stake than meets the natural eye. Balthasar and Barth viewed the Jewish-Christian schism with spiritual vision and recognized the implications of its reversal.

Something extraordinary has occurred in recent centuries among Jews who believe in Jesus. Through them an exit ramp may lead off the highway of schism, with signs pointing back to the road not taken long ago. May all members of the *ekklēsia* be blessed with eyes to see, ears to hear, and hands to turn the wheel.

---

42. Balthasar, *Martin Buber*, 99–100.
43. Cited in van Buren, *A Theology of the Jewish-Christian Reality*, Part 2, 251–52.

CHAPTER 6

# The Community of Jewish Disciples of Jesus

Standing and Serving as a Priestly Remnant

*Drawing upon Scripture, Jewish and Christian liturgy, and key theological sources, Kinzer analyzes the distinguishing features of both Israel and the ekklēsia as well as the ekklēsia's composition as a community of Jews and gentiles. He reflects specifically on the priestly vocation of Jewish followers of Jesus, helpfully mapping a spectrum of what covenant fidelity looks like for this subset of both Israel and the ekklēsia. Kinzer argues that we need to understand this group as having a very specific calling of witness and testimony to the way in which God has bound these two groups together, representing the core reality of each community to the other and the fact that they can only properly be understood with reference to one another.*[1]

---

1. This chapter originated as a paper delivered at the Hashivenu Forum, a Messianic Jewish think tank, in 2011. An adapted version (directed to the wider sphere of Jewish disciples of Jesus) was then presented at the 2011 meeting of the Helsinki Consultation on Jewish Continuity in the Body of the Messiah in Paris, France, which addressed the theme "*Am Israel*—Our People." The original version was published in *Kesher* 28 (2014) 79–101; this chapter is a revised version of the *Kesher* article.

## JEWISH AND CHRISTIAN COMMUNITY

Franz Rosenzweig

IN MY BOOK *POSTMISSIONARY Messianic Judaism*, I argued that the identity of the Christian church is inseparable from that of the Jewish people. I also argued that the identity of the Jewish people is inseparable from the person of its crucified and risen Messiah, Jesus of Nazareth. It follows that the Jewish people and the Christian church are so intimately bound together that it is impossible to adequately understand one without also understanding the other. We distort our presentation of Jewish community and Christian community when we treat them as two separate topics that can be studied independently.[2]

In the history of Jewish and Christian thought, few have attempted to look systematically at the Jewish people and the Christian church in this way. The greatest thinker to do so has been Franz Rosenzweig. In *The Star of Redemption*, Rosenzweig employs the image of stellar fire to convey the indissoluble connection between these two communities and their complementary characters and roles. The Jewish people constitutes the burning core of the star, folded in on itself as a dynamic singularity; the Christian community, in all its multiplicity, comprises the rays of heat and light that radiate ever outward.

According to Rosenzweig, both communities exist for the purpose of bearing witness (*das Zeugnis*). Ultimately, their joint testimony is to God and to God's self-revelation, which each community has received. Rosenzweig often depicts this witness against the backdrop of the temporal nature of human existence; each community witnesses to eternity (*die Ewigkeit*)—eschatological time—and its proleptic accessibility in the present age. As the eternal people (*das ewige Volk*) the Jewish community embodies the eternal life (*das ewige Leben*), whereas the Christian church is the eternal way (*der ewige Weg*). Only together in God, as the wholeness of the star of redemption, do they make up the eternal truth (*die ewige Wahrheit*). Rosenzweig thus utilizes Jesus's self-designation from John 14:6 (the way, the truth, and the life) to characterize these two interdependent communities of witness.

To convey the distinctive manner in which each community bears witness and the implications for its distinctive communal character,

---

2. For an illustration of a treatment of Jewish and Christian history which seeks to avoid this distortion, see Sandgren, *Vines Intertwined*.

Rosenzweig exploits cognate forms of the German verb *zeugen*. The root verb can mean either "bear witness" or "generate, beget." Derived forms remove the ambiguity: *bezeugen* means "bear witness," while *erzeugen* means "generate, beget." Let us see what Rosenzweig does with these words and concepts:

> The bearing witness for eternity [*Das Zeugnis für die Ewigkeit*], which in the eternal people [i.e., the Jewish people] is furnished by the begetting [*die Erzeugung*] must be furnished as real bearing witness [*Zeugnis*] on the eternal way [i.e., by Christians]. . . . Instead of the fleshly flowing on of the one blood which testifies [*bezeugt*] to the ancestor in the begotten grandson [*im gezeugten Enkel*], here the pouring out of the Spirit in the uninterrupted stream of baptismal water from one to the other must establish the mutual participation of bearing witness [*die Gemeinschaft des Zeugnisses*]. . . . The mutual participation [*Die Gemeinschaft*] becomes one through the testified faith [*den bezeugten Glauben*]. . . . [The Christian] knows his own life is on the way that leads from the [first] coming to the coming again of Christ.[3]

The Jewish people bears witness to its own "eternity" by transmitting its biological life from one generation to the next. In contrast, the Christian church must be reborn over and over again through the waters of baptism, which enable those who are born biologically with an existence outside the church to become spiritual participants in its community of witness (*Gemeinschaft des Zeugnisses*).

Rosenzweig further explains the difference in the two forms of witness by examining the role faith (i.e., that which is confessed and believed) plays in each:

> This knowledge [i.e., that one's life takes place on the path that leads from the first to the second coming of Christ] is faith. It is faith as content of a bearing witness [*eines Zeugnisses*]. It is faith in something. It is exactly the opposite to the faith of the Jew. His [the Jew's] faith is not content of a bearing witness [*eines Zeugnisses*], but product of begetting [*Erzeugnis einer Zeugung*]. He who is begotten as Jew [*Der als Jude Gezeugte*] bears witness to his faith [*bezeugt seinen Glauben*] by continuing to beget [*fortzeugt*] the eternal people. He does not have faith in something, he is himself the having of faith; he is faithful in an immediacy that no Christian dogmatic can ever afford for itself. This having

---

3. Rosenzweig, *The Star of Redemption*, 362–63. Original German from Raffelt, *Der Stern der Erlösung*.

faith sets little value on its dogmatic fixing; it has existence—this is more than words. But the world is entitled to words. A faith that wants to win the world must be faith in something.... And this is exactly the main point of the Christian faith. It is dogmatic in the highest sense, and must be so. It cannot renounce its words. On the contrary: it cannot have enough to do with words, it cannot invent enough words. It would really have to have a thousand tongues. It would have to speak all languages. ... So the Christian faith, with bearing witness [*der zeugnisablegende christliche Glaube*], is the first begetter [*erst der Erzeuger*] of the eternal way in the world, whereas the Jewish faith follows in the steps of the eternal life of the people as begotten product [*als Erzeugnis*].[4]

When Christians bear witness (*bezeugen*) to their faith in Christ by confessing it publicly and verbally in fulfillment of their missionary calling, they beget (*erzeugen*) the eternal way in the world by enabling those outside the church to enter its eschatological community of witness. Christian faith must be verbal and conceptual, focused perpetually on a cognizable object (i.e., the person of Christ) external to the witnessing community. As such, *this faith gives birth to the community*. In contrast, Jews have no outwardly oriented missionary calling (beyond serving as the source of life and light for the church in its missionary labor). Faithful Jews do not have faith in some cognizable object external to themselves; instead, *their faith derives from their lived existence as a community and is equivalent to that existence*. In consequence, they bear witness (*bezeugen*) to their faith in the God of Israel by begetting (*erzeugen*) Jewish children.

For Rosenzweig, the Jewish people are a particular biological community, a natural family, adopted by God to bear lived witness to eternal life in the midst of a temporal world. The Christian church, on the other hand, is a universal spiritual community united by bonds of faith that is called by God to bear verbal witness to the eternal way in the midst of that same temporal world. Without the eternal way of the Christian church, the eternal life of the Jewish people remains an isolated island in a sea of paganism. Without the eternal life of the Jewish people, the eternal way of the Christian church degenerates into gnostic philosophy, a set of ideas abstracted from the concrete particularities of real earthly existence.

This manner of depicting the Jewish-Christian distinction has been controversial among Jews since Rosenzweig. Many prefer to see Judaism

---

4. Rosenzweig, *The Star of Redemption*, 363.

as a universal religion along the lines advocated by Maimonides.⁵ According to this view, conversion to Judaism is a sensible if not a necessary course of action for non-Jews. Judaism stands as a superior rival to Christianity, rather than its complement. Other Jewish thinkers accept the particularity of Jewish peoplehood and its inherently biological character, but reject any notion that the Jewish people are dependent on the Christian church for the realization of Israel's universal mission. A few, adopting a radical fringe position, even question whether gentiles share equally with Jews in humanity, and merit the same basic protections (such as the right to life).⁶ In each of these views, Judaism and the Jewish people stand independent of Christianity and the Christian church.

Nevertheless, there are influential Jewish voices who have adopted an approach similar to that of Rosenzweig. Among Jewish theologians, the most prominent is Michael Wyschogrod.⁷ Among Jewish historians, the most noteworthy is Daniel Boyarin.⁸ Both Wyschogrod and Boyarin emphasize the particular embodied character of the Jewish people and resist attempts to treat Judaism as a universal religion along the lines of Christianity. Both also appreciate the positive and complementary role Christianity can play as a universal community bearing witness to the God of Israel. Beyond this, each finds it impossible to explore the meaning of Jewish communal identity apart from an exploration of Christian communal identity.

## Israel: One, Holy

While some prominent Jewish and Christian thinkers have adopted a vision of the Jewish people and the Christian church resembling that of Rosenzweig, this vision finds little or no expression in the corporate worship or popular consciousness of the two communities. Nevertheless, we discover in their most central liturgical and creedal affirmations of self-identity a parallel formulation whose implications have not been adequately considered or assimilated by either group.

---

5. For a forceful presentation of this position, see Neusner, *Recovering Judaism*.

6. See the controversy in Israel early this century over the book, *Torat Hamelekh*. Ben-Shimon, "The Murder Midrash," 14–17.

7. Wyschogrod, *The Body of Faith* and *Abraham's Promise*.

8. Boyarin has written extensively from this perspective. See, for example, *Carnal Israel*, *A Radical Jew*, *Dying for God*, and *Border Lines*.

The Nicene Creed refers to the church as "one, holy, catholic, and apostolic." These four attributes, linked together as one phrase, have become the classical way of describing the Christian church. The Creed makes no explicit reference to the people of Israel, and this omission reflects the supersessionism that characterizes the dominant theology of the early church.[9] While a supersessionist interpretation of the Creed's articulation of ecclesial self-identity undoubtedly captures the intent of most of those in the early church and afterwards who recited it as part of their liturgical confession of faith, I will argue for an alternative interpretation that takes account of a parallel formulation from the Jewish liturgy.

At the heart of the Jewish liturgy, recited twice daily, stands the *Shema*. The opening line of the *Shema* consists of an acknowledgment of Israel's God as one. In the blessing that precedes and prepares for the recitation of the *Shema*, the divine unity serves as the basis and goal for a corresponding unity among those who confess it—initially, in the heart of each Jew ("unify our heart to love and fear your Name"), and then in the community of dispersed Jews throughout the world who are to be gathered together as one ("bring us in peace from the four corners of the earth, and lead us upright to our land"). As a result of God's action to establish Israel in spiritual and physical unity, Israel will acknowledge in eschatological fullness the unity of the divine Name ("draw us near to your great Name in truth, to acknowledge you and your unity in love").

The linkage between God's oneness and Israel's oneness becomes even more explicit in *Shomer Israel*, a short intercessory poem found in the penitential service recited on most days after the morning and afternoon *Amidah*. This poem pleads with God to preserve Israel, and does so with reference to the *Shema*:

> Protector of Israel, protect the remnant of Israel;
> Do not let Israel perish—those who say "*Shema* Israel."
> Protector of a nation that is one (*goy echad*), protect the remnant of a nation that is one;
> Do not let perish a nation that is one—those who acknowledge the unity of your Name [by saying] "Adonai is our God, Adonai is one."[10]

As in the blessing before the *Shema*, the oneness of Israel derives from the oneness of the God who has chosen Israel and finds expression and

---

9. For a fuller analysis of the Nicene Creed, see chapter 2 of this volume.
10. All translations from the siddur are mine, unless otherwise noted.

confirmation in Israel's acknowledgment of God's oneness in its daily recitation of the *Shema*.

What is meant here by *goy echad*? If the *Shema* itself is a guide, the phrase refers to Israel's uniqueness in the eyes of God. Just as Israel worships Adonai as its only God, so Adonai singles out Israel as his own special possession. This is why reference to Israel's identity as a *goy echad* provides the prayer with such compelling petitionary force: if we are truly your unique people in all the earth, how can you possibly permit us to perish from the earth? At the same time, the phrase may also suggest the common national identity shared by all Jews. Though Israel be scattered to the four corners of the earth, yet it is one and the same people wherever it resides—and this oneness will be confirmed on the day God gathers it together from the earth's ends to its own land. In the meantime, this common identity finds expression daily when Jews throughout the world say, "*Shema Israel, Adonai Elohaynu, Adonai echad.*"

The same connection between God's oneness and Israel's oneness is found in the blessing for Shabbat inserted in the *Amidah* of the Shabbat *Minchah* service:

> You are one, and your Name is one,
> And who is like your people Israel (*mi ke'amcha Israel*),
> a nation one (*goy echad*) in the earth.

The first clause employs the language of the *Shema* to honor Adonai as Israel's only sovereign and the world's only God. The second clause honors Israel as a people uniquely related to the world's only God, in language drawn directly from 1 Chronicles 17:21: "And who is like your people Israel, a nation one in the earth." Here we discover the biblical source for the phrase *goy echad* that plays such a central role in *Shomer Israel*.

The sages of the Talmud already discern a relationship between the *Shema* and 1 Chronicles 17:21. In a vivid flourish of anthropomorphic midrash, they suggest that God wears *tefillin*, just as God's people wear *tefillin*. The *tefillin* worn by Jews carry within them the text of the *Shema*, in which Adonai is acknowledged as Israel's only God. What text lies in God's *tefillin*? According to Rav Hiyya bar Avin, the heavenly *tefillin* contains 1 Chronicles 17:21—God's reciprocal acknowledgment of Israel as a people set apart as to be God's unique possession.[11] As Adonai is one God, so Israel is one people.

---

11. b. *Berachot* 6a.

We now move on to our second basic designation for Israel. A liturgical unit associated with the *Shema* is the *Kedushah*—the threefold angelic confession of God's holiness. The *Kedushah* is found initially in the first blessing before the *Shema*. The liturgy introduces the *Kedushah* with the following words:

> All [i.e., the angels] accept upon themselves, one from another, the yoke of the kingdom of heaven, granting permission to one another to sanctify the One who formed them, in serene spirit, pure speech and sweet melody. All, as one [*ke'echad*], proclaim his holiness, saying in awe: holy, holy, holy.[12]

The phrase "accept the yoke of the kingdom of heaven" is a well-known rabbinic idiom referring to the act performed by Israel in the recitation of the *Shema*.[13] Thus, what Israel does on earth by reciting the *Shema* is enacted in heaven when the angels recite the *Kedushah*. In both cases, God is acknowledged as the only universal sovereign. And in both cases, the unity of those rendering the acknowledgment is a condition and a consequence of its fulfillment.

The term "holy" designates God as unique, set apart, distinct in character and power from all else that is. The first blessing before the *Shema* stresses also the holiness of those angels who confess God's holiness: "May You be blessed, our Rock, King and Redeemer, Creator of holy beings."[14] Applied to creatures, the term "holy" refers to a status of belonging to God in a special way, of being set apart from other creatures for divine use, and of participating in a creaturely manner in God's unique character and authority. The word thus has much in common with the word "one" as it is employed in the *Shema* and in liturgical and midrashic materials related to the *Shema* that speak of Israel as a *goy echad*.

Returning to *Shomer Yisrael*, we should not be surprised, therefore, to discover that the third stanza refers to the *Kedushah* and deals with the holiness of God and the holiness of Israel.

> Protector of a holy nation [*goy kadosh*],
> protect the remnant of a holy people [*'am kadosh*];
> Do not let perish a holy nation [*goy kadosh*],
> those who repeat the threefold holiness to the Holy One.

---

12. Sacks, *Koren Siddur*, 92–94.
13. See, for example, m. Berachot 2:2.
14. Sacks, *Koren Siddur*, 92.

The phrase *goy kadosh* derives from the divine words to Moses at the inauguration of the Sinai covenant and is there associated with the phrase *mamlechet kohanim* ("kingdom of priests").[15] The synonymous phrase *'am kadosh* appears in a parallel passage in Deuteronomy 7:6, which speaks of God's loving choice of Israel. Like the angels in heaven, God calls Israel to fulfill on earth a priestly role, living as a holy people set apart for worship and for bearing witness to the holiness of the divine Name. Since God has chosen Israel in love for such a crucial role, how can the Holy One let the holy nation perish?

God is one, and so Israel is one. God is holy, and so Israel is holy. These nearly identical statements, in nearly identical form, are likewise found in the Shabbat *Amidah* for the afternoon *Minchah* service when it is recited privately. We already saw the beginning of the fourth blessing:

> You are one, and your Name is one,
> And who is like your people Israel (*mi ke'amcha Yisrael*),
> a nation one (*goy echad*) in the earth.

The words immediately preceding these in the private recitation of the *Amidah* are as follows:

> You are holy, and your Name is holy,
> And holy ones praise you daily, Selah.
> Blessed are You, *Adonai*, the holy God.

The opening words of the fourth blessing are formulated to echo the words of the blessing that precedes it. God is holy, and God's Name is holy, and holy ones (the angels in heaven, Israel on earth) perform priestly service by acknowledging God's holiness in praise. God is one, and God's Name is one, and a nation that is one celebrates its unique calling by delighting in the holy rest of Shabbat.

Because God is holy and unique, so the people God has chosen for priestly service in the world is also holy and unique. It is truly a *goy* (nation) and an *'am* (people)—a particular ethnic unit joined by kinship, culture, and political life, and demonstrating visible continuity through time. However, it is unique among all the nations and peoples of the earth, for it has been singled out for God's special priestly service. As a nation and a people, it bears witness to the Holy One who has called it into being and who sustains it through its historical journey. In all its fleshly particularity, it endures as the eternal people (*das ewige Volk*).

---

15. Exod 19:6.

## The Community of Messiah: Catholic, Apostolic

Assuming a vision of Israel's oneness and holiness similar to that found in later Jewish liturgy, the book of Ephesians proclaims that God has acted in Israel's Messiah to include those from the nations in an expanded eschatological commonwealth of Israel. Ephesians teaches a high view of Israel's status and calling, but it roots that unique dignity among the nations in God's eternal election and blessing in the Messiah.

> Blessed be the God and Father of our Lord Jesus the Messiah,
> who has blessed us [Israel] in Messiah
> with every blessing of the Spirit in the heavenly places,
> even as he chose us [Israel] in him before the foundation of the world,
> that we [Israel] should be holy and blameless before him....
> In him [Messiah] ... we [Israel] who first hoped in Messiah
> have been destined and appointed to live for the praise of his glory.[16]
> (Eph 1:3-4, 11-12)

Even before the incarnation, Messiah dwelt with Israel as the destined realization of God's eschatological promise and Israel's hope. As a consequence, those remote from Israel were remote from Messiah.

> Therefore remember that at one time you from among the nations...
> were separated from Messiah, alienated from the commonwealth of Israel,
> and strangers to the covenants of promise,
> having no hope and without God in the world.
> (Eph 2:11-12)

Now, through the death and resurrection of Jesus the Messiah and the gift of his Spirit, those from the nations have been assigned a place with the holy ones of Israel:

> So then you [from the nations] are no longer strangers and sojourners,
> but you are fellow citizens with the holy ones [i.e., Israel]
> and members of the household of God,

---

16. All biblical translations are mine, unless otherwise noted. For more on reading these verses from Ephesians 1 as referring to Israel, see McRay, *Paul: His Life and Teaching*, 339-40; Kinzer, *Searching Her Own Mystery*, 69-73; and Schumacher, "The Addressees of Ephesians," 233-47.

> built upon the foundation of the apostles and prophets,
> Messiah Jesus himself being the cornerstone [or capstone],
> in whom the whole structure is joined together and grows into
>    a holy temple in the Lord.
> (Eph 2:19–21)

Through Jesus, these former pagans have been joined to Israel without becoming Jews and the result is an expanded and reconfigured people of God that continues to express Israel's oneness (Eph 4:4–6) and holiness, but in a new form suited to the dawning of the messianic age.

The book of Ephesians would concur with the Nicene Creed that the eschatological multinational expansion of Israel is one and holy. Its oneness and holiness is an extension of the oneness and holiness of the Jewish people, which is itself eternally rooted in the oneness and holiness of God and God's Messiah. The reconciliation of those from the nations with the Jewish people bears witness to the power of God's messianic shalom. However, their reconciled unity does not annul their distinct identity as Jews and non-Jews, but instead requires such distinction in perpetuity so that their joint witness to reconciliation will endure for all ages.

The book of Ephesians would also concur with the Nicene Creed that the eschatological people of God are catholic and apostolic. The word "catholic" means universal or general. In contrast to the Jewish people, whose identity is essentially particular and circumscribed, the community of the Messiah encompasses those from among all the nations of the world. But just as God's infinity does not negate but instead embraces created finitude (as seen preeminently in the incarnation), so the catholicity of the expanded people of God does not abolish but instead sustains and elevates the particularity of Israel. The Jewish people remain at the center of this new catholic reality as a distinct national entity, a sanctified community of kinship and common ethnicity. But the circle of oneness and holiness has now been widened to include all those from the nations who are reconciled with the God of Israel and the Israel of God. Within this widened circle, all are holy—with distinctions in role but no distinctions in access or proximity to God differentiating Jew from Greek, male from female.[17]

In the early centuries of the common era, the term "catholic" was employed to distinguish the faith and life of the authentic *ekklēsia* from

---

17. According to Cardinal Jean-Marie Lustiger, the very term "catholic" refers to the identity of the *ekklēsia* as a twofold community of Jews and gentiles. See Lustiger, *The Promise*, 6, 125; Duchesne, *Cardinal Jean-Marie Lustiger*, 15.

her allegedly fraudulent rivals by focusing on the sectarian and schismatic character of the latter. The true *ekklēsia* could be discerned by determining which Jesus communities throughout the known world maintained relationships of mutual recognition. This was a legitimate criterion of ecclesial discernment. Sadly, by failing to grasp the way the catholic and apostolic community was rooted in Israel's oneness and holiness, the multinational expression of the twofold *ekklēsia* adopted a vision of catholicity that negated rather than elevated the particularity of the Jewish people. As such, it damaged its own vaunted catholicity.

The catholic character of the community of the Messiah derives from its apostolic foundation. As Ephesians 2 proclaims, those who formerly were "strangers and sojourners" are now fellow citizens with the Jewish people in an expanded eschatological Israel that is "built upon the foundation of the apostles and prophets." Ephesians presents Jesus as the keystone rather than the foundation. Why the special emphasis on the apostles? Since Ephesians everywhere exalts the preeminence of Messiah Jesus, we may not read this text as detracting from his unique dignity. On the contrary, to stress the foundational character of the apostles is to point the way to Messiah Jesus. They are the ones authorized by Jesus to be his representatives and he announces through them his message of shalom to the nations (Eph 2:17).[18] The authentic messianic *ekklēsia* is both catholic and apostolic.

Just as the principle of catholicity points to the spatial-geographical continuity of the messianic *ekklēsia*, so the principle of apostolicity points to its temporal continuity. No less than the Jewish people who are its point of origin, the messianic *ekklēsia* is a structured human community that transmits its life continuously from one generation to the next. However, in the two cases the modes of transmission differ. As Rosenzweig perceived, the Jewish people—founded on the twelve sons of Jacob—transmits its life through the begetting (and rearing) of children. In contrast, the messianic *ekklēsia*—founded on the twelve apostles of Jesus—transmits its life through the proclamation of its apostolic faith. But just as the catholicity of the messianic *ekklēsia* assumes and elevates the particularity of the Jewish people (rather than negating it), so the apostolic continuity of the *ekklēsia* likewise confirms the genealogical

---

18. For more on the apostolic character of the *ekklēsia* in Ephesians and its dependence on the Jewish identity of the apostles, see Kinzer, *Searching Her Own Mystery*, 65–82.

continuity of the Jewish people and its enduring national witness to the God of Israel.

The apostolic character of the messianic *ekklēsia* points to its historical source: the person, work, and teaching of a crucified and risen Jew and his foundational commissioning of emissaries—all of them Jewish. The apostolic character of the messianic *ekklēsia* also points to her ongoing mission to receive and enrich the apostolic message transmitted across the generations and to carry that message to all the peoples of the earth. In this way, the apostolic character of the *ekklēsia* establishes its catholic character. It does so both by welcoming all nations into its house and by binding those nations to the heritage of Israel—that community of kinship and ethnicity set apart to be one and holy.

Our reinterpretation of the Nicene vision of the *ekklēsia*—one, holy, catholic, and apostolic—reveals a twofold *ekklēsia* bound forever to the Jewish people. But what does this say about the nature and role of the community of Jewish disciples of Jesus, both in its original first-century context and (in revived form) in the ever-changing circumstances of the twenty-first-century world?

## THE COMMUNITY OF JEWISH DISCIPLES OF JESUS

### A Priestly Remnant

As a nation that is "one" and "holy," the Jewish people corporately have a priestly vocation. Do the Jewish followers of Jesus have a special priestly calling within that priestly people? The New Testament does not teach this explicitly, but it hints that such is the case.

Romans 11 opens with the question, "has God rejected his people?" Paul denies this notion, but in order to do so he must explain why the people of Israel as a whole have not embraced Jesus as the Messiah. He begins by presenting himself, an Israelite and an apostle of the Messiah, as a sign of God's continuing fidelity to Israel (11:1). He then points to his fellow Jewish Jesus-followers, whom he calls "the remnant" and "the chosen," as a similar sign (11:5-7). After offering reasons why God "hardened" the rest of the Jewish people in their response to Jesus, Paul argues that this hardening is temporary and that Israel's future attachment to Jesus will usher in the eschaton (11:15). As an assurance of Israel's destined redemption, he states: "If the dough offered as first fruits is holy, so is the whole lump" (Rom 11:16 RSV).

The logic of Paul's argument in Romans 11 suggests that the term "first fruits" refers back to the Jewish Jesus-followers of verses 5–7. In halakhic terms, the offering of first fruits does not sanctify the remaining dough but instead releases it for secular use.[19] However, the offering of first fruits fits into a wider pattern within the Torah according to which a part is devoted to God as representative of the whole. The Aaronic priesthood constitutes a prime example of this pattern in which the holiness of the representative part confirms and sustains the holiness of that which it represents—the entire people of Israel. Similarly, Jewish Jesus-followers perform a priestly service on behalf of their fellow Jews by representing them before God. As a consequence, all Israel retains its sacred status, in hope of the day of redemption when in fullness it will acknowledge its returning Messiah.

This priestly understanding conditions Paul's use of the term "remnant." A strict notion of remnant involves the substitution of a part for the whole. Following a judgment that destroys or disqualifies an unfaithful majority, a faithful minority—the remnant—takes their place.[20] Priestly election likewise singles out a minority, but it does so for the purpose of representing and sanctifying rather than *replacing* the whole. Paul does not portray Jewish disciples of Jesus in strict remnant terms, but instead as a priestly remnant which *represents* but *does not replace* the Jewish people.

A priestly reading of Romans 11:16 draws support from a curious Pauline idiom. In several texts, Paul refers to the Jesus community of Jerusalem as "the holy ones" (Rom 15:25–26, 31; 1 Cor 16:1; 2 Cor 8:4; 9:1, 12). Elsewhere, Paul applies this term to Jesus-followers in general (e.g., Rom 1:7; 1 Cor 1:2). However, here the word appears to have a special association with the Jewish disciples of Jesus of the Holy City—the true messianic "first fruits."[21] In light of Romans 11:16, we may understand this terminology as implying that the Jewish Jesus community, especially

---

19. Because of this, Benjamin Gordon argues that Paul is not thinking here of the custom of setting aside a small portion of dough for a priest (Num 15:18–20), for in that situation the rest of the loaf is not sanctified but is instead released for normal consumption. Gordon proposes that Paul is instead thinking of a situation in which sacred and unsacred produce are mixed, in which case the unsacred become sacred. See Gordon, "On the Sanctity of Mixtures," 356–59.

20. See Meyer, "Remnant," 669–71.

21. See Tomson, *Paul and the Jewish Law*, 80 (see especially n112). John McRay argues that this use of "holy ones" to refer specifically to Jewish Jesus-followers is common in Ephesians (see McRay, *Paul: His Life and Teaching*, 346–48).

as it was embodied in Jerusalem, constituted a sanctifying first fruits not only for the Jewish people, but also for the *ekklēsia* from among the nations (see Jas 1:18). They performed a priestly function on behalf of the entire people of God.

As an apostle of Jesus and a Jew, Paul himself fulfills this priestly role on behalf of the nations by bringing them the good news:

> Because of the grace given to me by God, to be a liturgical servant (*leiturgos*) of Messiah Jesus in the priestly labor of the good news of God, so that the offering of the those from the nations may be acceptable, sanctified by the Holy Spirit.
> (Rom 15:15–16)

Here the non-Jewish followers of Jesus are the offering that Paul is presenting to God. However, in later verses dealing with the contribution he is bringing to the Jerusalem assembly on behalf of these non-Jews, Paul modifies the metaphor:

> At present, however, I am going to Jerusalem, in service to the holy ones [i.e., the Jerusalem Jesus community]; for Macedonia and Achaia have been pleased to share their resources (*koinōnia*) with the poor among the holy ones at Jerusalem. They were pleased to do this, and indeed they owe it to them; for if those from the nations have come to share (*koinōneo*) in their spiritual blessings, they ought also to be of liturgical service (*leiturgeō*) to them in material things. (Rom 15:25–27)

The Jewish disciples of Jesus in Jerusalem have "shared" their spiritual treasure with those from the nations; in gratitude, those from the nations are now reciprocating by "sharing" their material treasure. As a parallel expression for this "sharing" of material resources, Paul says that those from the nations are performing "liturgical service" by sending material gifts to the Jerusalem community. The reciprocal nature of the "sharing" noted by Paul implies that the "liturgical service" was likewise reciprocal—that the Jerusalem Jesus community had also performed priestly liturgical service for those from the nations by sharing with them their spiritual treasure, the good news of God. In accordance with this inference, Paul's priestly liturgical service for those from the nations (described in Romans 15:15–16) manifests the priestly function of the Jerusalem community, and presumably of the Jewish Jesus-followers as a whole.

In Romans 15, Paul emphasizes the apostolic dimension of the priestly vocation of the first Jewish disciples of Jesus. They had received and transmitted the message of the good news. However, more is involved here. When enumerating the chief privileges of the Jewish people in Romans 9:4-5, Paul brings his list to a climax with these words: "To them belong the patriarchs, and from them, according to the flesh, comes the Messiah." The sanctified kinship bond with both the patriarchs and the Messiah does not in itself assure the eternal destiny of individual Jews, but it does distinguish the entire people of Israel as a nation set apart for special divine service. The "flesh" has its own necessary and proper role to play. We should not be surprised, therefore, to discover that those who are joined to Messiah Jesus in *both* flesh and Spirit—the chosen ones from among the chosen ones—are also summoned to a distinctive priestly vocation. According to this calling, they serve as an effective sign of the enduring *oneness* and *holiness* of Israel in Messiah Jesus, and of the *catholic* continuity in space and the *apostolic* continuity in time of the messianic *ekklēsia*.

While the significance of a fleshly connection to Jesus occupies only a subordinate place in Paul's letters, it appears to have been far more prominent in the thinking of other early Jesus-followers. Richard Bauckham has underlined the central role played by the relatives of Jesus in the first-century Jesus movement, especially in its Jewish sphere.[22] James, leader of the Jerusalem community, was Jesus's brother. According to Hegesippus, the successor to James was Simeon, cousin of Jesus. Bauckham suggests that Simeon's election reflected "a kind of dynastic feeling, to which it seemed right that the leadership of the church should remain in the hands of relatives of Jesus."[23] Such an emphasis on immediate kinship to Jesus among his Jewish disciples makes sense if they likewise saw significance in the less immediate kinship to Jesus shared by all Jews. If God could employ physical descent as a condition for priestly service in the Jerusalem Temple and as a condition for the royal service of the Messiah himself (Rom 1:3), might he not also set apart for special service those united to Messiah by bonds of both faith and kinship?

In addition to treating James with reverence, early tradition in the Jesus movement stressed his priestly role. This is evident in an account from Hegesippus, preserved by Eusebius:

---

22. Bauckham, *Jude and the Relatives of Jesus*, 86–94.
23. Bauckham, *Jude*, 88, 125–33.

> He was called the "Just" by all men from the Lord's time to ours, since many are called James, but he was holy from his mother's womb. He drank no wine or strong drink, nor did he eat flesh; no razor went upon his head; he did not anoint himself with oil, and he did not go to the baths. He alone was allowed to enter into the sanctuary, for he did not wear wool but linen, and he used to enter alone into the temple and be found kneeling and praying for forgiveness for the people, so that his knees grew hard like a camel's because of his constant worship of God, kneeling and asking forgiveness for the people.[24]

Hegesippus combines Nazirite and priestly elements in his description of James. The brother of Jesus is even presented as resembling the high priest on Yom Kippur, who prays in the sanctuary—where he alone is permitted to enter—for the forgiveness of the nation.[25] While its historical value regarding James is questionable, this early tradition supports our contention that James and the Jerusalem community were viewed widely in priestly terms.

Our conclusion at this point is simple: any sustained reflection on the meaning of the community of Jewish disciples of Jesus must account for the priestly dimension of their identity and assign it a position of central importance.

## Diverse Modes of Priestly Service

The New Testament texts examined above suggest that a priestly vocation extends to all communities of Jewish disciples of Jesus. However, these texts also differentiate among such communities, demonstrating an awareness of the diverse manifestations of the one priestly calling.

All of the Jewish followers of Jesus portrayed in the New Testament lived as full members of the Jewish community. However, they did so in different ways, depending on their geographical locations and their particular callings. Thus, James and the Jerusalem assembly of Jesus-followers displayed an unambiguous attachment to Jewish communal life. They worshipped at the Temple alongside the rest of the Jewish community, presenting their prayers and offerings and learning Torah in the Temple courts. Most likely, they had only limited contact with non-Jews, welcoming Jesus-followers from the nations as guests but not expecting

---

24. Eusebius, *Ecclesiastical History* (II:23), 1:171.
25. For commentary on this text, see Painter, *Just James*, 125–27.

many to remain as residents in the Holy City. James and the Jerusalem assembly of Jesus-followers represented the corporate witness of the messianic *ekklēsia* to Israel that its election and destiny were summed up in Messiah Jesus. They also represented the corporate witness to all non-Jewish followers of Jesus that the messianic *ekklēsia* existed only as an eschatological extension of Israel's national life.

In contrast, Paul and his Jewish colleagues (such as Barnabas, Silas, and Timothy) spent substantial amounts of time with non-Jews. Like James and his Jerusalem assembly, they related to Jewish communal institutions as their own, attending the synagogue and recognizing the legitimacy of its authorities.[26] However, their particular task consisted of carrying the message of Jesus to the nations of the earth. They also announced the good news to fellow Jews in the diaspora, but this was not their immediate and primary vocation (Rom 1:5, 13-15; 15:15-16; Gal 1:16; 2:9), though the ultimate redemption of Israel appears to have been their long-term goal (Rom 11:13-14). In their work with non-Jews, they stressed the ongoing importance of the Jewish people and fostered identification with the community of Jesus-followers in Jerusalem. This was the purpose of the offering for the "holy ones" in Jerusalem, which occupied so much of Paul's attention (Rom 15:25-33; 1 Cor 16:1-4; 2 Cor 9:1-15; Gal 2:10).

We know less about Peter, but he seems to occupy a middle-ground between James and Paul. In the initial period following the resurrection of Jesus, Peter presides over the Jerusalem community of Jesus-followers and focuses exclusively on bearing witness to Jesus before the Jewish people. He is the main spokesmen for the community before the Temple governors. In Paul's account of an important conference in Jerusalem, Peter takes the lead (along with James and John) as the apostle bringing the good news to "the circumcision (Gal 2:7-9)."

On the other hand, according to Acts 10 Peter is the one who opens the door for the proclamation of the good news to non-Jews by traveling to Caesarea and immersing Cornelius. Paul reports that there are some among the Corinthian Jesus-followers who claim special loyalty to Peter (1 Cor 1:12; 3:22). Paul also informs us that Peter traveled on apostolic journeys with a wife (1 Cor 9:5). These Pauline references to Peter do not state that Peter worked and lived among non-Jews in his travels, but it is likely that his audience included both Jews and non-Jews. Paul's account

26. Otherwise, Paul would not have submitted to synagogue discipline, as he evidently did (2 Cor 11:22-24).

of his dispute with Peter at Antioch reveals that Peter attempted to walk a middle path between the way of James and that of Paul (Gal 2:11–14). The first letter of Peter hints at a Roman provenance for its composition, and early tradition reports that Peter died there as a martyr (1 Pet 5:13). This is consistent with a picture of him as traveling extensively and laboring among both Jews and non-Jews.

The New Testament thus suggests that groups of Jewish disciples of Jesus in the first century adopted a variety of different modes of communal interaction depending on their geographical locations and the particular apostolic roles they were called to play. They all lived as faithful Jews, but faithfulness demanded different behavior in diverse relationships and contexts. For James and the Jerusalem community, called to demonstrate the rootedness of the messianic *ekklēsia* in the people of Israel and to bear witness to Israel's future redemption in Jesus, covenant faithfulness meant immersion in the heart of Jewish communal life and scrupulous adherence to widely accepted halakhic norms. For Paul and his apostolic team, called to champion the eschatological expansion of the commonwealth of Israel among the nations of the world in Messiah Jesus, covenant faithfulness required the halakhic flexibility incumbent on every diaspora Jew whose life involved substantial contact with non-Jews. For Peter and his associates, called to a service of unity on behalf of the twofold messianic *ekklēsia*, covenant faithfulness meant keeping all relational channels open—with the wider Jewish community, with James and the Jerusalem assembly, and with Paul and the mission among the nations.

While tensions existed among those called to diverse modes of priestly service as Jewish disciples of Jesus, all acknowledged their interdependence. Paul implies that his own priestly service among those from the nations is an extension of the priestly service of the "holy ones" in Jerusalem and he places a priority on raising funds for those "holy ones." James affirms the Pauline mission and sees it as a sign that God is truly rebuilding the fallen booth of David—i.e., that God is restoring Israel under the reign of the promised Son of David (Acts 15:13–18). Most clearly of all, Peter's role as unifier depended on the success of both James and Paul. These three apostles may have exasperated one another, but they could not do without one another.

Having examined the interrelated nature of Jewish and Christian community and the first-century precedents for a community of Jewish disciples of Jesus, we are now ready to consider our own situation in the twenty-first century.

## PRIESTLY COMMUNITY IN THE TWENTY-FIRST CENTURY

Given the distinctive character of the community of Jewish disciples of Jesus, how shall we approach the challenges that face us today? I will offer five recommendations.

### 1. The Ways of James, Peter, and Paul

In accordance with the apostolic diversity of Jewish modes of life and service seen above, we would be wrong to assume that there is one normative expression of community appropriate for all Jewish disciples of Jesus. While all communities of Jewish disciples of Jesus will be committed *both* to Jewish covenant fidelity and the welfare of the wider Jewish world *and* to the twofold messianic *ekklēsia* and its universal mission among the nations, each community will have its own emphasis based on its location, capabilities, and calling.

The primary vocation of Messianic Jewish communities today falls within the James to Peter spectrum. Like James, we are summoned to live within the Jewish world as witnesses to God's enduring fidelity to Israel in Messiah Jesus and as priestly representatives of those among whom we live. This is the most difficult but also the most crucial aspect of our calling. It means that most Messianic Jewish communities should be situated in areas of high Jewish population density, and that we must do all that is in our power to participate in the life of the wider Jewish community.

Like Peter, Messianic Jews are also summoned to live as agents of unity, binding together the *ekklēsia* of the nations and the Jewish people. This requires meaningful relationship with the Christian church. But the point of the relationship is not to reside in the church's own sphere for the sake of shaping its internal life. Instead, the point is to unveil for the church the mystery of its identity as a participant in the eschatological blessings of an expanded Israel and to actualize that truth in the church's life through mutual love and communal interchange.

Some Jewish disciples of Jesus are also be called to the Pauline task of being a "light to the nations"—in our context, of immersion in the life of the Christian church in order to teach those from the nations about Jesus from a Jewish perspective. Some of these Jewish disciples of Jesus may identify as Messianic Jews, but generally they are content with the more fitting self-designation "Jewish Christians." In principle, if not in actual practice, this path should be the exception for Jewish disciples of Jesus rather than the rule. This is necessarily the case because the ways of James and Peter are a condition for the success of the way of Paul. Without thriving communities of Messianic Jews living faithfully within the wider Jewish world and without a unifying link between these communities and the church, the mission of Jewish disciples of Jesus within the Christian church will inevitably become only another expression of the inner life of the church. Without such thriving communities, it will also be impossible for Jewish disciples of Jesus who walk in the way of Paul to sustain a Jewish life for themselves or their families.

## 2. Priestly Identity

As we have seen, the fundamental vocation of the Jewish people is to be a holy nation, a priestly people. This entails existing as a community of sanctified kinship and culture. Similarly, the fundamental vocation of the community of Jewish disciples of Jesus is to be the priestly first fruits of Israel's eschatological destiny. Thus, an essential condition for fulfilling our vocation is existence as a community of sanctified Jewish kinship and culture.

## 3. Priestly Remnant

As we have also seen, Paul only employs the term "remnant" in a qualified manner. The community of Jewish Jesus-followers is a *priestly* remnant, representing rather than replacing the people as a whole. The priestly election of the remnant secures the holy and elect status of the rest, rather than their condemnation.

This implies that we cannot view the community of Jewish disciples of Jesus as the only true and valid expression of the people of Israel or of the messianic *ekklēsia*. We are neither Israel recovered from its "backsliding" nor the "restored first-century church" purified of its "paganism." Instead, we are but eschatological first fruits who stand before God on behalf of Israel and the church, who stand before Israel as witness to the sanctifying presence of Jesus in its midst, and who stand before the church as witness to the sanctifying presence of Israel in its midst.

## 4. Priestly Service

Observance of the Torah does not constitute Jewish community, but it does provide the shape of the community's priestly service. The most fundamental task of a priest is the worship of God, and worship is at the heart of the Torah.

As an eschatological priestly remnant, we offer our worship to God through Jesus in the Spirit. As an eschatological priestly remnant of the Jewish people, we offer worship to God in accordance with the Torah, both as written and as carried in the life of the Jewish people through history. As an eschatological priestly remnant of the Jewish people bound in love also to the *ekklēsia* from the nations, we offer worship to God as representatives of the one and holy people of Israel, the fiery core that through Messiah becomes a flaming catholic and apostolic star.

## 5. Priestly Sodality

Full participation in a Messianic Jewish community demands special dedication and commitment. It may not be appropriate for all Jews who have heard and answered the call of the Messiah.

To explain this, we may draw upon Ralph Winter's missiological distinction between a modality and a sodality.[27] A modality is a group comprised of a full range of human beings—old and young, male and female, married and single. It has leaders and followers, strong and weak, able and disabled. There are no membership restrictions other than a willingness to abide by the standards of the group, and the objective of the group is simply to live its life in a particular way.

In contrast, a sodality is a group with a focused vocation, with membership restricted to those who will be able to contribute to the fulfillment of that vocation. Sodalities require a higher level of commitment than do modalities. Winter sees the first-century communities of Jesus-followers as modalities, while he views Paul's apostolic team as a sodality. He also argues that monasteries, religious orders, and missionary

---

27. Winter, "The Two Structures of God's Redemptive Mission," 244–53.

societies demonstrate the fruitfulness of the sodality model throughout Christian history.

Sodalities of this sort are not service organizations composed of employees or volunteers who commit a segment of their week for a limited period of their life to accomplish a narrowly defined task. Instead, they are communities of people who have joined together in family-like relationships of mutual commitment and responsibility to fulfill a calling that is particular but that embraces the entirety of their lives.

As a representative part of the people and not the whole, as a part with a particular priestly calling that involves formidable challenges and imposes multiple hardships, Messianic Jewish communities should be viewed as sodalities rather than modalities. They are not for everyone. A Messianic Jewish community must be a priestly remnant of Jews and Jewish families—how else can they hope to represent the people of Israel? They must be a priestly community of Jews and Jewish families who embrace or are being drawn to Messiah Jesus—how else can they represent Israel in Jesus before God, or Jesus to Israel, or Israel to the Christian church? They must be a priestly community of leaders rather than followers—how else will they be able to maintain their convictions in the midst of fierce opposition? They must be a priestly community of stable mature families and individuals—how else will they be able to make the sacrifices required to fulfill their priestly commission? Finally, they must actually be *communities*—not fluid collections of individuals and families who meet occasionally to fulfill their own needs or perform a task, but people bound together in long-term family-like relationships. How else can they be priestly representatives of a sanctified extended family?

There is also a need for extra-local sodalities that bring together Jewish disciples of Jesus who are walking the different paths of James, Peter, and Paul. That is the aim of Yachad BeYeshua, an international interconfessional fellowship of Jewish disciples of Jesus, established in 2018.[28]

## CONCLUSION

We cannot ignore the vast discrepancy between the picture drawn in this chapter of the community of Jewish Jesus-followers and the reality that most of us live. Search though we might, we can find no roadmap to

---

28. See Spitzer, "Covenant Partners," 268–80. Spitzer draws upon a previously published version of this chapter in order to present the mission and identity of Yachad BeYeshua.

guide us to our destination. Nevertheless, if this formulation accurately expresses the calling of Jewish disciples of Jesus, then the One who calls us is also the One who will guide us and who will sustain us on the journey.

We ourselves may never reach the destination. That may be for a future generation. But in order for them to complete the journey, we must take the next step. As Rabbi Tarfon tells us, "You are not obliged to finish the task, but neither are you free to neglect it" (Avot 2:21). And so, with eyes open to our calling and our need, let us exercise our priestly gift in Messiah Jesus.

CHAPTER 7

# The Torah and Jews in the Christian Church

Covenantal Calling and Pragmatic Practice

> *To live as a Jew within the context of the Christian church is a formidable challenge. Drawing from his own experience and demonstrating a keen sensitivity to the manifold tensions inherent in this endeavor, Kinzer offers a practical and constructive proposal for how to increasingly embrace Jewish life within Christian communal settings.*[1]

## DIFFERENTIATED DISCIPLESHIP AND COVENANTAL CALLING

IN MY BOOK *POSTMISSIONARY Messianic Judaism* (*PMJ*), I argued that Jewish believers in Jesus have a covenantal calling to observe the basic practices of the Torah directed specifically to Jews, including circumcision, Shabbat, holidays, and *kashrut* (the Jewish dietary laws). While discipleship to Jesus fulfills the core intention of the Torah for both Jews and gentiles, according to apostolic teaching and precedent that discipleship takes different forms for Jews and gentiles. This thesis of differentiated discipleship for Jewish and gentile followers of Jesus is relatively uncontroversial in the Messianic Jewish congregational movement, but

---

1. This chapter was originally presented in Berlin, Germany at the 2012 Helsinki Consultation on Jewish Continuity in the Body of Messiah and has not previously been published. For more about the Helsinki Consultation, see appendix B.

in almost all other ecclesial settings a homogenous pattern of Jewish and gentile discipleship goes unquestioned.

For Jews in the Christian churches, this issue involves far more than assessing the truth-value of theoretical doctrinal propositions. It is loaded with existential challenges and normally evokes intense resistance. For some, Jewish identity was never of great significance and their initial attraction to Jesus reflected their alienation from the Jewish community and Jewish tradition. For others, Jewish identity was always important but was understood in strictly secular and cultural terms, divorced from its covenantal moorings in the Torah. In either case, the thesis proposed in *PMJ* suggests that faith in Jesus calls such Jews to rethink their Jewish identity and practice. Ironically, for those who hear this call, faith in Jesus reverses its past function in the history of the church: instead of signaling the doorway out of Jewish life, it serves as the portal back to robust commitment to the Jewish people and its spiritual heritage.

Like all divine calls, this entails both responsibility and opportunity. As responsibility, it opens our eyes to the enduring mission of the Jewish people in the world and of our particular role as Jewish disciples of Jesus in carrying out that mission. From this perspective, the call to follow Jesus *in a Jewish manner* is a gift to the church and to the world, regardless of the benefit it brings to us as individuals. As opportunity, however, the call to a distinctively Jewish form of discipleship opens for us new avenues to the realization of our own particular identity in the Messiah. As the Chasidic tradition has recognized, there is such a thing as a *yiddishe neshama*, a Jewish soul, and that soul requires a certain type of nutrition if it is to flourish. The Torah and the Jewish practices it inculcates provide nutrition for the Jewish soul awakened by the call of Messiah Jesus.

But it is exceedingly difficult for Jews in the Christian churches to hear and discern this call to a distinctively Jewish form of following Jesus. As they mature theologically and spiritually, they may come to recognize the enduring importance of the Jewish people in the divine economy and to rejoice in the privilege of being born a Jew. Upon further study and reflection, they may even develop an appreciation for the spiritual heritage of the Jewish people and for the Torah, which is central to that heritage. But formidable obstacles stand in the way of adopting the distinctive practices of Jewish life rooted in the Torah. These obstacles are not abstract and theoretical in nature, but concrete and practical. They result from the fact that the churches currently contain no communal space that nurtures and sustains Jewish life.

## A PROGRESSIVE, PRAGMATIC, AND PERSONAL APPROACH

What is most needed is for Christian leaders to rethink the relationship between Jewish identity and Christian identity, between Jewish life and Christian life. Until such rethinking occurs, Jews in the church will find it difficult to respond to their covenantal calling in accordance with the basic practices of the Torah directed specifically to Jews. Nevertheless, "difficult" does not mean "impossible"—as long as we understand basic Jewish practice in *progressive*, *pragmatic*, and *personal* terms rather than as an abstract all-or-nothing categorical imperative. Jews within the church should not wait for ecclesial authorities to act institutionally; within the limits imposed by the teaching and order of their church bodies, they should take initiative and seek to respond to the divine calling.

What do I mean by a *progressive*, *pragmatic*, and *personal* approach to Jewish practice?

- By *progressive*, I refer to a dynamic approach that emphasizes learning and growth rather than perfect conformity to an absolute standard. From this perspective, a Torah-observant life is not so much a settled state that one attains but a continual process, like the imitation of Jesus, which is its messianic fulfillment. The question for those taking a progressive approach to Torah practice is not "am I keeping all the *mitzvot* related to Shabbat?" Instead, the question is "am I growing in my observance of Shabbat? Am I keeping more of the *mitzvot* today than I was a year ago?"

- By *pragmatic*, I refer to a realistic approach that takes account of all the circumstances and responsibilities of life and then aims to follow basic Torah practices within the constraints imposed by those realities. The question for those taking such a pragmatic approach to Torah practice is not "am I scrupulously following all the traditional rules of *kashrut*?" Instead, the question is "am I following as many of the traditional rules of *kashrut* as I can without failing in my duty to love my family, friends, and fellow parishioners, and without bringing my household to financial ruin?"

- By *personal*, I refer to a relational approach that treats the *mitzvot* not as abstract laws or principles but as practices expressing the relationship of a Jew to God and to fellow Jews.[2] The question for

2. I am using the term "personal" here with its classical theological sense in mind.

those taking such a personal approach to Torah practice is not "am I achieving my goal of complying with an ideal standard of observance?" Instead, the question is "am I responding appropriately to God's gracious gift to me as a Jewish follower of the Messiah? Is my Jewish observance drawing me closer to Jesus and enabling me to know him better? Am I drawing closer to other Jews through my practice, and in a way that does not endanger my existing relationships with non-Jewish brothers and sisters in the Messiah?"

As soon as we adopt a *progressive*, *pragmatic*, and *personal* approach to Torah practice, Jewish life within the church becomes a possibility—though still a daunting task.

The difficulty of the task might also be thought to derive from uncertainty regarding what the Torah actually teaches about Jewish life for believers in Jesus. Indeed, once a Jewish disciple of Jesus advances in Torah observance, challenging questions do arise. But at the beginning these questions are largely irrelevant. When one's normal pattern has been to eat without any reference to *kashrut* or to treat Saturday as a day for work, errands, chores, or shopping (as is the case for most Jews in a church context), questions about the applicability of particular rabbinic ordinances are beside the point. We do not know whether Jesus and the Twelve mixed meat and dairy; we *do know* that they did not eat pork or shellfish. We do not know whether Jesus would consider electricity equivalent to fire and prohibit initiating its use on Shabbat; we *do know* that Jesus set aside his hammer and saw on Saturdays and devoted the day to study, teaching, prayer, and synagogue attendance. For beginners in Jewish practice, the first steps—indeed, the first miles—lack ambiguity. Halakhic controversy concerning the outlines of the path only develops as one walks a healthy distance beyond its starting point.

In reality, the task is daunting mainly because the churches provide no communal space in which to undertake it nor any encouragement to do so. Furthermore, the situation is even more complicated than this way of depicting it might suggest. The problem is not just an absence of space or encouragement but a continual conflict of calendars, priorities, and relationships. How am I to observe Shabbat when the calendar of my church includes activities on that day (such as fasting) that conflict with

---

The Greek word *hypostasis* was employed in Nicene theology to refer to the three persons of the Triune God. The personal or hypostatic identity of each of the persons of the Triune God are entirely determined by their relations to the other two. Thus, personal identity is equivalent to relational identity.

its spirit? How am I to refrain from secular occupations on Shabbat and attend Jewish services when my church expects me likewise to refrain from such occupations and attend Christian services on the Lord's Day? How am I to celebrate Purim when it falls during Lent, or even on Ash Wednesday? How am I to rejoice on the day of Passover and hold a luscious fun-filled seder when it falls during Holy Week? How am I to avoid eating any products containing leaven during the Passover season when it falls during Easter week and I am involved in multiple festive meals with Christian friends and family? How am I to participate in events within the Jewish community when I have so many conflicting time commitments within the Christian community? How am I to maintain the rules of *kashrut* when I am invited to meals at the homes of my Christian friends or when I participate in communal meals at church? How am I to do any of these things that involve my family when my spouse is not Jewish and has no interest in building a Jewish family life?

For Jews in non-liturgical Protestant settings with a less densely textured church life, some of the above challenges will not arise. But many will remain. I have Jewish friends who are part of a charismatic church where I live. Their teenage son was part of the church youth group and the group held a marvelous event: they spent a day together fasting and praying for the poor. Unfortunately, the day they picked to do this was a Saturday! Similarly, it is common in the United States for churches to sponsor fundraising events of various sorts on Saturdays—a day in which observant Jews have no contact with money! It is just as common to do other work projects for the church (or the needy) on Saturday. These examples should suffice to show that Jews in non-liturgical churches are not exempt from the sorts of impediments to Jewish practice that I am concerned with here.

The force of these practical challenges should not be minimized. They raise questions that are not only practical in nature but also ethical. We have covenantal responsibilities as Jews but we also have responsibilities to our immediate and extended families and to those in our church communities whose lives are intertwined with our own. Much of the stress we experience as citizens of the twenty-first century results from competing responsibilities and interests—immediate family, in-laws, work, church, school, study, exercise, recreation, engagement with the arts. Now we add Judaism to this already complicated mix! For those of us who are conscientious about maintaining our commitments, this is a recipe for anything but a tranquil life.

I do not intend here to propose a practical solution to these dilemmas. Each situation is different, each person is different, and no universally applicable formula for resolution exists. Instead, I want only to suggest a place to begin: *Jews in the churches should take as their starting point the frank acknowledgment of the legitimacy of the competing claims on their lives, including the call to follow Jesus in a distinctively Jewish way.* This is a formidable challenge in itself. Faced with competing claims on our time, energy, resources, and passion, we may be tempted to alleviate our moral discomfort by denying the legitimacy or importance of one or more of those claims. I am urging my fellow Jewish followers of Jesus who are loyal members of Christian churches to resist this temptation. If we are Jews, then we have a call from God to *live as Jews*. But that is not the only call we have.

From this starting point, the way forward becomes a matter of gradually incorporating elements of Jewish practice into our lives. Adopting a *progressive*, *pragmatic*, and *personal* approach to such practice, our focus will be on growing into a deeper Jewish life and on doing so in a way that is beneficial rather than damaging to ourselves and to those around us. As with all attempts at reconciling competing commitments and responsibilities, we are certain to experience frustration and feelings of inadequacy. But living fruitfully with such tension and incompleteness is a mark of spiritual and human maturity. The fragmentation of our lives is but a reflection of the fragmented world in which we live and the fragmented people of God of which we are part. To bear that pain with patience is to share in the sufferings of our Messiah.

Given our circumstances, the *personal* (or relational) aspect of our approach to Jewish practice deserves special attention. To remove Torah-based Jewish practice from its relational context in Jewish communal life is to strip it of much of its intended meaning. Yet, the absence of Jewish communal life in the church is the greatest challenge we are facing. The conclusion I reach from this dilemma is simple: *the first and highest priority for Jewish believers in Jesus who are seeking to live a distinctively Jewish form of discipleship is to build relationships with other Jews.* More urgent than observing Shabbat, keeping kosher, or praying from the *siddur* is to join or build a Jewish relational context in which these practices gain much of their meaning. Such a context might involve a small group of Jewish church members meeting regularly for study or celebration. It might involve Jewish church members developing connections to Messianic Jewish congregations. It might entail finding a setting in the wider

Jewish community which is able to tolerate the respectful presence of an eccentric Jew (who also identifies as a Christian). Whatever form it takes, the road to a distinctive pattern of Jewish discipleship begins with forging Jewish relational connections, both as a fundamental expression of our distinctive covenantal calling and as the necessary context for all further Jewish practice.[3]

## MY OWN EXPERIENCE

The subject of this chapter is one that I have struggled with in my own life. For the last three decades, I have participated in the Messianic Jewish congregational movement. However, for the two previous decades (from 1971 to 1993), I lived as part of an ecumenical Christian community. It was predominantly a community of families, but I was a member of an ecumenical celibate religious order within the wider family-community. The community and the religious order each involved a Catholic majority, but a substantial number of Protestants also participated. There were other Messianic Jews in the family-community, but I was the only Jew in the religious order.

The family-community and the religious order each developed a rich liturgical life based on the calendar of the Western church. Our spiritual life followed an annual cycle that flowed from Advent to Christmas to Lent to Holy Week to Easter Week to Pentecost. Similarly, our weekly pattern of life revolved around the Lord's Day, which the community honored as a day of worship, rest, and refraining from secular pursuits. Each morning, our household of celibate men would rise at a common time, have breakfast, chant psalms together in a room set aside for worship, and then devote two hours to personal prayer and study. Each evening, we would gather once again to chant psalms before eating dinner together. We would meet a final time to pray before going to sleep.

I was not only a participant in this life but at the age of twenty-four I became one of its leaders. As an assistant to one of the community founders, I helped shape the liturgical life described above. Together we composed a ceremony for the beginning of the Lord's Day that families used on Saturday evenings and other holiday prayers that could be employed

---

3. It is this conviction, shared by many Messianic Jews and Jewish Christians, that led in 2019 to the formation of Yachad BeYeshua, an international and ecumenical fellowship of Jewish disciples of Jesus. See www.yachad-beyeshua.org.

throughout the year.[4] There are Christian communities around the world that still employ the home liturgies I co-authored in the 1970s.

From the beginning of my participation in this community in 1971, I knew that my primary vocation was to serve the Messiah in the midst of the Jewish people. But it took many years to discern what that service should look like in daily practice and to realize the complications posed to such practice by my commitment to an ecumenical Christian community. With the agreement of my religious superior, I began in 1974 to attend a traditional synagogue on Saturday mornings. I would return at noon to my household of Christian brothers and join with them for two hours of chores before beginning the Lord's Day with corporate prayer and a Saturday evening meal. It did not take long for the incongruity of this pattern to dawn on me. But at first, I did not know what to do about it.

In 1978, after a period of study and prayerful reflection (under the guidance of my superior), I decided that I needed to move toward a Torah-observant life, without any clear notion of what that would mean. I immediately refrained from all meals that contained pork products or shellfish. I returned to the study of Hebrew, which I had begun as a university undergraduate. I stopped doing chores on Saturday afternoons and arranged to do them at another time during the week. I taught myself to lay *tefillin* and began praying the daily morning service from the *siddur*. I had now begun a journey that involved the observance of two liturgical calendars and participation in two religious communities with two densely textured spiritual traditions. It was not easy, but it was what I needed to do to be faithful to my calling.

As noted above, there were a number of Jews in the wider family-community. In the mid-1970s, we began to celebrate a Passover seder together. This led to other holiday events and eventually to a monthly Shabbat dinner. In 1981, a set of Jewish families from the community moved into a common neighborhood and our religious order established a household for me in the same locale. To the surprise of many, a Jewish relational network began to take shape in the midst of an intensely committed Christian community.

I was motivated to persevere in this difficult journey by the conviction that Jesus had called me to it. It was a responsibility, a fundamental expression of the particularity of my discipleship as a Jew rather than an

---

4. Many decades after its in-house publication, a book called *Family Worship* still appears on the Amazon website when my name is entered as part of an author search.

optional extra that I could choose or ignore as I pleased. But I was also motivated by the opportunity it provided to nurture my Jewish soul. In inexplicable ways, Jewish life touched me in my depths. When I prayed in Hebrew, I sensed my words soaring to heaven. When the ark was opened during the Torah service at synagogue, I sensed the powerful presence of Jesus, the Torah incarnate, along with the holy angels. When I fasted on Yom Kippur, I could almost see Jesus in the heavenly holy of holies, presenting his wounds before the Father and interceding on behalf of Israel and the entire world. I experienced Jewish practice as sacramental, as a vehicle through which Jesus revealed himself to me and through which he also revealed my own identity as a Jew.

Adopting a *progressive, pragmatic,* and *personal* approach to Torah observance in the midst of a Christian community, I grew as a Jew and as a human being. I learned to live with tension and ambiguity and I came to realize through experience that the perfect can become the enemy of the good. Then, in 1993, a split within the community brought my life to a crossroads and led its Jewish members to embark on a new course—the formation of a Messianic Jewish congregation. While my path diverged from that of my Christian brothers, the friendships forged within the community remain with me to this day, as does the commitment to an ecumenical vision of unity for the divided people of God.

While the shift from ecumenical community to Messianic Jewish congregation reduced some of the tensions I had experienced, I do not want to suggest that a similar move is advisable for all Jews within the Christian churches. My circumstances were unique to me, just as the circumstances of others are unique to them. I gained much in the move, but I also lost much. Others lost far more; the change in course was only possible because of a tragic crisis and rupture that damaged many lives. With thirty-plus years hindsight, I am convinced that I ended up taking the path that was right for me. But I do not regret devoting the previous twenty years to a life of prayer, service, and community-relationship in an ecumenical Christian context.

I have carried with me into Messianic Jewish congregational life this *progressive, pragmatic,* and *personal* approach to Torah observance. Every year, I grow in Jewish practice. It took me many years after 1993 to incorporate all three daily services of prayer—*Shachrit, Minchah,* and *Ma'ariv*—into my normal rhythm of life. And every year I face new challenges to my ritual practice, from family commitments and institutional responsibilities—challenges that must be faced pragmatically and not dogmatically.

## CONCLUSION

Over the past quarter-century, I have been part of a group of Messianic Jewish leaders who are seeking to foster Torah observance among Jewish believers in Jesus and who together have adopted a *progressive, pragmatic,* and *personal* approach to achieving this end. Our association is called the Messianic Jewish Rabbinical Council (MJRC). While the MJRC mainly seeks to provide guidance for members of the Messianic Jewish movement, the materials it has produced are also relevant to Jewish followers of Jesus in the Christian churches who have become conscious of their covenantal call as Jews and who are seeking practical wisdom on how to fulfill that call.[5]

If a significant number of Jewish followers of Jesus awaken to their covenantal call as Jews and seek ways to help one another live out that call with wisdom and compassion, this fact will in itself alert the leaders of the Christian churches of a pastoral need requiring their attention. Spurred to action, these leaders might then look for ways to nurture Jewish life in their midst. The suffering perseverance of the pioneers could pave a path for future generations of Jewish followers of Jesus to walk with less ambivalence as Jews and as disciples of the Jewish Messiah.

The Christian church and the Jewish people in this world are divided and at times opposed one to the other. This renders precarious the situation of those seeking to be loyal to both. Nevertheless, it is our conviction that Jesus himself stands in that precarious position. His loyalty to one does not negate his loyalty to the other. As his disciples, we can do no better than stand with him and welcome the worldly tension and eschatological peace that come from his firm and loving embrace.

---

5. For more on the MJRC, see www.ourrabbis.org and appendix A of this volume.

CHAPTER 8

# Jewish Disciples of Jesus and the Healing of the Twofold Tradition
## Eight Theses

> *The Christian church and the Jewish people have historically defined themselves in contradistinction and mutual exclusion from one another, which leaves Jewish followers of Jesus without a clear roadmap for navigating each tradition and what authority it might have for faith and discipleship. Kinzer presents eight theses that outline how Messianic Jews and Jewish Christians ought to approach and assess their own praxis in light of the two divinely inspired traditions that bear upon them.*[1]

JESUS, THE LIVING TORAH, is the ultimate authority in shaping the way of life of his Jewish disciples and in giving it a distinctively Jewish character. But how do we receive our resurrected Rabbi's guidance? What role does Christian tradition play in the process? What role does Jewish tradition play? These questions cannot be answered in a single and uniform manner for all Jewish disciples of Jesus. Perhaps that is the most significant conclusion in this chapter—but its meaning will only become clear in what follows.

---

1. This chapter was originally presented in the Netherlands at the 2014 Helsinki Consultation on Jewish Continuity in the Body of Messiah and has not previously been published. For more details on the Helsinki Consultation, see appendix B.

My views on the role of Torah observance for Jewish disciples of Jesus are well known.[2] I have argued that the distinctive Jewish practices commanded in the Torah that have defined the way of life of the Jewish people since the destruction of the Temple (e.g., Shabbat observance, the holidays of the Jewish calendar, ritual circumcision of male children on the eighth day of life, and the dietary laws) remain obligatory for Jews who have accepted Jesus as Israel's Messiah.[3] Just as well-known are my views on the essential role of Jewish religious tradition in determining how these practices should be configured.[4] I have argued that it is a hopeless and fruitless task to attempt to observe naked biblical commandments apart from the clothing they have received in the course of Jewish history.[5] Search though we may through the Bible, the ecumenical councils, the church fathers, Thomas Aquinas, Martin Luther, or John Calvin, we will not learn how to observe a Passover seder, how to build a valid *sukkah*, how to slaughter a chicken or a cow in a way that renders it fit for Jewish consumption, or how to make ritual fringes for a four-cornered garment.

Some have interpreted my writings as advocating an Orthodox Jewish lifestyle for all Jewish disciples of Jesus, though I have stated unequivocally that this is not the case.[6] Other forms of modern Judaism participate alongside Orthodox Judaism in the organic development of the Torah and we can learn something from them all. Furthermore, we must claim our own measure of halakhic authority as a prophetic movement for Jesus among the Jewish people.[7] The decisions we reach must

---

2. See Kinzer, *Postmissionary Messianic Judaism*.

3. See Kinzer, *Postmissionary Messianic Judaism*, 49–96.

4. See Kinzer, *Israel's Messiah and the People of God*, esp. ch 3.

5. See Kinzer, *Postmissionary Messianic Judaism*, 235–62, and *Israel's Messiah and the People of God*, 29–61.

6. See Kinzer, *Israel's Messiah and the People of God*, 61, 186–87.

7. "Any Messianic Jewish version of the Oral Torah must recognize two legitimate halakhic authorities in tension—those recognized by the Jewish community as a whole, and those presiding over its messianic sub-community. Our halakhic authority to bind and loose is prophetic in nature, just as Yeshua's own authority derived not from institutional office but from messianic empowerment. When the requirements inherent in the faith of Yeshua conflict with the norms of rabbinic tradition and the institutions of the wider Jewish community, then we must find a way to be true to Yeshua while maintaining respect for the community and its tradition" (Kinzer, *Israel's Messiah and the People of God*, 61).

take account of Jewish tradition but at times they will depart from existing precedent and break new ground.[8]

The approach to these matters advanced in my writings has received a wide hearing in the Messianic Jewish movement. Many remain unconvinced, but the approach has been adopted in large part by one leadership organization, the Messianic Jewish Rabbinical Council, and in that context it is being tested in the concrete details of congregational life. At this point, the approach appears feasible and fruitful in such a setting.

In contrast, it seems clear that my conclusions regarding Torah praxis and Jewish tradition are practically unworkable for most Jewish Christians (those Jewish disciples of Jesus whose primary ecclesial context is a Christian church rather than a Messianic Jewish group or a traditional mainstream synagogue). This is especially the case for Jews in historical churches, which possess a rich and densely textured liturgical life, but to a great extent it also applies to Jewish Christians in more free-form Protestant settings. How, for example, can adherence to the Jewish calendar of holidays be reconciled with a conflicting Christian calendar?

If Jewish Christians are to express and preserve their identity as Jews, they will need to adopt a different approach to Jewish tradition from the one I have advocated for Messianic Jews. What might such an approach look like and how might it resemble or diverge from a Messianic Jewish approach? That is a question that has never been addressed.

A second question arises that I have only addressed in past writings in the most general terms. What role should *Christian* tradition play in the development of Messianic Jewish life? If the appropriation of Jewish tradition poses a formidable challenge for Jewish Christians, so the appropriation of Christian tradition raises analogous concerns for Messianic Jews. Most Messianic Jews fail to see any relevance of the Christian tradition for their lives, just as most Jewish Christians find little of enduring significance for themselves in Jewish tradition. If we Messianic Jews want Jewish Christians to reconsider the matter of Jewish tradition, then we should likewise be open to the reconsideration of Christian tradition.

In what follows, I will propose eight theses regarding the Jewish and Christian traditions and their particular significance for Jewish disciples of Jesus. Here I am not attempting to argue on their behalf; I will simply set them forth as a basis for discussion, so as to provide public

---

8. To understand better the character of the halakhic process that I propose for the Messianic Jewish community and the type of halakhic conclusions it might reach, see appendix A in this volume.

clarification of my views and to stimulate further communal dialogue on these questions.

## THESES 1–4: THE JEWISH AND CHRISTIAN TRADITIONS

### Thesis #1: The One Twofold People of God and of the Messiah

> *The Jewish people and the Christian church together form the one people of God, and Jesus dwells among them both (albeit in different ways) as the mediator of the presence of the Father.*

I understand the Christian church to be as much a visible and historical community as the Jewish people. I also understand the Jewish people to be as much a spiritual and transcendently moored reality as the Christian church. We must avoid any simplistic differentiation between the two that identifies one as visible and earthly, the other as invisible and heavenly.

The assertion that Jesus dwells among the Jewish people as well as the Christian church is central to my past writing and should need little further explanation here. I acknowledge the differences in the mode of his indwelling, and these differences are manifested (though not precisely specified) in the way each tradition speaks of the community's relationship to the divine presence. Thus, the Christian spiritual tradition focuses especially on the baptized individual and emphasizes the way Jesus (through the Holy Spirit) lives "in" each one of them. The Jewish tradition, on the other hand, focuses on the Jewish people as a whole or on its communal expression in particular times and places, and emphasizes the way the *Shekhinah* (i.e., the divine presence) dwells "among" or "in the midst of" them.

This first thesis deals with ecclesiology/Israelology rather than tradition. That is because the meaning and function of tradition must be understood as an aspect of the life of the people of God as it transmits its life from one generation to the next. Thus, any discussion of tradition must begin with ecclesiology/Israelology, just as ecclesiology must begin with Christology/Messianology and pneumatology.

### Thesis #2: Tradition and the Spirit

> *Jesus, the living Torah, guides his people by means of the Holy Spirit, who is the fundamental principle of Scripture and tradition*

> *(with the latter referring to both the apostolic tradition and the Oral Torah). Thus, the Spirit—like Jesus, whose presence the Spirit mediates—also dwells among both communities, albeit in different ways.*

Jesus underlines the connection between himself, the Spirit, and the apostolic tradition at his final meal with his disciples before his death:

> I have said these things to you while I am still with you. But the Advocate, the Holy Spirit, whom the Father will send in my name, will teach you everything, and remind you of all that I have said to you. . . . I still have many things to say to you, but you cannot bear them now. When the Spirit of truth comes, he will guide you into all the truth; for he will not speak on his own, but will speak whatever he hears, and he will declare to you the things that are to come. He will glorify me, because he will take what is mine and declare it to you. (John 14:25–26; 16:12–14)

Michael Wyschogrod speaks about the Oral Torah in a similar fashion: "The oral law is that part of the law carried in the Jewish people. . . . [T]he Torah enters the being of the people of Israel. It is absorbed into their existence and they therefore become the carriers or the incarnation of the Torah."[9] Though the authoritative texts of the rabbinic tradition bear witness to the Oral Torah, the two are not equivalent, for the Oral Torah is a living reality that can never be confined to or fully contained in writing. Thus, in Jewish tradition, the relationship between the Oral Torah and the Written Torah is analogous to the relationship between the Holy Spirit and the Incarnate Word in Christian tradition. And just as the Incarnate Word is the source and principle of the Written Torah, so the Holy Spirit is the source and principle of the Oral Torah.

## Thesis #3: The Freedom of the Spirit-Inspired Tradition

> *"Where the Spirit of the Lord is, there is freedom" (2 Cor 3:17). The Spirit brings freedom by granting access to the Father through the Son, and by imparting strength for the observance of the divine word, but also by bestowing upon the community the gift of wisdom to understand and apply the divine word in ever new settings. In this process, the work of the Spirit empowers the community to become a free, creative, and responsible partner with Jesus in the unfolding of divine revelation.*

---

9. Wyschogrod, *The Body of Faith*, 210.

In both Jewish and Christian theology, spiritual freedom entails the capacity to fulfill one's divinely founded vocation as an active agent rather than a passive instrument. The twofold tradition of the one people of God manifests and bears witness to such free, active, and creative human participation in the process of transmitting, interpreting, applying, and embodying the divine word.

## Thesis #4: The Tragic Legacy of Schism

> *While Jesus has acted by means of the Spirit to shape the bilateral tradition of the one twofold people of God, the Jewish and Christian traditions have each developed in a partial and one-sided manner as a result of the tragic schism that has rent this people asunder.*

From an early period, the Jewish community and the Christian church became locked in a debilitating conflict characterized by rivalry, animosity, and mutual reactivity. The tendency of each community to define itself in opposition to the other displayed in perverse fashion the interlocking nature of their communal identities and destinies.

The wholeness of "catholic" tradition consists of these two traditions, purified of their mutual negations and complementing one another without losing their distinctive properties. The Chalcedonian definition of Christology captures well the best way of conceiving of their proper relationship: they are to be "undivided" and yet "unconfused." Those who recognize this truth must labor to appreciate the strengths and weaknesses of each tradition so that each partner can learn from the other without forfeiting its particular calling.

## THESES 5–8: JEWISH DISCIPLES OF JESUS AND THE TWOFOLD TRADITION

## Thesis #5: The Freedom of Jewish Disciples of Jesus for the Healing of the Tradition

> *The emergence in our day of a community of Jewish disciples of Jesus is a new work of the Spirit who has granted to this developing body the authority to fashion an appropriate way of life that can contribute to the healing of the twofold tradition. To fulfill this calling, Jewish disciples of Jesus must bring together what has been*

> *separated and by the guidance of the Spirit draw from both traditions what each can supply for this purpose. However, the mode of engaging with each of the two traditions will differ for Jewish Christians and Messianic Jews.*

As noted already in thesis #3, the freedom given by the Spirit entails a capacity to participate actively in the unfolding of the divine purpose. The way this freedom is expressed depends upon one's particular setting and calling. Jewish disciples of Jesus in the twenty-first century find themselves in a new situation with new opportunities and dangers that demand a creative engagement with both the Jewish and the Christian traditions. For us, the freedom of the Spirit is a commission and a charge as much as it is a gift, and the charge demands faithful immersion in both traditions and innovative developments anticipated by neither.

By virtue of their divergent ecclesial settings, Jewish Christians and Messianic Jews begin with distinct and contrasting relationships to the twofold tradition. Nevertheless, neither is free to disregard, disrespect, or deny the significance of that part of the tradition that is secondary rather than primary in establishing its own identity.

### Thesis #6: Messianic Jews and the Twofold Tradition

> *Messianic Jews should begin with the consensus practices and way of life of observant Jews and then assess and adapt them in light of the theological and practical wisdom gained through the New Testament and the living tradition of the church. Messianic Jews should also receive the distinctive sacraments of the renewed covenant as transmitted in the life of the church and seek to practice them in forms adapted from Jewish tradition.*

In developing their way of life, Messianic Jews should take as their starting point the Jewish tradition as it has developed over the past two millennia. A starting point—but not an end point. Just as the apostles interpreted creatively the biblical tradition in light of the life, work, and teaching of Jesus and the guidance of the Spirit, so Messianic Jews should do the same for the post-biblical Jewish tradition. The result will be a recognizably Jewish way of life with innovations reflecting the messianic distinctive. That messianic distinctive should be rooted in the New Testament and the tradition of the church.

To take the Jewish tradition as a starting point means that practices acknowledged by the full spectrum of observant Jews require no further justification to be accepted as authoritative. Departure from such practices, on the other hand, does require justification. In some cases, departure will undoubtedly be warranted, but the warrant must be articulated and of a weight proportional to the significance of the practice that is being modified.

While providing a starting point that can be adopted or adapted, the traditional Jewish way of life does not provide all that Messianic Jews need in order to be faithful disciples of the Messiah. Jesus instituted certain new practices among his disciples whose concrete pattern and full theological significance can only be learned through engagement with the tradition of the church. While receiving these practices from the church with gratitude, Messianic Jews must also exercise their freedom in the Spirit by fashioning for these practices new forms drawn from Jewish tradition.

## Thesis #7: Jewish Christians and the Twofold Tradition

> *Jewish Christians should begin with the consensus practices and way of life of their particular ecclesial traditions and then assess and adapt them (within the limits permitted by their ecclesial authorities) in light of the theological and practical wisdom gained through classic rabbinic texts and the living tradition of the Jewish people. Jewish Christians should also receive the distinctive signs of holiness* (kedushah) *and election as transmitted in the life of the Jewish people and seek to express them in forms accessible to their ecclesial communities.*

Just as Messianic Jews take the Jewish tradition as their starting point, so Jewish Christians take the Christian tradition as their starting point. And, once again, the starting point is not the end point. Many Christian thinkers are already engaged in the process of retrieving the Jewish roots and character of their respective ecclesial traditions in conversation with Jewish scholars and the ongoing Jewish tradition; Jewish Christians should draw from the fruit of their labors.

While providing a starting point for the fashioning of a distinctively Jewish mode of Christian discipleship, the traditional Christian way of life cannot provide all that Jewish Christians need in order to be faithful Jews as well as faithful Christians. Distinctive Jewish expressions of holiness and election, which have been lost in the Christian church, have been preserved among the Jewish people, and their concrete pattern and full theological significance can only be learned through direct engagement with Jewish tradition. While receiving such signs of holiness and election with gratitude, Jewish Christians should also exercise their freedom in the Spirit by developing ways of expressing these signs that fit their particular ecclesial contexts.

## Thesis #8: Messianic Jews and Jewish Christians Together

> *While Messianic Jews and Jewish Christians have much in common and can learn much from one another, their ways of living out Jewish discipleship to Jesus will vary because of their differing relationships to the Jewish and Christian traditions. They cannot develop a common halakhah, nor should they seek to do so. However, they can seek to develop a relationship of ecumenical brotherhood and sisterhood in which they support one another in their common commitment to the healing of the twofold people of God and its twofold tradition. This relationship will also enable them to speak publicly with one voice about this common commitment so that the church, the Jewish people, and the world might hear and be blessed.*

Messianic Jews and Jewish Christians differ from one another in vocation and way of life. But they also need one another. This shared conviction led a group of Messianic Jews and Jewish Christians to form the Helsinki Consultation in 2010. Similarly, it led the members of the Consultation to organize a Congress of Jewish Disciples of Jesus in Dallas in 2018. That gathering eventuated in the 2019 formation of Yachad BeYeshua, an international ecumenical fellowship of Jewish disciples of Jesus. Yachad BeYeshua exists to unite Jewish disciples of Jesus in loving fellowship as a witness to God's faithfulness to Israel and the church.

The prayer of the members of Yachad BeYeshua is that the God who raised Jesus from the dead may, by his Spirit, raise up in our day a dynamic and visible ecumenical community of Jewish disciples of Jesus as a prophetic sign and catalyst for the healing of the twofold people of God and its twofold tradition.

CHAPTER 9

# Jewish Disciples of Jesus
## The Sacrament of Messianic Communion

> *Drawing on the thought of Orthodox Christian thinker Lev Gillet, Kinzer reflects upon the unique vocation of Jewish followers of Jesus in their relationship to both the wider Christian church and the wider Jewish people. Following Gillet, Kinzer challenges us to see not only the church's mission to the Jews but also Israel's mission to the church as theologically significant in God's overarching plan of revelation and redemption.*[1]

## THE BASIC QUESTION

THIS CHAPTER SEEKS TO address the question, "what, in God's providential design, is our distinct vocation as Jewish disciples of Jesus?"

The fact that we are asking the question is itself noteworthy. From the fourth century to the modern era, the question could hardly have arisen, since baptism was assumed to nullify the existential significance of Jewish identity for the one baptized. Even apart from baptism, Jewish identity had lost its positive theological significance in the divine plan as a result of the new economy inaugurated by the crucified and risen Christ. Consequently, the Jewish people (along with its obsolete religious tradition) and the Christian church (along with its divinely bestowed religious

---

1. This chapter was originally presented in Moscow, Russia at the 2015 Helsinki Consultation on Jewish Continuity in the Body of Messiah and has not previously been published. For more details on the Helsinki Consultation, see appendix B.

tradition) were understood to constitute mutually exclusive realms. This principle of mutual exclusivity, accepted also by the Jewish world (with a radically different perspective on its meaning), seemed self-evident to all. It no longer seems so, at least to many of us. The fact that Jewish disciples of Jesus are asking about their distinct vocation means that they no longer find this longstanding presupposition to be axiomatic.

The principle of mutual exclusivity, which formerly rendered this question unaskable, points to an even more basic question: *If the Jewish people/tradition and the Christian church/tradition do not constitute mutually exclusive realms, with one occupying a positive pole and the other a negative, how do we conceive of their relationship and their relative status in God's providential design?* A common answer to this question offered by Jewish Christians in the modern era has been to validate Jewish identity while also *subordinating it* to Christian identity as its destined fulfillment. In this view, the Jewish people retain a unique status among the nations of the world and that status is perfected rather than annulled when Jews affirm their calling by receiving baptism. At the same time, the Jewish religious tradition and way of life are largely left behind as the church's religious tradition and way of life are embraced. The Jewish people have enduring theological significance, but only in relation to the Christian church and her more perfect identity and vocation.

But the *subordination* of Judaism to the church is not the only possible answer to the question concerning the proper relationship between the two communities. Other views began to emerge in the early twentieth century which proposed a *coordination* of these two traditions. One perspective of this sort (originating with Franz Rosenzweig) rendered Jewish Christian identity problematic or meaningless by confining the salvific significance of Jesus to his mediation on behalf of gentiles. However, a rival perspective coordinated the two traditions *on the basis of a high Christology with universal significance* and proposed this coordination as the ultimate justification for Jewish Christian identity. One of the most articulate exponents of this latter position was an Orthodox Christian priest from France who was steeped in the theological and spiritual world of Russian Christianity—Fr. Lev Gillet. I would like to explore his thinking on this topic, for he lays a solid foundation for answering the question of the vocation of Jewish disciples of Jesus.

## COMMUNION IN THE MESSIAH

When I first read Lev Gillet's *Communion in the Messiah* almost three decades ago, I was shocked that such a book on Jewish-Christian relations could be written by an Orthodox priest in the middle of the Second World War. I was not then familiar with the writings of Vladimir Soloviev (with whom Gillet identified) or Sergei Bulgakov (who was Gillet's friend), and so this author's profound appreciation of Judaism seemed to be a *creatio ex nihilo*. Though I now have a better grasp of the historical context that made his work possible, I still marvel at its prophetic insight.

Gillet's primary concern is not with the Judaism of the Bible, but with the historical reality of the Jewish spiritual tradition over the past twenty centuries. He makes the audacious claim that Jewish tradition as a whole is part of God's unfolding revelatory work in the world:

> The whole message of Israel is an authentic part of God's Revelation and can be, without the abolition of a single jot, brought together with the message of Jesus. Nothing of the true Jewish tradition—from Hillel to modern Hasidism—needs to be altered in order to adjust itself to the Gospel: it needs only to be complemented.[2]

Gillet thus *coordinates* Jewish and Christian tradition, treating the former as a necessary partner for the latter. This does not make Jesus superfluous for Jews, for Gillet insists that the gospel is "the fruit and completion and crown of Judaism." Where he differs from most Christian missionaries to the Jews is in his assertion that the "Judaism" that Jesus "crowns" consists not merely of the "Old Testament," but includes also the entirety of post-biblical Jewish religious tradition:

> Do missionaries bring to Jews the Gospel *as* the crown of their faith, when they consider as non-existent or unimportant the whole of the Jewish tradition of belief and worship which accompanies and supplements the Old Testament? To bring to the Jews the crown of their faith means to show them the continuity between Christianity and the whole line of Jewish religious thought, rabbinical as well as Scriptural. . . . There is nothing, absolutely nothing, in Jewish belief that a Jew turned Christian ought to reject. Christianity is, in relation to Judaism, a completion and a fulfillment.[3]

---

2. Gillet, *Communion*, 186. The book was originally published in 1942.
3. Gillet, *Communion*, 180, 196.

From these citations, we see that Gillet emphatically subordinates Judaism *to Jesus and "the Gospel"*—but he refuses to subordinate Judaism to the historical reality of the Christian church.

But is that church not the mystical "body of Christ"? How can Gillet ascribe such value to Jewish spiritual life even when it has not yet been "crowned" by faith in the gospel? To answer this question, Gillet draws upon the thinking of his Catholic contemporary Jacques Maritain, who proposed that the Jewish people are likewise a *corpus mysticum* (i.e., a mystical body).

> The *corpus mysticum Christi* is not a metaphor; it is an organic and invisible reality. But the theology of the Body of Christ should be linked with a theology of the mystical Body of Israel. This is one of the deepest and most beautiful tasks of a "bridge theology" between Judaism and Christianity.[4]

Maritain had distinguished the historical planes on which these two mystical bodies function, with the Jewish people serving "secular history" and the church "sacred history." Gillet rejects this facile distinction, contending that faithful Jews "belong to sacred history and achieve a redeeming work in the *diaspora*."[5] This perspective on the Jewish people as a *corpus mysticum* enabled Gillet to perceive Jewish suffering—which had reached an unprecedented crescendo in the period in which he wrote—as a realization of Isaiah 53:

> If we do ascribe a religious significance and purpose to the existence of the Jews, we must consider their sufferings as part of this purpose, . . . we must interpret Israel's woes in the light of the teaching about the Suffering Servant. . . . By its many sufferings, Israel may help the consummation of the divine purpose in history.[6]

Gillet thus affirms the traditional Jewish reading of Isaiah 53 (i.e., the servant is Israel), but only in conjunction with the traditional Christian reading (i.e., the servant is Jesus). The life of the Jewish people in history is bound inextricably to its crucified and risen Messiah.

To describe the character of Israel's enduring relationship to Jesus, Gillet employs the concept of *communion*. While he observes that most Jews have lost an expectation of a personal messiah, he also asserts that

---

4. Gillet, *Communion*, 215.
5. Gillet, *Communion*, 157.
6. Gillet, *Communion*, 160.

they have retained the hope of a coming messianic kingdom, a hope that inspires among them the practical pursuit of righteousness, justice, and peace. In this hope and pursuit, Gillet contends, faithful Jews experience communion with Messiah Jesus, albeit in a partial and mysterious manner:

> There is no action whatever, sincerely made for the sake of the Messianic Kingdom, which is not made for and in the Messiah. There is no Messianic communion which is not a communion in the Messiah. The Jews who work for the Kingdom may perhaps not know with Whom they have to do. When the Messianic Kingdom appears, they will learn the truth and the Messiah will manifest Himself.[7]

So, despite appearances to the contrary, pious Jews are not cut off from Jesus. Furthermore, and also despite appearances to the contrary, many Christians experience a constricted communion with Jesus because they fail to recognize him as a *Jewish* Messiah and because they have lost a vision of the messianic kingdom that he establishes.

> The Christian attitude in relation to Messianism is rather strange. Christians believe in a personal Messiah. Notwithstanding this belief, they are far less messianically-minded than the Jews. Their lack of Messianic consciousness takes two forms. They have largely lost the sense of Jesus' Messiahship. And they have, largely also, lost the Messianic vision.[8]

This defect in Christian communion with the Messiah—combined with Israel's real yet hidden communion with the same Messiah—results in a *coordination* of the roles of the Jewish people and the church of the nations as two bodies jointly *subordinate* to Jesus. Moreover, their partial yet genuine communion with Jesus the Messiah also brings the two bodies into a partial yet genuine communion with one another.

> What about the pious Jew who (without any guilt) has not accepted Jesus? What about the pious Christian entirely unconscious of his Jewish inheritance? Is there no communion between them? They communicate, to a certain extent, in the Messiah. . . . This communion is partial and implicit. God will make it someday total and explicit.[9]

---

7. Gillet, *Communion*, 107.
8. Gillet, *Communion*, 104.
9. Gillet, *Communion*, 196.

This vision of Jewish and Christian coordination, founded in and directed toward "communion in the Messiah," is also reflected in Gillet's conception of mission. While retaining the notion of a Christian mission to the Jews, he places it in a context of mutuality that transforms its meaning.

> We think (and in this we differ from most Christian missionaries) that the word "mission," used in connection with Israel, has a twofold meaning: there is, and there ought to be, a mission of the Christian Church to Israel; but there is also a Mission of Israel to the Christian Church, and this (as we think) divinely appointed mission must not be overlooked.[10]

> Israel is nowadays used and will, to a greater extent still, be used in the service of the Revelation. The people of the Law and the Prophets is perpetually sent (*missus, missio*) by God to the Christian Church in order to witness to certain truths and powers.[11]

This mutual mission has as its goal *full and explicit communion* with the Messiah, and with one another.

> A Jew who accepts (not only intellectually) Jesus as Messiah enters into communion with the Messiah *as Jesus*, and with the community of the followers of Jesus. Reciprocally, a Christian who becomes aware of the Jewish contents of his own faith and inwardly responds to this new awareness enters into communion with Jesus *as Jewish Messiah* and invisibly with the Messianic community of Israel, insofar as the Messiah displays an immanent activity inside it. Thus the Mission—the two-fold Mission—ends in communion.[12]

The Jewish and Christian communities are sent by God to one another that together they might fulfill a common mission in the world as servants of the Messiah. When the Christian mission succeeds in enabling individual Jews (if not entire communities) to "accept Jesus as Messiah," what then? Consistent with his coordinated vision of Jewish and Christian "communion in the Messiah," Gillet rejects the view that Jews should be absorbed and assimilated within the existing churches, surrendering their distinctive identity and vocation.

---

10. Gillet, *Communion*, 172.
11. Gillet, *Communion*, 191.
12. Gillet, *Communion*, 196.

> Generally speaking, we are very far from considering the adhesion of a Jew to one of the Gentile Christian Churches as an ideal solution. It may sometimes be the only possible one, but we do not think it either normal or desirable. The appearance and diffusion of a Jewish Christianity, inside the Church universal, is, as we believe, the only true solution.[13]

For many Jewish disciples of Jesus today, "adhesion . . . to one of the Gentile Christian Churches" still seems to be the only practical option. While acknowledging this fact, may we not also agree with Gillet that such an arrangement is neither "normal or desirable"?

What does Gillet have in mind when he speaks of "Jewish Christianity"? In his estimation, Jewish Christianity could legitimately develop along two distinct ecclesiological lines. The first he calls "unsynagogued Jewish Christianity."[14] He defines this as "a Jewish Christianity which has broken its ties with the Synagogue." The term "Synagogue" here refers not to a particular local Jewish congregation, but instead to the Jewish community as a whole, especially as embodied in its life of common worship. Such a form of Jewish Christianity would exist either as an autonomous branch of one of the historical Christian churches or as an independent Christian church. The second possible ecclesiological expression of Jewish Christianity he terms "synagogued Jewish Christianity."[15] In this model, Jews who believe in Jesus would seek to remain as much as possible within the Jewish community and to express their religious life in traditional Jewish forms. In his openness to various models and in his vision of "Jewish Christianity" as "inseparably linked with the development, among Christians, of a new ecumenical consciousness,"[16] Gillet's thought anticipates the convictions of the Helsinki Consultation on Jewish Continuity in the Body of Messiah and Yachad BeYeshua, the ecumenical fellowship of Jewish disciples of Jesus which emerged from the Helsinki Consultation.[17]

Thus, Lev Gillet *coordinates* the Jewish and Christian religious traditions in *subordination* to a high Christology (or, more precisely, high "Messianology"). He then employs this coordination/subordination as the fundamental justification for the restoration of what he calls "Jewish

13. Gillet, *Communion*, 191.
14. Gillet, *Communion*, 206.
15. Gillet, *Communion*, 206–8.
16. Gillet, *Communion*, 209.
17. For more details on the Helsinki Consultation, see appendix B.

Christianity." In so doing, he lays a sound foundation for our attempts to answer the question, what is the role of Jewish disciples of Jesus in the providential purposes of God?

## A SACRAMENTAL CALLING

Jewish disciples of Jesus have experienced the life-transforming reality of the God of Israel through the person and work of Jesus. Consequently, we properly subordinate all things of this world to our Messiah—including our Jewish identity. It is easy, then, to equate Jesus with his church (not only in its dimension as a universal mystical reality but also as a concrete historical phenomenon) and to draw the conclusion that our identity as part of the Jewish people should likewise be subordinated to our identity as part of the church. In recognizing the indissoluble connection between Jesus and his church, we do justice to the church's reality as the mystical body of Christ. But in subordinating our identification with the Jewish people to our membership in the church (considered empirically), we fail to do justice to Israel's reality as a *corpus mysticum* in communion with the Messiah.

Our ecclesial location as Jewish disciples of Jesus varies greatly. Many of us live as members of what Gillet calls "one of the Gentile Christian Churches."[18] Some in that circumstance also participate regularly in ecclesial groupings that Gillet would consider "Jewish Christian" in character. Others among us live as members of Messianic Jewish congregations which would be categorized by Gillet as expressions of "unsynagogued Jewish Christianity." Some in that circumstance also are involved regularly in the wider Jewish community of our region and thus exemplify in modest form what Gillet calls "synagogued Jewish Christianity." We all have some contact and relationship with the "Gentile Christian Churches," and most of us also have some contact and relationship with the mainstream Jewish world (if only through our extended families).

On a practical level, rarely will any of us perfectly coordinate our commitments and participation in these two bodies. One will almost always be subordinated to the other. Which body is so subordinated will vary among us. This accords with our particular life circumstances and vocations. Nevertheless, as Jewish disciples of Jesus, we may all learn from Gillet that such necessary practical expressions of subordination

18. Gillet, *Communion*, 191.

should not be universalized and interpreted by us in ways that set one community and tradition over the other. All must be subordinated to the Messiah, but the two forms in which the community of the Messiah is expressed are mutually ordered in a complementary rather than a hierarchical manner. When Jewish Christians associate only with other Jewish and gentile Christians, they may lose sight of this fact. When Messianic Jews associate only with other Messianic and mainstream Jews, they may likewise lose sight of this fact. When Jewish Christians and Messianic Jews gather together, the reality of the coordinated twofold *corpus mysticum* is far more difficult to ignore.

So, what is our calling as Jewish disciples of Jesus? Drawing from the work of Gillet, I propose that our significance lies not in who we are in ourselves but instead in our role as witnesses to the coordinated calling of the Jewish people and the Christian church in communion with the Messiah and with one another. In ways that vary according to our particular circumstances, we express the twofold mission in which Israel challenges the church and the church challenges Israel. We are called to be instruments and efficacious signs of the messianic communion that God desires for the twofold people of God, and for all creation—sacraments of that communion, which is now only partial and implicit. May this communion in the Messiah be perfected soon, speedily and in our day.

CHAPTER 10

# "Physician, Heal Yourself"
## Baptized Jews and the Wounded People of God

> *Alongside the larger body of Kinzer's work, many of the chapters in this volume point to the theological significance and important ecclesiological contributions of Jewish followers of Jesus. However, the positive and hopeful aspects of their existence is not the whole story. Here Kinzer unpacks the painful and treacherous actions of Jewish followers of Jesus from the past, and we would be remiss not to include this shadow side of history in our understanding of the influence of Jews within the body of Messiah. Jews who follow Jesus today are heirs of this unfortunate history and embracing this sad truth is key to living out their unique vocation.*[1]

## BAPTIZED JEWS AS AGENTS OF HEALING

The twentieth century provides us with an impressive list of Jewish disciples of Jesus whose lives and labors have contributed to the cause of reconciliation between the church and the Jewish people. John Connelly has documented the essential role played by Jewish Catholics such as Johannes Oesterreicher, Annie Krause, Raïssa Maritain, Brunno Hussar, and Gregory Baum in the revolution in Catholic-Jewish relations that

---

1. This chapter was originally presented in Krakow, Poland, at the 2017 Helsinki Consultation on Jewish Continuity in the Body of Messiah and has not previously been published.

culminated in *Nostra Aetate*.² Their mantle was taken up in the post-conciliar period by the archbishop of Paris, Cardinal Jean-Marie Lustiger.

The Eastern church featured the extraordinary witness of Fr. Alexander Men.³ Reflecting on his one short encounter with Fr. Alexander, Cardinal Lustiger wrote the following: "When I found myself face to face with Fr. Alexander Men, I felt I had known him all my life. He seemed like a brother, a friend who would always be close to me, despite the fact that we only spoke for perhaps ten minutes.... My memory of the event has taken the form of a strong, beautiful vision of a meeting in the mystery of the suffering and raised Messiah, a mystery that we both contemplated together."⁴ Cardinal Lustiger recognized a kindred Jewish soul with a kindred mission. Neither of these men specialized in the field of Jewish-Christian relations, but their teaching and their lives pointed the way to a more hopeful future for the two communities that each loved and honored.

Among Jewish disciples of Jesus in the Protestant world, Paul Philip Levertoff stands out. Levertoff served as an ordained Anglican priest but was also one of the most distinguished scholars of Jewish mysticism of his time.⁵ In the 1930s, he attempted to alert British Christians about the suffering of German Jews.⁶ It was largely through Levertoff's influence that Fr. Lev Gillet in 1942 wrote *Communion in the Messiah*—one of the finest books on Jewish-Christian relations ever published.⁷

We can learn much from reflecting on the lives of these exemplary figures. Their stories reinforce the thesis proposed in the previous chapter and articulated also in *Searching Her Own Mystery*: "If we [Jewish disciples of Jesus] embrace our Jewishness as a spiritual vocation ... we become a sacramental sign of the spiritual bond joining the *ekklēsia* to genealogical-Israel."⁸ As a "sacramental sign," Jewish disciples of Jesus are able to function as a "means of grace," a source of healing and spiritual renewal for both the *ekklēsia* and the Jewish people.

---

2. "From the 1840s until 1965, virtually every activist and thinker who worked for Catholic-Jewish reconciliation was not originally Catholic. Most were born Jewish" (Connelly, *From Enemy to Brother*, 5).

3. See Hamant, *Alexander Men*.

4. Hamant, *Alexander Men*, 209–10.

5. See Levertoff, *Love and the Messianic Age*.

6. See Behr-Sigel, *Lev Gillet*, 233–34.

7. Gillet, *Communion in the Messiah*.

8. Kinzer, *Searching Her Own Mystery*, 175.

However, a danger lurks if these are the *only* stories of baptized Jews that we recall. We may then conclude falsely that the historical trauma of post-Constantinian Jewish-Christian relations was inflicted exclusively by nefarious "others." In that scenario, we baptized Jews are innocent newcomers who now ride to the rescue in order to save our hapless comrades. If that is the story we tell ourselves, we are deluded as to the nature of the historical burden and the attitude that is required from those who are to bear it.

In reality, baptized Jews have played a significant and ignoble role in this historical tragedy. If we do not face that fact honestly, we will never understand the revulsion many of our Jewish kin feel in our presence or the concerns about us held by many gentile Christians committed to Jewish-Christian dialogue. My aim in this chapter is to remind Jewish disciples of Jesus of this unpleasant history so as to encourage humility as we bear witness to "the mystery of the suffering and raised Messiah"—who rules in the midst of both Israel and the church, reconciling each to the other in his own person.

## BAPTIZED JEWS AS SOURCE OF TRAUMA

The medieval period is the nadir of Jewish-Christian relations. It is the era of crusades (with their associated Jewish pogroms), host-desecration and blood libels, coercive disputations, the burning of Jewish books, forced baptisms, expulsion of entire Jewish communities, the Inquisition, and the *auto de fe*. With their inside knowledge of Jewish affairs, baptized Jews facilitated many of these developments. From one angle, they can be viewed as victims of the rivalry and fear that plagued both communities. But it does no service to those baptized Jews when we negate their dignity as responsible and culpable agents. And it does no service to us twenty-first-century baptized Jews when we deny the burdensome legacy we have received from them, our spiritual forbears.

A few well-known examples should suffice.[9] Nicholas Donin was a Parisian Jew who was baptized and entered the Franciscan order in the 1230s. He incited the persecution of Jews in France and convinced French authorities to burn copies of the Talmud.[10] Two or three decades

---

9. For reflection on the historical context of the figures and incidents described in these paragraphs, see Cohen, *Living Letters of the Law*, 317–63; Endelman, *Leaving the Jewish Fold*, 17–48.

10. See http://www.jewishencyclopedia.com/articles/5277-donin-nicholas-of-la-rochelle.

later, a Jew from Montpelier was baptized and entered the Dominican order. Taking the name Pablo Christiani, he engaged in a famous disputation with Nachmanides in Spain, denounced the Talmud, and convinced King Louis IX of France to require Jews to wear distinctive badges.[11] Joshua HaLorki (Geronimo de Santa Fe/Hieronymus de Sancta Fide), a fifteenth-century Spanish Jew, followed a similar path, participating in disputations and authoring articles such as "*Tractatus Contra Perfidiam Judæorum*" and "*De Judæis Erroribus ex Talmuth*."[12] Johannes Pfefferkorn was a German Jew baptized in the first decade of the sixteenth century. He published many anti-Jewish pamphlets, including one called "*Der Judenfeind*" (the Jewish enemy). Pfefferkorn persuaded the emperor to order the destruction of all non-biblical Jewish books.[13]

These baptized Jews saw their past religious life as no better than paganism. Their journey from Judaism to Christianity was an exodus from darkness to light. Solomon Halevi (Paul of Burgos), a fifteenth-century Spanish rabbi who became a bishop, expressed well their spiritual vision:

> I was ... brought up in Jewish blindness and incredulity; while learning Holy Scripture from unsanctified teachers, I received erroneous opinions from erring men, who cloud the pure letter of Scripture by impure inventions. ... But when it pleased Him whose mercies are infinite to call me from darkness to light, and from the depth of the pit to the open air of heaven, the scales seemed as it were to fall from the eyes of my understanding.[14]

Such insider testimony confirmed the anti-Jewish prejudice of the Christian world and added fuel to a fire that was already flaming out of control.

The most egregious anti-Jewish church practices of the medieval period faded away in the modern West. However, Christian anti-Jewish sentiment remained and continued to feed on the testimony of learned insiders who made the exodus from Judaism to the church. A renowned example of such a baptized Jew is Alfred Edersheim (1825–89), an Anglican priest whose writings on the New Testament continue to enjoy a wide readership. In his magnum opus, *The Life and Times of Jesus the Messiah*, Edersheim has this to say about the Talmud: "If we imagine something

---

11. See http://www.jewishencyclopedia.com/articles/4365-christiani-pablo.

12. See http://www.jewishencyclopedia.com/articles/8035-ibn-vives-al-lorqui-of-lorca-joshua-ben-joseph.

13. See http://www.jewishencyclopedia.com/articles/12081-pfefferkorn-johann-joseph.

14. Cohn-Sherbok, *Messianic Judaism*, 9.

... full of digressions, anecdotes, quaint sayings, fancies, legends, and too often of what, from its profanity, superstition, and even obscenity, could scarcely be quoted, we may form some general idea of what the Talmud is."[15] Edersheim's assessment of rabbinic Judaism as a whole is no more flattering. It is not merely *inferior* to Christianity, but *contrary* in its essence:

> The one [i.e., Rabbinism] developed the Law in its outward direction as ordinances and commandments; the other [i.e., Jesus] in its inward direction as life and liberty. Thus Rabbinism occupied one pole—and the outcome of its tendency to pure externalism was the Halakhah. . . . The teaching of Jesus occupied the opposite pole. Its starting-point was the inner sanctuary in which God was known and worshipped.[16]

> Thus as between the two . . . it may be fearlessly asserted that as regards their substance and spirit, there is not a difference, but a total divergence, of fundamental principle between Rabbinism and the New Testament, so that comparison between them is not possible. Here there is absolute contrariety.[17]

Generations of devout English-speaking Christians have learned about Judaism from Alfred Edersheim. While his writings are less inflammatory than those of his medieval forbears, they still keep the fire burning.

In the East, the medieval spirit endured. No more perfect embodiment of that spirit can be found than the figure of Jacob Brafman and the notorious volume he authored, *The Book of the Kahal*. In the early nineteenth century, the Russian government related to Jewish communities as corporate entities. The leadership structure in each Jewish community was called a *kahal*. The *kahals* were responsible for the conscription of Jewish youth into the Russian army and as such were resented by many Jews. In 1844, this system of administration was dismantled by the Russian authorities. Jacob Brafman was a Jew who struggled against the *kahals* in the final years of their existence. His resentment led him to

---

15. Edersheim, *The Life and Times*, 103. On the other hand, Edersheim acknowledged that the Talmud has its bright spots: "When we bear in mind the many sparkling, beautiful, and occasionally almost sublime passages in the Talmud, but especially that its forms of thought and expression so often recall those of the New Testament, only prejudice and hatred could indulge in indiscriminate vituperation" (Edersheim, *Life and Times*, 104)

16. Edersheim, *Life and Times*, 106.

17. Edersheim, *Life and Times*, 107.

flee Judaism and enter the Orthodox Church. In the 1860s, he worked as a spy for the Russian government within the Jewish world. In 1869, he published *The Book of the Kahal*, in which, as Gregory Yuri Glazov puts it,

> he contended that the *kahal*, though abolished in 1844, continued to exist as a secret organization, controlling the world's Jews by Talmudic fanaticism and Hasidic obscurantism and seeking to exploit the world's economy under the guise of religious organizations and charities. . . . Printed at public expense and sent to all government offices to guide Russian officials in dealing with Jewry, it became the most successful and influential Judeophobic work in Russian history, making Brafman the grandfather of all save the occult elements of the *Protocols of the Elders of Zion*.[18]

It is disheartening to learn that some of the most vicious anti-Jewish tropes of the modern era have their roots in the writings of an embittered baptized Jew.

Brafman followed the medieval model of Christian anti-Jewish activism in which religious attacks on Judaism were combined with slanderous charges of immoral conduct leveled against Jewish communities. This was a potent concoction and, as in the medieval period, resulted in horrific violence against Jews. In contrast, the modern Western approach exemplified by Alfred Edersheim focused exclusively on the deficiencies of Jewish religious practice. While less threatening to life and limb, the Western attitude of baptized Jews did nothing to heal the wounds opened by their medieval ancestors.

In general, the example of baptized Jews in the last hundred years has been more edifying. The individuals mentioned at the beginning of this chapter were exceptional in their dedication and talents, but they represent an orientation shared by many contemporary baptized Jews. In some quarters, however, older attitudes have endured. I have heard reports from reliable sources that a pioneering figure of late twentieth-century Christian missions charged that "Judaism is a false religion." An Israeli Jewish Christian leader went on the record with the following:

> Rabbinic legalism has destroyed the spirit of the Law and rendered it ineffective. . . . The Law is viewed by Judaism by way of legalistic literalism, which takes it out of the realm of morality and into the realm of a commercial transaction: if I do this and that, you will do this and that for me. . . . In the hands of the

18. Solovyov, *The Burning Bush*, 70.

rabbis, the Law has been transformed into an instigator of human pride and self-satisfaction.[19]

Such comments hearken back to an earlier era in which baptized Jews drew upon their insider knowledge to heap contempt on their religious origins and glorify their newly acquired faith.

## EMBODYING RECONCILIATION

Some Messianic Jews advance an opposite but only slightly less damaging view. In their teaching, Christianity is the "false religion." Christmas and Easter are considered pagan holidays and the entire Christian tradition is nullified. Judaism is the one true faith and all nations are called to adopt it. Such thinking takes us no further along on the road to healing and reconciliation.

As a leader in the Messianic Jewish movement, I have witnessed too many triumphalist celebrations in which we Jewish disciples of Jesus are the key to the restoration of the church, the salvation of Israel, and the redemption of the world. In such settings, the church and Israel are sometimes portrayed as wandering in thick darkness, waiting for us Messianic Jews to come to the rescue. Of course, such claims of self-importance should not be taken at face value; they make psychological sense only when viewed against the backdrop of Messianic Jewish marginality and ostracism. To sustain our precarious existence, we Messianic Jews must believe we are fulfilling an essential role in the divine plan. I believe that this is indeed the case, but the part assigned to us is not that of the *one true church* or the *one true Israel*. We are to be humble servants of messianic reconciliation, not conquerors overthrowing rival kingdoms.

For my Jewish Christian friends, the temptation is to understate rather than underline their distinctive Jewish identity. But this plays into a more traditional *Christian* triumphalist narrative in which Judaism pales in comparison with Christian faith and the voice of the Jewish people sounds an indecipherable note amid the universal chorus of the nations.

In either case, we have forgotten our checkered history, the history of baptized Jews. The leaders of the Jewish community have not forgotten. They do not behold us as we really are but see on our faces the masks

19. Maoz, *Judaism Is Not Jewish*, 157–58.

of Nicholas Donin, Pablo Christiani, Geronimo de Santa Fe, Johannes Pfefferkorn, Paul of Burgos, and Jacob Brafman.

Remembering that history, we will forsake all triumphalism, recognizing that the traumatic tale of Jewish-Christian relations cannot be externalized. It is *our* history, not the history of others. *We are the Jews who suffered; we are the Christians who persecuted; we are the baptized Jews who betrayed our families.*

But we are also the baptized Jews of the past hundred years who have charted a different course. Following the example set by Cardinal Lustiger, Fr. Men, and Reverend Levertoff, we have a unique role to play in the drama of reconciliation. That role requires that we identify loyally with the Jewish people as our people and also with the community of those who confess the name of Jesus. *The reconciliation that we proclaim is one that we must first embody. The wounds of history are inscribed on our own limbs, and we will only become the healer of others by first being healed ourselves.*

# PART III.

*Eschatology as Zionology:
The Jewish Jesus
and the Culmination of History*

CHAPTER 11

# The People and Land of Israel in Lukan Eschatology

> *Pushing back against prevailing understandings of Luke-Acts, Kinzer argues that the land of Israel and the city of Jerusalem are essential pillars in Luke's theological narrative. According to Kinzer, the unfinished geographical trajectory of Luke-Acts parallels its unfinished soteriological story, both pointing toward an eschatological redemption of the people of Israel, centered in the restored land of Israel. As Kinzer argues, it is only within this larger narrative arc that the gospel's outward expansion can be properly understood.*[1]

At no point do the earliest Christians view the Holy Land as a locus of divine activity to which the people of the Roman empire must be drawn. They do not promote the Holy Land either for the Jew or for the Christian as a vital aspect of faith. ... The early Christians possessed no territorial theology. Early Christian preaching is utterly uninterested in a Jewish eschatology devoted to the restoration of the land. The kingdom of Christ began in Judea and is historically anchored there but it

---

1. An abbreviated version of this chapter was presented in April 2015 at Georgetown University as part of a conference sponsored by the Institute on Religion and Democracy. The theme of the conference was "People of the Land: A 21st Century Case for Christian Zionism." An expanded version of the conference paper was published under the title "Do the People of Israel and the Land of Israel Persist as Abiding Concerns in Luke's Two Volumes?" alongside the other conference papers in McDermott, *The New Christian Zionism*, 141–65.

is not tethered to a political realization of that kingdom in the Holy Land.[2]

THESE WORDS OF GARY Burge place him in the mainstream of Christian scholars. It is commonplace for specialists in Christian theology and Scripture to assert that the land of Israel loses its theological significance in the New Testament. Minimally, it seems self-evident to most that the theme of the land as a particular geographical location (as opposed to an eschatological symbol representing the entire world) lacks prominence in the New Testament texts.

I will argue in this chapter that Luke-Acts displays an orientation to the city of Jerusalem that contradicts these standard conclusions.[3] According to Luke-Acts, Jerusalem possesses a unique status not only because "the kingdom of Christ" is "historically anchored" there, but even more because that kingdom will achieve its eschatological consummation within its walls. This means that the land of Israel also retains its unique status for Luke-Acts, for the city of Jerusalem functioned from the time of the post-exilic prophets as a symbol for the land as a whole, as well as for the people destined to inherit it.[4] It is no accident that the modern movement to restore corporate Jewish life in the land took the name "Zionism," for Zion (i.e., Jerusalem) represents the entire land of Israel.

Gary Burge recognizes the importance of Luke-Acts for any treatment of this topic, and rightly highlights a set of verses from the first chapter of Acts:

> So when they had come together, they asked him, "Lord, is this the time when you will restore the kingdom to Israel?" He replied, "It is not for you to know the times or periods that the Father has set by his own authority. But you will receive power when the Holy Spirit has come upon you; and you will be my witnesses in Jerusalem, in all Judea and Samaria, and to the ends of the earth." (Acts 1:6–8)

2. Burge, *Jesus and the Land*, 59.

3. The arguments presented in this chapter are more fully elaborated in Kinzer, *Jerusalem Crucified*.

4. "Isaiah, like Ezekiel, reorients the blessing of Abraham so that it comes to center almost exclusively on Jerusalem, on Mount Zion. . . . What had formerly been attributed to the land as a whole is now transferred to the city and the holy mountain. . . . Like Ezekiel, Zechariah uses the traditional formulas associated with the promise of the land, but he has centered them solely on Jerusalem and Judah" (Wilken, *The Land Called Holy*, 15–16, 18).

Burge interprets these words of Jesus as a denial of the validity of the disciples' question: "Jesus' correction of the apostles should not be taken to mean that Jesus acknowledges the old Jewish worldview and that its timing is now hidden from the apostles. Instead, Jesus is acknowledging their incomprehension. He in effect says, 'Yes, I will restore Israel—but in a way you cannot imagine.'"[5]

This reading of Acts 1 draws support from two structural features of the book of Acts. First, Acts 1:8 signals the geographical structure of the book as a whole. The volume begins in Jerusalem, moves on to Judea and Samaria, and then concludes in Rome (the "ends of the earth"). This structure suggests that Jerusalem is important only as the site of ecclesial origins; it represents the honored past but not the glorious future. In the words of Burge, "the work of this messianic era is not centripetal but centrifugal: moving away from the center, Jerusalem, while remembering where it came from."[6] Second, many commentators see the tone and content of the book's final scene in Rome as implying a definitive judgment on the Jewish people, a judgment that deprives them of their covenantal privileges. The destruction of Jerusalem that will occur in the years immediately following this final scene confirms the decisive nature of this judgment. Thus, for the author of Luke-Acts, Jerusalem and the Jewish people represent the *ekklēsia*'s past, but her future belongs with the nations of the world.

I will first examine these two structural features of the Lukan writings and argue that their significance has commonly been misunderstood. I will then return to Acts 1:6–8 and offer my own interpretation of these crucial verses.

## "HE SET HIS FACE TO GO TO JERUSALEM" (LUKE 9:51)

Luke underlines the thematic centrality of Jerusalem for his two-volume work by structuring his narrative geographically, with Jerusalem as its pivot. No other book in the New Testament adheres to such a defined geographical pattern as a primary principle of organization. This author also gives more attention to the destiny of Jerusalem than any other New Testament writer. An examination of the geographical structure of

---

5. Burge, *Jesus and the Land*, 61.
6. Burge, *Jesus and the Land*, 62.

Luke-Acts and of Luke's teaching concerning Jerusalem will provide clues regarding the message that the two volumes convey.

## The Geographical Structure of the Gospel of Luke

Among the four Gospels, only Luke begins in Jerusalem—and not merely in Jerusalem, but at the heart of the city, the holy Temple, where the future father of John the Baptist offers incense and receives an angelic visitation (Luke 1:5–23). While both Matthew and Luke describe Jesus's birth near Jerusalem in Bethlehem (Matt 2:1–12; Luke 2:1–70), only Luke depicts the presentation of the infant Jesus in the Temple, accompanied by the prophetic blessings of Simeon and Anna (Luke 2:22–38). Only Luke among the canonical Gospels provides readers with a story of Jesus as a youth, and that story recounts the boy's visit to Jerusalem and his lingering in the courts of the Temple (Luke 2:41–51). Thus, Luke's two-chapter introduction centers on the city of Jerusalem and its Temple.

In chapter 3, the book shifts its focus to Galilee and for the next seven chapters it follows generally the order of events recorded in the Gospel of Mark. Near the end of chapter 9, Luke begins a new section of his narrative which combines material from the double tradition (i.e., units shared by Luke and Matthew but not by Mark) with material unique to Luke. The new section begins in this way: "When the days drew near for him to be taken up, he set his face to go to Jerusalem" (Luke 9:51). The next nine chapters of Luke's "special section" (Luke 9:51—18:14) take the form of an extended travel narrative encompassing Jesus's final journey to Jerusalem. The material itself is only loosely geographical in character, consisting of parables and stories that usually lack an intrinsic connection to the journey. Nevertheless, Luke has chosen to organize the material around this Passover pilgrimage with occasional editorial reminders of the geographical context (e.g., Luke 13:22; 17:11). In this way, the central section of Luke's narrative, which occurs outside Jerusalem, employs the Holy City as its point of orientation and source of structural unity.

As in all four Gospels, the events of Luke's passion narrative occur in Jerusalem and its immediate environs. However, only Luke restricts resurrection appearances to the Jerusalem region and only Luke includes the dominical command requiring the disciples to remain in the city (Luke 24:49). The Gospel ends as it began—in the Jerusalem Temple, with a community of Jews worshipping the God of Israel (Luke 24:53).

Among the canonical Gospels, only Luke begins in Jerusalem, ends in Jerusalem, and orients its central narrative around a journey *to* Jerusalem. This geographical structure underlines Luke's unique concern for the Holy City and its enduring theological significance.

## The Geographical Structure of the Book of Acts

The book of Acts likewise orders its narrative according to a geographical pattern centered in Jerusalem and, as already noted, that pattern finds explicit articulation in Acts 1:8: "You will be my witnesses in Jerusalem, in all Judea and Samaria, and to the ends of the earth."

Like the Gospel of Luke, the book of Acts begins in Jerusalem, with a community centered on the Temple (Acts 2:46; 3:1–10; 4:1–2; 5:12, 20–21, 42). The story develops as the message of Jesus radiates outward—first to the towns of Judea and Samaria, then with reference to Damascus.[7] In Acts 10, Peter proclaims the good news to Cornelius and his household in the coastal city of Caesarea. In Acts 11, the reader learns that persecution in Jerusalem has led some disciples to Phoenicia, Cyprus, and Antioch (Acts 11:19). From Antioch, Paul begins his travels (Acts 13:1–3), wending his way through Asia Minor (Acts 13:4—14:26), and eventually crossing over to Europe (Acts 16:9–10) and establishing Jesus-believing communities in Greece. The story concludes with Paul in Rome, the capital of the Empire.

The geographical outline of Acts 1:8 and the above summary of the narrative of Acts leave out a particular detail that has profound implications for our interpretation of the geographical structure of Acts: while radiating steadily outward, *the story continually reverts back to Jerusalem*. Paul encounters Jesus on the road to Damascus and then *returns to Jerusalem* (Acts 9:26–29). Peter proclaims Jesus to Cornelius in Caesarea and then *returns to Jerusalem* (Acts 11:2). A congregation arises in Antioch and then in a time of famine *sends aid to Jerusalem* (Acts 11:27–30). Paul and Barnabas journey from Antioch to Asia Minor and then *return to Jerusalem* for the central event in the book—the Jerusalem council (Acts 15:2). From Jerusalem, Paul travels with Silas to Greece and then *returns to Jerusalem* (Acts 18:22).[8] Paul completes his final missionary journey

---

7. On the spread of the movement to Judea and Samaria, see Acts 8:1, 4–25; on the city of Damascus, see Acts 9:1–2, 10, 19.

8. The Greek text of Acts 18:22 says merely that "Paul went up and greeted the church" (see KJV, RSV, NIV). However, commentators generally recognize that Luke

and then *returns to Jerusalem* where he is arrested (Acts 21:17—23:11). While this feature of the geographical structure of Acts is often ignored by commentators, Robert Brawley is a notable exception:

> Although Acts begins in Jerusalem and ends in Rome, it is inaccurate to conclude that Jerusalem falls out in favor of Rome. The narrative in Acts actually reciprocates between Jerusalem and the extended mission. . . . Even when Paul is in Rome, his memory reverts to Jerusalem to reiterate his fate there (28:17). Hence, Acts does not delineate a movement away from Jerusalem, but *a constant return to Jerusalem*. In the geography of Acts emphasis repeatedly falls on Jerusalem from beginning to end.[9]

If indeed Acts 1:8 is a geographical outline of the book, then its language supports this conclusion, for it characterizes Rome as being located at "the *ends* of the earth." Given the city's overwhelming political, military, economic, and cultural dominance within the first-century world inhabited by Luke, applying this phrase (even by implication) to Rome comes as a shock. For Luke, Rome may be the capital of a gentile empire that rules much of the earth, but it was neither the *center* nor the true capital of the world.[10] That honor belonged to Jerusalem alone.

This assessment finds further confirmation in the geographical structure of the list of Jews gathered for the holiday of Pentecost (Acts 2:5, 9–11). Richard Bauckham has analyzed this list, and the results are striking:

> Luke's list of the nations and countries from which the pilgrims attending the festival of Pentecost had come (Acts 2:9–11) provides a much more authentically *Jerusalem* perspective on the

---

is employing the traditional Jewish idiom ("to go up") for a journey to Jerusalem. The translators of the NRSV were so confident of this interpretation that they incorporated it into their English text: "When he had landed at Caesarea, he went up *to Jerusalem* and greeted the church, and then went down to Antioch." I. Howard Marshall concurs with this understanding of the verse and also notes its significance: "When he [Luke] goes on to say that *Paul went up and greeted the church*, this is usually understood as a reference to going up to Jerusalem and seeing the church there. . . . If this is a correct assumption, it means that each of Paul's missionary campaigns concluded with a visit to Jerusalem, so that Paul's work began from and ended in Jerusalem in each case" (Marshall, *Acts*, 301–2).

9. Brawley, *Luke-Acts and the Jews*, 35–36 (emphasis added).

10. "Luke rejoices that the word of God and the good news about the Jewish messiah and king Jesus flow out of Zion to the rest of the world, conquering even Rome, which, vis-à-vis Jerusalem, lies at the extremities of the earth, not at the center" (Oliver, *Torah Praxis After 70 CE*, 28).

> Diaspora. The order in which the names occur has perplexed interpreters. In fact, if we take the trouble to plot the names on a map of the world as an ancient reader would have perceived it, we can see that Luke's list is carefully designed to depict the Jewish Diaspora with Jerusalem at its centre.... The names in Acts 2:9–11 are listed in four groups corresponding to the four points of the compass, beginning in the east and moving counterclockwise.... The first group of names in the list... *begins in the far east and moves in towards Judaea*, which is then named. Recognizing that Judaea is in the list because it is the centre of the pattern described by the names is the key to understanding the list. The second group of names... is of places to the north of Judaea, and follows *an order which moves out from and back to Judaea*, ending at the point from which one might sail to Judaea. The third group of names... moves west from Judaea through Egypt... and Libya to Rome, *and then back to Judaea* by a sea route calling at Crete. Finally, a single name (Arabs) represents the movement south from Judaea, presumably indicating Nabataea, immediately due south of Judaea.[11]

Not only does this list depict Jerusalem as the center of the world; it also follows the same rhythm of outward and inward movement that characterizes the entire narrative of Acts. Reading Acts 1:8 in light of Acts 2:9–11 and in light of the overall structure of Acts, we might say that the Pentecost list portrays the historical spread of the good news in accordance with Acts 1:8, whereas the narrative of the book of Acts focuses on one particular strand of that greater story—the strand associated with the controversial figure of Paul. In both the greater story of the advance of the good news and the more circumscribed story of Paul, Jerusalem is the heart from which the blood flows and to which it invariably returns. Contrary to Burge's claim, the centrifugal movement of the narrative of Acts is continually balanced by a centripetal movement.

## The Judgment/Redemption of Jerusalem and the Puzzle of Luke-Acts

This movement of outward-flow and inward-return continues until we reach the final chapter of Acts, at which point the movement is cut off mid-cycle. The story concludes in Rome, at "the ends of the earth," with no return to Jerusalem. If Jerusalem had only functioned in the narrative

---

11. Bauckham, "James and the Jerusalem Church," 419 (emphasis added).

as a point of origin, as Burge suggests, then an ending in Rome would be natural and fitting. However, as we have seen, Jerusalem plays a much more prominent role in the geographical structure of Acts than this simple linear scheme would suggest. It is Luke's center and Rome is but the periphery. Has that center now forfeited its privileged status? Has the former periphery now taken its place?

To answer this question, we must return to the Gospel of Luke and reflect on a puzzling feature of its narrative that provides essential insight on the meaning of its companion volume. I refer to the Gospel of Luke's preoccupation with the destruction of Jerusalem in 70 CE and its hints of Jerusalem's future redemption. While the Jewish war with Rome looms in the background of each of the canonical Gospels, Luke's orientation to this event is unique among the four of them.

First, Luke is unique in his portrait of Jesus's sympathy for the suffering that Jerusalem will undergo. Like Matthew, Luke depicts Jesus's frustrated longing for Jerusalem's repentance: "Jerusalem, Jerusalem, the city that kills the prophets and stones those who are sent to it! How often have I desired to gather your children together as a hen gathers her brood under her wings, and you were not willing!" (Luke 13:34). But in Luke this verse follows a warning from the Pharisees to Jesus that Herod seeks to kill him (Luke 13:31–33)—a warning that distances these Pharisees from Herod's malicious intent and portrays them as quasi-allies of Jesus.[12] In contrast, Matthew positions this saying (Matt 23:37–39) as the climax of a fierce *denunciation* of the Pharisees which holds them culpable for the blood of the prophets (Matt 23:34–36); the Matthean context undercuts the pathos accentuated in the Lukan setting and inherent in the words themselves.[13]

Luke also emphasizes this pathos by including two incidents in his Gospel that are absent from Matthew, Mark, and John—one describing Jesus's public entrance into Jerusalem and the other portraying his public departure. When Luke recounts Jesus's triumphal procession into the Holy City, he alone among the Gospel writers informs us that Jesus wept as he contemplated the suffering she would experience forty years later

---

12. See Tomson, "*If this be from Heaven . . .*," 223; Brawley, *Luke-Acts and the Jews*, 84, 102.

13. The Matthean version of this saying is typical of the book's polemical attitude toward the Pharisees. As I have argued elsewhere, Matthew's polemics derive in large part from the author's ideological proximity to Pharisaic thought (see Kinzer, *Postmissionary Messianic Judaism*, 247–55). They do not imply a view of the Jewish people or the land of Israel that diverges radically from what is found in Luke-Acts.

at the hands of the Romans (Luke 19:41-44). When Luke describes Jesus's humiliating exit from the city under the whip of Roman soldiers, he alone among the Gospel writers tells us of the women who follow along wailing for him (Luke 23:27), and of Jesus's response to them—a response that again anticipates the future suffering of Jerusalem:

> But Jesus turned to them and said, "Daughters of Jerusalem, do not weep for me, but weep for yourselves and for your children. For the days are surely coming when they will say, 'Blessed are the barren, and the wombs that never bore, and the breasts that never nursed.' Then they will begin to say to the mountains, 'Fall on us'; and to the hills, 'Cover us.' For if they do this when the wood is green, what will happen when it is dry?" (Luke 23:28-31)

Luke includes more of these proleptic flashes of impending judgment than the other Gospels, but in doing so the author evinces no sense of joy or vindication at Jerusalem's tragic fate. In pondering the city's day of judgment, the Lukan Jesus weeps.

A second unique feature of Luke's orientation to the destruction of Jerusalem in 70 CE appears in his account of Jesus's eschatological discourse (Luke 21:5-36). In Mark and Matthew, this discourse so combines and compresses references to the *imminent* destruction of Jerusalem and the *ultimate* distress of the eschaton that the two events are inextricably entangled. This overlay of one event upon the other is especially evident in Mark 13:14-20:

> But when you see the desolating sacrilege [*to bdelugma tēs erēmōseōs*] set up where it ought not to be (let the reader understand), then those in Judea must flee to the mountains; someone on the housetop must not go down or enter the house to take anything away; someone in the field must not turn back to get a coat. Woe to those who are pregnant and to those who are nursing infants in those days! Pray that it may not be in winter. For in those days there will be suffering, such as has not been from the beginning of the creation that God created until now, no, and never will be. And if the Lord had not cut short those days, no one would be saved; but for the sake of the elect, whom he chose, he has cut short those days.

The "desolating sacrilege"—or, more literally, "the detestable thing of desolation"—alludes to the apocalyptic prophecies of Daniel (Dan 9:27; 11:31; 12:11) and their description of an idolatrous altar or image erected in the Temple; the phrase thus refers to an event immediately preceding the resurrection of the saints and the transformation of heaven and earth. In contrast, Luke's version of these verses distinguishes clearly between what will happen in Jerusalem in 70 CE and what will happen when Jesus returns.[14]

> When you see Jerusalem surrounded by armies, then know that its desolation [*erēmōsis*] has come near. Then those in Judea must flee to the mountains, and those inside the city must leave it, and those out in the country must not enter it; for these are days of vengeance, as a fulfillment of all that is written. Woe to those who are pregnant and to those who are nursing infants in those days! For there will be great distress on the earth and wrath against this people [*laos*]; they will fall by the edge of the sword and be taken away as captives among all nations [*ethnē*]; and Jerusalem will be trampled on by the gentiles [*ethnōn*], until the times of the gentiles [*ethnōn*] are fulfilled. (Luke 21:20-24)

Luke transforms Mark's reference to the desecration of the Temple (*to bdelugma tēs erēmōseōs*) so that it becomes a description of the "desolation" (*erēmōsis*) of the entire city. The sign that leads the disciples to flee is no longer an idolatrous altar but instead the sight of Jerusalem surrounded by Roman armies. The Markan text implies a cosmic distress, whereas the Lukan version speaks of "wrath against *this people*" (i.e., the Jewish people who inhabit Jerusalem). Most significantly, *the world in its unredeemed form—and the Jewish people—remain in existence after this event*, for not all of the inhabitants of Jerusalem are slain but some are "taken away as captives among all the gentiles [*ethnē*]," and "Jerusalem will be trampled on by the gentiles [*ethnōn*], until the times of the gentiles [*ethnōn*] are fulfilled."[15] This concluding statement about Jerusalem implies that an extended period of time will elapse between the destruction

---

14. N. T. Wright famously interprets the entirety of Mark 13 as referring to the destruction of Jerusalem in 70 CE (see Wright, *Jesus and the Victory of God*, 339-68). His argument for this position has convinced few scholars. Dale Allison's trenchant critique of this reading of Mark 13 represents the trustworthy consensus of New Testament scholarship. See Allison, "Jesus and the Victory of Apocalyptic," 126-41. Wright's response to this critique is found in the same volume, 261-68.

15. It is unfortunate that the NRSV translates *ethnē* in v. 24a as "nations" and then renders the two uses of *ethnōn* in v. 24b as "gentiles." This obscures the connection between the two halves of the verse, which preserves throughout the distinction between the Jewish people (the *laos* of v. 23b) and the gentiles who are the agents and the locus of their exile.

of the city by the gentiles and the end of the age (which will occur only *after* "the times of the gentiles are fulfilled").

The above text from Luke 21 also displays the third unique feature of Luke's orientation to the destruction of Jerusalem. Verse 24 states that "Jerusalem will be trampled on by the gentiles, until [*achri*] the times [*kairoi*] of the gentiles are fulfilled." Robert Tannehill considers this verse in light of other Jewish literature of the period, and draws the most reasonable conclusion:

> That Jerusalem or the sanctuary has been or will be "trampled on" is a repeated theme in ancient Jewish writings.... This trampling of Jerusalem will last only "until the times of the Gentiles are fulfilled." We are not told explicitly what will happen then, but if we return to the other texts that speak of this trampling, we find the expectation *that Jerusalem will be restored.*[16]

This interpretation of Luke 21:24 receives further support from a similar use of *achri* ("until") in Peter's Temple speech in Acts 3:

> And now, brethren, I know that you acted in ignorance, just as your rulers did also. But the things which God announced beforehand by the mouth of all the prophets, that His Christ would suffer, He has thus fulfilled. Therefore repent and return, so that your sins may be wiped away, in order that times [*kairoi*] of refreshing may come from the presence of the Lord; and that He may send Jesus, the Christ appointed for you, whom heaven must receive until [*achri*] the period of restoration [*apokatastasis*] of all things about which God spoke by the mouth of His holy prophets from ancient time. (Acts 3:17–21 NASB)

I will comment further on this passage below, but at this point I only note its connection to Luke 21:24. The "times [*kairoi*] of the gentiles"—referring to exclusive gentile sovereignty over Jerusalem resulting from Israel's rejection of the prophetic message—will give way to the "times [*kairoi*] of refreshing" when Israel repents and welcomes "the Christ [i.e., Messiah] appointed for you." The resurrected Messiah will remain in the heavenly sphere "*until* [*achri*] the period [*chronoi*] of restoration [*apokatastasis*] of all things about which God spoke by the mouth of His holy prophets"—which is apparently equivalent in meaning to "*until* [*achri*] the times [*kairioi*] of the gentiles are fulfilled." According to Albrecht Oepke, the

---

16. Tannehill, *Luke*, 305–6 (emphasis added). The "other texts" to which Tannehill refers include Zechariah 12:3 (LXX) and the Psalms of Solomon 17:21–24.

verbal form of *apokatastasis* becomes in the Septuagint and Josephus a technical term "for the restoration of Israel to its own land."[17] From its context, the noun form in Acts 3:21 evidently includes this meaning.

Luke is thus unique among the Gospels not only in its emphasis on Jerusalem's coming destruction but also in its anticipation of the city's future restoration. This theme occupies an especially prominent place in the Lukan infancy narrative, where Simeon and Anna's encounter with the child Jesus satisfies their longing to see the beginning of "the redemption of Jerusalem" (Luke 2:38) and the "consolation of Israel" (Luke 2:28). Since the hope for Jerusalem's redemption resounds at the beginning of the Gospel but is not in fact attained in the course of the events recounted in Luke's two volumes, attentive readers recognize that Luke's story is incomplete.

Luke displays this sense of incompleteness—or, one might even say, of the temporary frustration of God's redemptive purpose—through the verbal connections linking two of his key texts. The first is the Song of Zechariah in Luke 1:69–79, uttered by the father of John the Baptist on the occasion of the child's circumcision. The song is a celebration of God's saving power at work in the fulfillment of God's promises to Israel. The object of praise is "the Lord God of Israel" (v. 68), and God's redeeming act is in accordance with the oath sworn to Abraham (v. 73) and the covenant established with the patriarchs (v. 72). In the births of John the Baptist and Jesus, God has "visited [*epeskepsato*] his people to redeem them" (1:68), "to give knowledge [*gnōsis*] of salvation to his people" (1:77), and "to guide our feet into the way of peace [*eirēnē*]" (1:79). God's work through John and Jesus will result in Israel being "saved" and "rescued" from its enemies [*echthroi*] (1:71, 73).

The second text is Luke's account of Jesus's weeping over Jerusalem before his triumphal entry to the city:

> As he came near and saw the city, he wept over it, saying, "If you, even you, had only recognized [*egnōs*] on this day the things that make for peace [*eirēnē*]! But now they are hidden from your eyes. Indeed, the days will come upon you, when your enemies [*echthroi*] will set up ramparts around you and surround you, and hem you in on every side. They will crush you to the ground, you and your children within you, and they will not leave within you one stone upon another; because you

---

17. Oepke, "*apokathistēmi, apokatastasis*," in *Theological Dictionary of the New Testament*, 388. See LXX Hos 11:11; Jer 16:15; 24:6; Jospehus, *Antiquities* 11:2, 63.

did not recognize [*egnōs*] the time of your visitation [*episkopē*] from God." (Luke 19:41-44)

While the language of these verses recalls that of the Song of Zechariah, the tone and content of the two texts are diametrically opposed. The ecstatic joy of the song has been transmuted into profound grief. John and Jesus came to bring Israel "the knowledge [*gnōsis*] of salvation," but the people "did not know [*egnōs*]" this salvation when it appeared. God has "visited [*epeskepsato*]" Israel for their good, but the people did not discern this "visitation [*episkopē*]." God had wanted to bring Israel "peace [*eirēnē*]" and rescue from "enemies [*echthroi*]," but Israel did not recognize "the things that make for peace [*eirēnē*]" and consequently will be surrounded and defeated by its "enemies [*echthroi*]."[18]

The contradictory tone and content of these two texts represent in vivid fashion the puzzling and paradoxical character of Luke's geographical structure and message. As the Jewish people's longed-for Messiah, Jesus comes to bring redemption to Jerusalem and consolation to Israel. Nevertheless, his mission results in the destruction of Jerusalem and Israel's second exile. Luke highlights both themes and sets them in jarring juxtaposition, rather than accentuating one and downplaying the other. Luke then proceeds to treat this destruction and exile as the beginning of an era—associated with "the gentiles"—which at some point in the future will come to an end. Finally, he implies in Acts 3:19-21 (and also in Luke 13:35) that Jesus will return in response to Jerusalem's repentance and corporate welcome. In this way the content of Luke and Acts supports our conclusion regarding the geographical structure of the latter book: the end of the book is not the end of the story. Luke intimates that the outward flow will once again be followed by an inward return and Israel's second Babylonian exile will culminate in a final pilgrimage to Zion.

Traditional interpreters such as Gary Burge have looked to the geographical structure of Luke-Acts in order to support their reading of Acts 1:6-8. Our examination of that structure in light of the Lukan teaching concerning the judgment and redemption of Jerusalem shows that the

---

18. Robert C. Tannehill notes the link between these two texts and the literary effect it produces: "The narrator intends to connect the arrival in Jerusalem with the birth narrative in order to highlight the tragic turn which the narrative is now taking. The great expectations in the birth narrative for the redemption of Israel and Jerusalem are not being realized in the anticipated way and with the anticipated fullness, because Jerusalem is failing to recognize the time of its visitation" (Tannehill, *The Narrative Unity of Luke-Acts*, 1:160).

opposite is the case. Far from confirming the traditional view of Acts 1, the geographical structure of the book effectively undermines that view. Luke tells a story that remains unfinished and that points forward to a day "when the times of the gentiles are fulfilled." In that day, Israel's Roman exile (anticipated by Acts 28:23–31) will come to an end, as did its earlier Babylonian exile, and "the ransomed of the LORD shall return, and come to Zion with singing" (Isa 35:10).

## "THIS SALVATION OF GOD HAS BEEN SENT TO THE GENTILES" (ACTS 28:28)

### The Traditional Reading

The ending of the book of Acts is significant not only because its scenes are set in Rome. Traditional commentators also underline the fact that the book ends with Paul's prophetic rebuke of the Jewish leaders of the city.

> The Holy Spirit was right in saying to your ancestors through the prophet Isaiah, "Go to this people and say, 'You will indeed listen, but never understand, and you will indeed look, but never perceive. For this people's heart has grown dull, and their ears are hard of hearing, and they have shut their eyes; so that they might not look with their eyes, and listen with their ears, and understand with their heart and turn—and I would heal them.' Let it be known to you then that this salvation [*sōtērion*] of God has been sent to the gentiles; they will listen." (Acts 28:25b–28)

Paul's citation of Isaiah 6 has been taken as marking the definitive dissolution of the Jewish people's covenantal status. Thus, Hans Conzelmann asserts, "Israel's turning away from salvation is final, as is clear in Paul's concluding statement in Acts 28:28."[19] While Joseph Tyson considers Luke's view of Judaism to be conflicted and complex, his assessment of Acts 28:28 echoes that of Conzelmann: "The text that exhibits such profound ambivalence in regard to Jews and Judaism [i.e., Luke-Acts as a whole] moves toward a resolution without ambivalence or ambiguity: an image of Jewish people as rejecting the gospel and thus as a people without hope."[20] If that is the case, then Luke envisions no eventual "return to

---

19. Cited in Tyson, *Luke, Judaism, and the Scholars*, 88.
20. Tyson, *Luke, Judaism, and the Scholars*, 144–45.

Jerusalem," and Burge is justified in reading Acts 1:6-8 as an instance of apostolic misunderstanding and dominical correction.[21]

This conclusion draws support from the way Luke structures his narrative of Paul's missionary expeditions. In his initial journey, Paul delivers a lengthy speech in the synagogue of Antioch of Pisidia in Asia Minor (Acts 13:16-41). At first, the Jewish audience welcomes Paul's message (Acts 13:42-43), but the following week they turn hostile. Paul's response anticipates his words to the Jewish elders of Rome, though he here cites Isaiah 49:6b rather than Isaiah 6: "It was necessary that the word of God should be spoken first to you. Since you reject it and judge yourselves to be unworthy of eternal life, we are now turning to the gentiles. For so the Lord has commanded us, saying, 'I have set you to be a light for the gentiles, so that you may bring salvation to the ends of the earth'" (Acts 13:46-47).

In his second missionary journey, Paul receives a vision beckoning him to leave Asia Minor in order to begin a new work across the Aegean (Acts 16:9-10). Paul eventually makes his way to Corinth, a city situated on an isthmus and described by Strabo in 7 BCE as "master of two harbors, of which the one leads straight to Asia, and the other to Italy."[22] Here Luke describes briefly a scene that resembles what occurred earlier in Antioch of Pisidia (in Asia) and what will occur later in Rome (in Italy): "Paul was occupied with proclaiming the word, testifying to the Jews that the Messiah was Jesus. When they opposed and reviled him, in protest he shook the dust from his clothes and said to them, 'Your blood be on your own heads! I am innocent. From now on I will go to the gentiles.' Then he left the synagogue and went to the house of a man named Titius Justus, a worshipper of God; his house was next door to the synagogue" (Acts 18:5-7).

Thus, Paul's declaration that he is "going to the gentiles" is recounted three times in three geographical settings that represent the crucial stages

---

21. Like Burge, Conzelmann contends that Jesus *will* restore the kingdom to a *redefined* Israel and the basis for his contention is Acts 28: "Acts i,6 speaks of the Kingdom being restored to Israel.... The emphatic passage, xxviii, 28... shows who now shares in this hope: salvation is passing to the Gentiles.... Luke thinks of the Christians, according to plan, taking over the privileges of the Jews as one epoch is succeeded by the next" (Conzelmann, *The Theology of St. Luke*, 163). In other words, the question of the apostles in Acts 1:6 is not in itself misguided; they only misunderstand the meaning of the term "Israel," which in the new dispensation refers to the church of the gentiles. Of course, this also implies a dramatic change in the nature of that kingdom (i.e., it will be non-geographical) and its restoration.

22. Cited by Hays, *First Corinthians*, 3.

of Paul's expanding apostolic sphere. As with the three accounts of Paul's vision on the road to Damascus (Acts 9:1–19; 22:6–16; 26:12–18) and the three accounts of Peter's encounter with Cornelius (Acts 10:1–48; 11:4–16; 15:7–9), the literary technique of threefold repetition emphasizes the importance of Paul's words in the eyes of the author.

Therefore, the traditional commentators have good reason to stress Paul's final words to the Jewish elders of Rome. But how does Luke understand these words and what is he trying to say through them? And how might they help us understand the words of Jesus at the beginning of the book of Acts (i.e., Acts 1:6–8)?

To answer these questions, I will first examine the intertextual network underlying Acts 28:28 and Acts 13:47, and then reflect on the impact of social context on the prophetic rhetoric of Paul's speeches.

## The Intertextual Network Underlying Acts 28:28

Paul's concluding words to the Jewish elders of Rome are as follows: "Let it be known to you then that this salvation of God [*to sōtērion tou Theou*] has been sent to the gentiles; they will listen" (Acts 28:28). The Greek word *sōtērion* is rare in the New Testament, appearing only five times. Three of those occurrences are found in Luke-Acts. The most important of the three, which illuminates the others, is Luke 3:4–6. Here Luke parallels Mark and Matthew by characterizing the mission of John the Baptist in terms of Isaiah 40:3, but then goes beyond Mark and Matthew by citing Isaiah 40:4–5 as well:

> As it is written in the book of the words of the prophet Isaiah,
> "The voice of one crying out in the wilderness:
> 'Prepare the way of the Lord,
> make his paths straight. [The citation of Isaiah 40 in Mark and Matthew ends here.]
> Every valley shall be filled,
> and every mountain and hill shall be made low,
> and the crooked shall be made straight,
> and the rough ways made smooth;
> and all flesh [*pasa sarx*] shall see the salvation of God [*to sōtērion tou Theou*].'" (Luke 3:4–6)

In Acts 28:28, Paul states that "the salvation of God" [*to sōtērion tou Theou*], which Israel is now failing to receive, will be experienced by gentiles. Yet, citing Isaiah 40:5, Luke 3 tells us that this "salvation" will be seen (i.e., experienced) by "all flesh." It thus appears that Acts 28:28 witnesses to only a partial fulfillment of Isaiah 40:5.

How does Luke understand the phrase "all flesh" (*pasa sarx*) in Isaiah 40:5 (LXX)? Who are those who are destined to "see the salvation of God"? Luke's intention becomes clear in the Song of Simeon, the remaining text in which the word *sōtērion* is found.[23]

> Master, now you are dismissing your servant in peace, according to your word;
> for my eyes have seen your salvation [*sōtērion*],
> which you have prepared in the presence of all peoples [*pantōn tōn laōn*],
> a light for revelation to the gentiles and for glory to your people Israel.
> (Luke 2:29-32)

Simeon's "all peoples" (*pantōn tōn laōn*) is equivalent to Isaiah's "all flesh" (*pasa sarx*), and the meaning of "all peoples" is then explained in the line that follows: the phrase refers to Israel and the gentiles (i.e., the nations) together. Verse 32 alludes to Isaiah 49:5-6:

> And now the LORD says, who formed me in the womb to be his servant,
> to bring Jacob back to him, and that Israel might be gathered to him,
> for I am honored in the sight of the LORD, and my God has become my strength—
> he says, "It is too light a thing that you should be my servant
> to raise up the tribes of Jacob and to restore the survivors of Israel;
> I will give you as a light to the nations,
> that my salvation may reach to the end of the earth."

God sends the servant to accomplish a dual mission: he is to be a "light to the nations" (i.e., gentiles), but also "to raise up the tribes of Jacob." Luke perceives these verses of Isaiah to be fundamental to the divine purpose and they give shape to his overall narrative. When Paul bears witness before King Agrippa, Isaiah 49:5-6 underlies his formulation of the mission of the risen Messiah conducted through his *ekklēsia*: "To this day I have had help from God, and so I stand here, testifying to

---

23. The importance of Isaiah 40 as an intertextual reference in the Song of Simeon is highlighted also by the way Luke introduces the figure of Simeon: "Now there was a man in Jerusalem whose name was Simeon; this man was righteous and devout, looking forward to the consolation [*paraklēsis*] of Israel" (Luke 2:25). The phrase "the consolation of Israel" alludes to the opening words of Isaiah 40: "Comfort, comfort [*parakleite, parakleite*] my people" (Isa 40:1 LXX).

both small and great, saying nothing but what the prophets and Moses said would take place: that the Messiah must suffer, and that, by being the first to rise from the dead, *he would proclaim light both to our people and to the gentiles*" (Acts 26:22–23, emphasis added). Even more telling is the explicit citation of Isaiah 49 in Paul's words to the Jewish community of Antioch in Pisidia, already noted above: "It was necessary that the word of God should be spoken first to you. Since you reject it and judge yourselves to be unworthy of eternal life, we are now turning to the gentiles. For so the Lord has commanded us, saying, 'I have set you to be a light for the gentiles, so that you may bring salvation to the ends of the earth'" (Acts 13:46–47).

While the Song of Simeon refers to both parts of the dual mission of the servant, and the reference to "all flesh" in Luke's citation of Isaiah 40:5 likewise asserts a comprehensive salvific purpose in the work of the Messiah (i.e., including both gentiles and the "tribes of Jacob"), Paul in Acts 13 ignores Isaiah 49:5–6a (which speaks of Israel) and mentions only Isaiah 49:6b (which speaks of the gentiles). As we have seen, this anticipates the final scene of Acts 28 in which Paul rebukes the Jewish elders of Rome and announces his "going to the gentiles."

The most reasonable conclusion to draw from this *intertextual* puzzle is identical to the one we reached regarding Luke's *geographical* puzzle: Luke never tires of asserting that the prophetic words of Scripture must be fulfilled, and Isaiah 40:5 ("*all flesh* will see the salvation of God")—understood in light of Isaiah 49:5–6 ("all flesh" = Israel + the nations)—takes a place of prominence in his reading of those prophetic words. Because of Israel's corporate resistance to the message of the Messiah, Jerusalem will be judged and only the gentile portion of Isaiah 49 will be realized in the immediate future. This is the significance of Paul's "going to the gentiles." However, Jesus has come not only as "a light for revelation to the gentiles"; he is also destined to bring "glory to your people Israel" (Luke 2:32). Isaiah 49:5–6a will come to pass, but only in a future beyond the events of 70 CE and Israel's second exile, when "the times of the gentiles are fulfilled" (Luke 21:24).[24] Just as in its original

---

24. Charles B. Puskas skillfully identifies the intertextual network discussed here and its relevance to the interpretation of Acts 28. Unfortunately, ignoring the evidence to the contrary, he thinks that Acts 28 indicates the fulfillment of the promises of Isaiah 40 for "all flesh," i.e., *both* gentiles and Jews: "Paul at Rome brings the universal significance of God's salvation in the person of Jesus, to its completion" (Puskas, *The Conclusion of Luke-Acts*, 103). This reading of Acts 28 fails to attend to the *lack of completion* that Luke conveys by ending his narrative in Rome, with Israel about to fall under divine judgment.

context Isaiah 6 pronounced a judgment and exile whose goal and result was to purify Israel and lead to its ultimate restoration, so Paul in Acts 28 cites these words of Isaiah with the same intent and meaning.[25]

## The Social Context of Paul's Prophetic Rhetoric in Acts

In order to understand Paul's rebuke of the Jewish leaders in Acts 28 and Luke's threefold description of Paul's "going to the gentiles," it is necessary to notice the social context in which Paul speaks. In this regard, Acts 28 sheds light on the earlier narratives in the book. Soon after Paul arrives in Rome, he invites the Jewish leaders of the city to visit him:

> Three days later [after arriving in Rome] he [Paul] called together the local leaders of the Jews. When they had assembled, he said to them, "Brothers, though I had done nothing against our people or the customs of our ancestors, yet I was arrested in Jerusalem and handed over to the Romans. . . . For this reason therefore I have asked to see you and speak with you, since it is for the sake of the hope of Israel that I am bound with this chain." (Acts 28:17, 20)

This is a formal gathering in which Paul addresses a set of communal representatives. His mode of address displays a rhetoric that emphasizes his relationship with these leaders as fellow members of the same people. He calls them his "brothers," refers to Israel as "*our* people" and to Judaism as "the customs of *our* ancestors," and speaks of his apostolic mission as oriented to "the hope of Israel." Luke then describes the discussion that ensued: "From morning until evening he explained the matter to them, testifying to the kingdom of God and trying to convince them about Jesus both from the law of Moses and from the prophets. Some were convinced by what he had said, while others refused to believe. So they disagreed with each other" (Acts 28:23b-25a).

Luke stresses the division of opinion that exists among these Jewish leaders; some accept Paul's message while others reject it. From Luke's brief summary description, the reader may assume that there are as

---

25. Justin Taylor takes a similar approach to Paul's use of Isaiah 6 in Acts 28: "As in the original context in the Book of Isaiah, it is a call to conversion [i.e., repentance] rather than a declaration of rejection" (Taylor, "Paul and the Jewish Leaders of Rome," 323). Moreover, Taylor argues that the Lukan Paul "who meets with representatives of the Jewish community in Rome in Acts 28 is in substantial agreement in his attitude to Israel with the Paul of Romans 9-11" (321).

many Jewish leaders in the former group as in the latter.²⁶ This is the social context in which Paul rebukes his audience by citing Isaiah 6 (Acts 28:25b–27) and announces his intention of "going to the gentiles" (Acts 28:28).

Why does Paul respond so negatively to what Christians today might consider a rather successful evangelistic encounter? His fierce reaction appears disproportionate to the mixed attitudes of his audience. This scene makes little sense if we view Paul's audience as a collection of Jewish individuals and Paul's aim in addressing them as the "salvation" of as many of them as possible. Instead, this assembly of prominent Roman Jews must have a corporate and representative function, and Paul's unattained goal in relation to them must likewise be defined in communal terms. Robert Tannehill interprets this scene in a way that takes account of these factors and explains the apparent disproportionality of Paul response: "The presence of disagreement among the Jews is enough to show that Paul has not achieved what he sought. He was seeking a communal decision, a recognition by the Jewish community as a whole that Jesus is the fulfillment of the Jewish hope. The presence of significant opposition shows that this is not going to happen."²⁷

In other words, the point of the passage is not that these leaders, as individuals or as a group, are definitively saying "no" to Paul's apostolic message. Instead, the point is that they are failing to definitively say "yes," i.e., to offer a communal welcome to the announcement of Israel's risen Messiah. The significance of such a "yes" becomes clear if we interpret Acts 3:19–21 (and Luke 13:35) as a prophetic promise that Israel's corporate repentance and reception of the apostolic message would trigger the events that culminate in Messiah's return. Paul's rebuke of this divided group of Jewish leaders should not then be taken as a sign that the Jewish people have forfeited their promised inheritance, but as implying the exact opposite: the Jewish people retain their unique covenantal status, a fact that increases both their responsibility when they fail and the cosmic blessing that ensues when they succeed.

---

26. As Taylor notes, "the text simply shows the group who heard Paul as divided: we are not even told that those who did not accept Paul's message were more numerous than those who did" (Taylor, "Paul and the Jewish Leaders of Rome," 315).

27. Tannehill, *The Narrative Unity of Luke-Acts*, 2:347.

Tannehill applies this same insight to the previous two incidents in which Paul faults Jewish communal recalcitrance and declares that he will henceforth "go to the gentiles":

> Paul's announcement that he is going to the Gentiles indicates a shift from a synagogue-based mission, addressed to Jews and to those Gentiles attracted to Judaism, to a mission in the city at large, where the population is predominantly Gentile. . . . Paul . . . has fulfilled his obligation to speak God's word to God's people. They are now responsible for their own fate. The pattern of speaking first to Jews and only later turning to the Gentiles testifies to Paul's sense of prophetic obligation to his own people. He is released from this obligation only when he meets strong public resistance within the Jewish community. Then he can begin the second phase of his mission within a city, a phase in which the conversion of individual Jews is still possible, although Paul is no longer preaching in the synagogue nor addressing Jews as a community.[28]

Paul must go to the Jewish community first, for they are the people of God, and the Messiah is in a unique way *their* Messiah. (Paul's commitment to this truth provides the theological rationale for the initial rhetoric of Acts 28:17-20, in which the apostle stresses his solidarity with the wider Jewish community and its leadership.) Once it becomes evident that the Jewish community in a region will fail to corporately acknowledge Jesus as the Messiah, Paul is free to speak to Jewish and gentile individuals and to form a distinct ecclesial body in that location. The transition from the first to the second phase of Paul's apostolic strategy in Acts means not that Israel forfeits its status, but that it exposes itself to divine judgment (as in past eras) and delays the ultimate arrival of both national and cosmic redemption.

By ending his two volumes with this scene in Rome, Luke signals that a new judgment—and a new exile—was about to befall the people of Israel. While individual Jews would continue to receive the message of Jesus, the Jewish community as a whole would for the immediate future withhold its corporate acclamation of Jesus as the one sent to be "the consolation of Israel." This does not, however, imply a definitive divorce of the Jesus movement from identification with that community nor a surrendering of hope for an eschatological reversal of that official communal

---

28. Tannehill, *The Narrative Unity of Luke-Acts*, 222–23.

response.²⁹ Far from undermining the thesis we have argued based on the geographical structure of Luke-Acts and its treatment of Jerusalem's coming judgment and redemption, this reading of Acts 28 offers further support for that thesis.

## "THE TIME WHEN YOU WILL RESTORE THE KINGDOM TO ISRAEL" (ACTS 1:6)

We are now ready to analyze Acts 1:6–8 itself. "So when they had come together, they asked him, 'Lord, is this the time [*chronos*] when you will restore [*apo-kathistēmi*] the kingdom to Israel?' He replied, 'It is not for you to know the times [*chronoi*] or periods [*kairoi*] that the Father has set by his own authority. But you will receive power when the Holy Spirit has come upon you; and you will be my witnesses in Jerusalem, in all Judea and Samaria, and to the ends of the earth'" (Acts 1:6–8).

One of the most striking features of this text is the way its language and meaning coincide with two interrelated passages examined above—namely, Luke 21:24 and Acts 3:17–21. The first of these passages speaks of "the times [*kairoi*] of the gentiles" as a temporal period intervening between the destruction of Jerusalem and its restoration. The addition of the word *kairoi* by Jesus in Acts 1:6 (the question of the apostles uses only the synonym *chronos*) may point the reader back to this crucial verse in the eschatological discourse and imply that the apostles have not yet understood that Jerusalem would be judged before being redeemed.

The second passage is found in Peter's speech in the Jerusalem Temple:

> And now, brethren, I know that you acted in ignorance, just as your rulers did also. But the things which God announced beforehand by the mouth of all the prophets, that His Christ would suffer, He has thus fulfilled. Therefore repent and return, so that your sins may be wiped away, in order that times [*kairoi*] of refreshing may come from the presence of the Lord; and that He may send Jesus, the Christ appointed for you, whom heaven must receive until [*achri*] the period [*chronoi*, lit. "times"] of

---

29. Tannehill adopts a view similar to that expressed here. Joseph Tyson endorses Tannehill's insight into the communal dimension of Paul's efforts among the Jewish people but he disagrees with Tannehill's suggestion that Israel's future is still open. Tyson thinks that Luke sees Israel as "a people without hope." As my entire argument shows, I find Tyson's contention unconvincing. See Tyson, "The Problem of Jewish Rejection in Acts," 126–27, and *Luke, Judaism, and the Scholars*, 142–45.

restoration [*apokatastasis*] of all things about which God spoke by the mouth of His holy prophets from ancient time. (Acts 3:17–21 NASB)

We have already noted the connection between the use of *achri* ("until") in verse 21 and the appearance of the same word in Luke 21:24 ("until [*achri*] the times of the gentiles are fulfilled"). At this point, we must attend to the parallels between these verses in Acts 3 and our main text, Acts 1:6–8. In both passages, the two roughly synonymous nouns, *chronoi* and *kairoi*, are paired. More significantly, Acts 1:6 employs the verb *apo-kathistēmi* (translated by the NRSV as "restore") while Acts 3:21 uses the cognate nominal form *apo-katastasis* (translated by the NASB as "restoration"). As noted above, Albrecht Oepke views the verb as a technical term in wider Jewish use "for the restoration of Israel to its own land." The language of the apostles' question to Jesus in Acts 1:6 is thus echoed by Peter's speech to the people of Jerusalem in Acts 3, with the same meaning in both cases: Peter tells the Jerusalemites that the kingdom will be restored to Israel (as a central and essential element in "the restoration of all things about which God spoke by the mouth of His holy prophets") when they acknowledge Jesus as Israel's returning king. This echo implies that Peter has not interpreted Jesus's answer in Acts 1:7–8 as a rejection of the legitimacy of the question.

The verses immediately following the opening dialogue between Jesus and his disciples in Acts 1 provide further confirmation of our thesis:

> When he had said this, as they were watching, he was lifted up, and a cloud took him out of their sight. While he was going and they were gazing up towards heaven, suddenly two men in white robes stood by them. They said, "Men of Galilee, why do you stand looking up towards heaven? This Jesus, who has been taken up from you into heaven, will come in the same way as you saw him go into heaven." Then they returned to Jerusalem from the mount called Olivet, which is near Jerusalem, a Sabbath day's journey away. (Acts 1:9–12)

What is meant by the revelation that Jesus "will come in the same way as you saw him go"? Verse 12 hints at the answer by telling us that the ascension occurred on the Mount of Olives. Luke's mention of the location points the reader to the eschatological prophecy of Zechariah 14: "For I will gather all the nations against Jerusalem to battle.... Then the Lord will go forth and fight against those nations as when he fights on a day of battle. On that day *his feet shall stand on the Mount of Olives*, *which lies before Jerusalem on the east; and the Mount of Olives shall be split in two from east to west by a very wide valley.* . . . *Then the* Lord *my God will come, and all the holy ones with him*" (Zech 14:2–5).

In light of Zechariah 14 and Luke's Jerusalem-centered cartography, we should interpret the phrase "in the same way" as including the physical site of the two events. Just as Jesus ascends now *from* the Mount of Olives, so he will descend at the end *to* the Mount of Olives. Just as he ascends now *from* Jerusalem, so he will descend at the end *to* Jerusalem. Jerusalem will suffer many things, just as Zechariah 12–14 foretells. But she will be consoled when her Lord comes to defend her at the end, his feet standing on the Mount of Olives. At that time the Lord will be welcomed by Jerusalem in a fitting manner, with her leaders and people taking up the cry uttered at Jesus's first coming only by his disciples: "Blessed is the king who comes in the name of the Lord" (Luke 19:38; see 13:35). This triumphal entry will be an occasion of messianic joy rather than lament (see again Luke 19:41–44).

Whether read in light of parallel verses in Luke and Acts, or in its own immediate context, or in relation to the ending or geographical structure of the books, or in connection to the wider Lukan teaching regarding Jerusalem's judgment and redemption, there is little evidence to suggest that Acts 1:6–8 should be read as anything but a dominical promise of the ultimate restoration of the kingdom to Israel in the Holy City of Jerusalem. Moreover, there is likewise little evidence to suggest that the "Israel" that is spoken of is an entity separate from the Jewish people. With the prophet Simeon, Luke continues to await the "redemption of Jerusalem."

## CONCLUSION

While necessary and richly suggestive, exegesis of Luke-Acts—or of any other New Testament texts—is not a sufficient ground for the cultivation of a twenty-first-century theological Zionism among the disciples of Jesus. The development of such a theological vision will also require (among other things) sustained and disciplined reflection on the identity of the *ekklēsia*, her relationship to the Jewish people, and her vocation in the realm of worldly politics; in addition, it will demand a theological and ethical assessment of a multitude of contingent facts of history.

The question I have addressed in this chapter is more circumscribed in character: Do the people of Israel and the land of Israel persist as abiding concerns in Luke and Acts? My answer is a resounding "yes." Exegesis of Luke-Acts *is* sufficient to undermine the arguments of those who assert that the New Testament delegitimizes the theological claims of the Jewish people in relation to the city of Jerusalem and the land of Israel. That is precisely the intent of the assertions of Gary Burge with which we began, and which we will again cite as we conclude:

> At no point do the earliest Christians view the Holy Land as a locus of divine activity to which the people of the Roman empire must be drawn. They do not promote the Holy Land either for the Jew or for the Christian as a vital aspect of faith.... The early Christians possessed no territorial theology. Early Christian preaching is utterly *uninterested* in a Jewish eschatology devoted to the restoration of the land. The kingdom of Christ began in Judea and is historically anchored there but it is not tethered to a political realization of that kingdom in the Holy Land.[30]

Luke-Acts refutes each of the above propositions: this two-volume work *does* "view the Holy Land as a locus of divine activity," *does* "promote the Holy Land . . . as a vital aspect of faith," *does* possess a "territorial theology," *is intensely concerned about* "a Jewish eschatology devoted to the restoration of the land," and—depending on the meaning assigned here to the word "political"—*is* "tethered to a political realization" of the "kingdom in the Holy Land."

The story told by Luke-Acts is unfinished. Its last *recorded* chapter is set in Rome, at the "ends of the earth." While yet unwritten, we know where the *final* chapter of the story will take place—and it will not be Washington, DC, Beijing, Brussels, or Moscow. When the outward flow of the apostolic mission has reached its appointed limit, the current will reverse and return to its center so that from there it might nurture the entire world. Then will be realized the words of the prophet: "On that day living waters shall flow out from Jerusalem, half of them to the eastern sea and half of them to the western sea; it shall continue in summer as in winter. And the LORD will become king over all the earth; on that day the LORD will be one and his name one" (Zech 14:8–9).

---

30. Burge, *Jesus and the Land*, 59.

CHAPTER 12

# Post-Supersessionist Eschatology
Welcoming Jesus at the Mount of Olives

> *In this essay, Kinzer places side by side an often-overlooked biblical motif (namely, the centrality of the land of Israel and the city of Jerusalem, particularly in Luke-Acts) and an interrelated pair of contemporary global and ecclesiological phenomena (namely, the founding of the modern state of Israel and the emergence of a distinctly Jewish segment of the body of Messiah). In doing so, he seeks to challenge common Christian sentiments about the "conversion of the Jews," positing instead that what is needed is a "conversion of the Christians" regarding Israel's irreplaceable role in the unfolding drama of divine redemption.*[1]

IN THE FIRST CHAPTER of this volume, I proposed a post-supersessionist messianology highlighting the ecclesiological implications of the role played by Jewish disciples of Jesus.[2] The chapter concluded with a brief

---

1. Kinzer presented two papers at an international symposium at the University of Vienna in July 2022: this chapter and an abbreviated version of chapter 1 in this volume. The focus of the symposium was "Jesus—Also the Messiah for Israel? The Messianic Jewish Movement and Christianity in Dialogue." The goal of the event was to foster theological engagement between European Christian scholars and leading Jewish disciples of Jesus, whether they self-identify as Messianic Jews, Jewish Christians, or Jewish Catholics. This article, along with the other papers from the symposium, is published in German (*Jesus—der Messias Israels?*, ed. Kinzer et al.) and is to be published in English (*Jesus—the Messiah of Israel?*, ed. Kinzer et al.).

2. See chapter 1 of this volume.

discussion of the traditional Christian motif of the eschatological "conversion of the Jews."

Most attempts at fashioning a post-supersessionist theology have given little attention to the events immediately preceding the second coming of the Messiah or to the distinctive role of genealogical Israel within the new age that his coming will inaugurate. There are good reasons for treading warily in this marshy terrain, which has long been inhabited by apocalyptic enthusiasts with little appetite for theological reflection or engagement with flesh-and-blood Jewish people. But, as with messianology, there is land here capable of bearing post-supersessionist fruit if properly drained and cultivated.

That is what I sought to do in my 2018 monograph, *Jerusalem Crucified, Jerusalem Risen*.[3] In the present article, I will summarize some of the results of that study, which focused on the role of the Jewish people and the land of promise in the eschatological vision of the Gospel of Luke and the Acts of the Apostles. As in *Jerusalem Crucified*, I will consider not only the Lukan teaching, but also historical events of the modern era that might be illumined by that teaching. My aim is to discern in these events the complex workings of divine providence, ever attentive to signs that might contain eschatological import.

## POST-SUPERSESSIONISM AND NON-SUPERSESSIONISM

But I will begin with a few words concerning the term "post-supersessionist." Kayko Driedger Hesslein prefers the term "non-supersessionist," arguing that the "post" prefix "implies that supersessionism is something that occurred and concluded in the past, and is no longer a concern in the present."[4] But that is not at all how the prefix functions in most contemporary English-language discourse. When we speak of postmodern sensibilities, we are not suggesting that modernist perspectives are obsolete and nonexistent. The same can be said for the terms postliberal, postconservative, postcritical, and postmissionary.[5] All of these terms

---

3. Kinzer, *Jerusalem Crucified*.

4. Hesslein, *Dual Citizenship*, 11n16.

5. On the term "postliberal," see Lindbeck, *The Nature of Doctrine*; on the term "postconservative," see Vanhoozer, *The Drama of Doctrine*; on the term "postcritical," see Ochs, *The Return to Scripture*; on the term "postmissionary," see Kinzer, *Postmissionary Messianic Judaism*.

assume that the older intellectual posture (X) transcended by "post-X" continues to exist and to exercise influence.

I prefer the term "post-supersessionist" to "non-supersessionist" because the latter suggests a mere negation of supersessionism. Non-supersessionist could easily be understood to mean anti-supersessionist. And, in fact, the earliest attacks on supersessionism had such a reactive character.[6] In particular, these early forays into non-supersessionist theology often rejected the high Christology of the ecumenical creeds as inherently hostile to Judaism and sought to build a new theological paradigm on the foundation of that rejection.

In contrast, the "post" prefix suggests a non-reactive posture that has learned from X but now seeks to go beyond it. Thus, postcritical approaches to Scripture accept the validity of historical-critical scholarship and benefit from its achievements while at the same time adopting canonical or theological modes of reading that offer a different angle of approach to the same texts. In keeping with such usage of the prefix, a post-supersessionist theology would be one that appreciates the wealth of Christian theological tradition and aims to correct its flaws by drawing upon previously untapped resources within the tradition. In particular, post-supersessionist theology—in contrast to early efforts at countering supersessionism—will view the high Christology of the ecumenical creeds as an asset rather than a liability.

## ESCHATOLOGY AND THE "CONVERSION OF THE JEWS"

Those seeking to move beyond supersessionism are rightly troubled by the triumphalist concept of an eschatological "conversion of the Jews." In chapter 1, I offered a perspective on this traditional Christian motif that sought to integrate its high Christology with a post-supersessionist perspective on the historical vocation of the Jewish people—a perspective that summons the Christian church to its own eschatological "conversion."

Traditional sources have generally based their hopes for an eschatological "conversion of the Jews" on a reading of the eleventh chapter of Paul's letter to the Romans. In *Jerusalem Crucified*, I provide a reading of Luke and Acts that furnishes a wider narrative canvas for considering the

---

6. For such a classic early attack on supersessionism, see Ruether, *Faith and Fratricide*. On the history of the term, see Azar, "Supersessionism," 1–25.

historical journey of the Jewish people and their eschatological meeting with "the Messiah appointed for [them]" (Acts 3:20). It is a reading that affirms the universal salvific role of Jesus, while at the same time supporting the covenantal integrity of Jewish life through the ages. It also raises new questions about the theological significance of the city of Jerusalem and the land of Israel.

My exploration of this motif can be summarized through an examination of four key texts in the Gospel of Luke and the Acts of the Apostles. The first of these texts is Luke 13:33–35:

> Yet today, tomorrow, and the next day I must be on my way, because it is impossible for a prophet to be killed outside of Jerusalem. Jerusalem, Jerusalem, the city that kills the prophets and stones those who are sent to it! How often have I desired to gather your children together as a hen gathers her brood under her wings, and you were not willing! See, your house is left to you. And I tell you, you will not see me until the time comes when you say, "Blessed is the one who comes in the name of the Lord."

Still in Galilee, Jesus here anticipates his arrest and execution in Jerusalem and portrays that event as continuous with Jerusalem's hostile response to a long line of prophetic messengers. He then adopts a prophetic voice, speaking in the first person on behalf of Israel's God who has longed for Jerusalem's obedience, only to be frustrated time and again. In grief over the resistance of his children, God will abandon the city and the Temple and render them vulnerable to enemy armies, just as in the destruction of the first Temple by the Babylonians—"See, your house is left to you." Nevertheless, as with the prophets Isaiah, Jeremiah, and Ezekiel, the message ends on a more hopeful note with a conditional promise of a divine return to Zion *after the divine departure in 70 CE*: "You [i.e., Jerusalem] will not see me until the time comes when you say, 'Blessed is the one who comes in the name of the Lord!'" God will come in glory to Jerusalem, but only after Jerusalem welcomes the one God sends.

In the second text, Jesus descends from the Mount of Olives (19:29, 37) and rides toward Jerusalem. As in the other gospels, he is acclaimed by the crowds with the words of Psalm 118 mentioned earlier in the conditional promise of Luke 13: "Blessed is the king who comes in the name of the Lord!" (v. 38). But unlike the other gospels, Luke states explicitly that the crowds reciting these words are "the whole multitude of the disciples" (Luke 19:37) who are accompanying him on the journey, *not the people of Jerusalem or their leaders.* The condition stipulated in the promise of Luke 13 has not been met, for those words were directed to the people and leaders of the capital. So, Jesus's entry to Jerusalem in Luke 19 does not fulfill God's saving promises to Israel, but only serves as a prophetic sign pointing to an as yet unrealized hope.

In the third text, the resurrected Jesus converses with his apostles before his ascension. They ask him, "Lord, is this the time [*chronos*] when you will restore [*apo-kathistēmi*] the kingdom to Israel?" (Acts 1:6). The verb employed here (*apo-kathistēmi*) was a technical term among Greek-speaking Jews, referring to the restoration of Israel's sovereignty in its own land.[7] Jesus tells them that the question cannot be answered because the timing of this restoration is not their business (v. 7). However, contrary to traditional interpretations, Jesus does not correct the underlying assumption that generates their question—namely, the expectation that Jesus will ultimately manifest himself in glory to Israel and rule over them as their King. After saying these words, Jesus ascends to heaven from the Mount of Olives (vv. 9, 12), and two angelic figures appear, saying, "Men of Galilee, why do you stand looking up toward heaven? This Jesus, who has been taken up from you into heaven, will come in the same way as you saw him go into heaven" (v. 11). Here we have an allusion to the eschatological prophecy of Zechariah 14: "For I will gather all the nations against Jerusalem to battle. . . . Then the Lord will go forth and fight against those nations as when he fights on a day of battle. On that day *his feet shall stand on the Mount of Olives*, which lies before Jerusalem on the east; and the Mount of Olives shall be split in two from east to west by a very wide valley. . . . *Then the* Lord *my God will come*, and all the holy ones with him" (Zech 14:2–5). In other words, what took place in the mode of prophetic sign on Palm Sunday (Luke 19)—the descent of Jesus from the Mount of Olives and his entry to Jerusalem—will occur at the end of the age in the mode of messianic fulfillment. In light of the message of Luke 13 and Luke 19, this implies that the city of Jerusalem and its leaders will in that day welcome the coming Messiah with the words shouted on Palm Sunday only by the disciples: "Blessed is the king who comes in the name of the Lord!"

What remains implicit in Acts 1 becomes explicit in our fourth text, Acts 3:17–21. Here Peter addresses a crowd of Jews in the Jerusalem Temple after the healing of a lame beggar.

---

7. See the previous chapter, 161n17, 173.

> Now brothers, I know that you acted in ignorance, just as your leaders did. But what God foretold through the mouth of all His prophets—that His Messiah was to suffer—so He has fulfilled. Repent, therefore, and return—so your sins might be blotted out, so times of relief might come from the presence of *Adonai* and He might send *Yeshua*, the Messiah appointed for you. Heaven must receive Him, until the time [*chronoi*] of the restoration [*apokatastasis*] of all the things that God spoke about long ago through the mouth of His holy prophets. (Acts 3:17–21 TLV)

Peter here interprets for the reader the scene depicted in the first chapter of Acts. Heaven "received" Jesus when he ascended from the Mount of Olives, but God will "send him" back to Jerusalem (via the Mount of Olives), for he is "the Messiah appointed for you" (i.e., for Jerusalem and the Jewish people). The purpose of his return to Jerusalem will be to "restore" the kingdom to Israel—the phrase and technical term (*apo-kathistēmi*) from Acts 1:6 interpreted here in Acts 3 as shorthand for "all the things that God spoke about long ago through the mouth of His holy prophets."[8] This will not happen, however, until Jerusalem and its leaders "repent" and "return"—that is, reverse the negative response to Jesus given in ignorance on Palm Sunday and its aftermath. In other words, Jerusalem will see the Messiah appointed for her when she says, "Blessed is the one who comes in the name of the Lord!"

This interlocking set of texts paints a picture of Israel's central role in the divine plan, a role that contrasts starkly with the traditional motif of the eschatological "conversion of the Jews." In the latter, the church displaces the Jews as the fulcrum of history and the end-time "conversion" only reinforces that displacement. In Luke and Acts, on the other hand, the Jewish people—and their capital city—retain their privileged place as the center of God's concern. History waits in sustained tension until they are united with the One appointed for them. The eschatological reconciliation of Israel with its King confirms the covenantal status that Israel never forfeited.[9] If the positive response of the Jewish people to the

---

8. Kinzer, *Jerusalem Crucified*, 35n3. The noun *apokatastasis* in Acts 3:21 is cognate with the verb *apo-kathistēmi* in Acts 1:6.

9. Rabbinic tradition likewise witnesses to the motif that the coming of the Messiah depends upon Israel's repentance. Perhaps the most colorful text in this regard is b. Sanhedrin 98a, which tells of Rabbi Joshua ben Levi's encounter with the Messiah at the gates of Rome. At the heart of the story is a messianic midrash on Psalm 95:7 ("O that today you would listen to his voice!"), which suggests that the Messiah will come

Messiah is a necessary and sufficient condition for his return, then Israel is the hinge on which God's purposes for the world turn.

## ESCHATOLOGY AND THE CITY OF JERUSALEM

The eschatological vision of Romans 11 speaks much of Israel but little of Jerusalem. For Luke and Acts, on the other hand, the city of Jerusalem and its leaders represent the Jewish people as a whole and the judgment or redemption of one is the judgment or redemption of the other. That is why the Mount of Olives plays such a pivotal role in these books. The Messiah is appointed for Jerusalem (and, thereby, for all Israel), and he must return to Jerusalem. However, he will only do so when Jerusalem is ready to welcome him with open arms. As on Palm Sunday, the welcoming party must begin at the Mount of Olives. That site was Jesus's earthly launching pad for his ascent to heaven and in the vivid pictorial imagery drawn from the prophet Zechariah, it is likewise the place he lands in order to make his triumphal entry into the city.

We do not know how this will be realized at the return of Jesus. The eschatological imagery of Scripture is intentionally elusive, defying literalistic hermeneutical frameworks that attempt to squeeze from the text predictive information. We never know exactly how prophetic texts will be fulfilled until the appointed fulfillment is before our eyes. But one thing is unmistakably clear: Luke and Acts view the city of Jerusalem and the land of Israel as intimately bound up with the history and destiny of the Jewish people. Jesus returns to the people of Israel by returning to Jerusalem, and his kingship is established over them by being established in this city.

Despite traditional views to the contrary, the geographical structure of Luke and Acts reinforces this thesis.[10] All commentators note the central role of Jerusalem in the Gospel of Luke, which begins in the city, ends in the city, and depicts the intervening drama in the form of Jesus's extended journey to the city. Acts likewise begins in Jerusalem, but from that point on the direction of movement is steadily outward, ending in Rome, the capital of the Empire. Commentators have traditionally understood this geographical structure as conveying a supersessionist message:

---

on the "today" when Israel as a whole "listens to his voice." See Allison, "Matt. 23:39 = Luke 13:35b," 75–84.

10. Kinzer, *Jerusalem Crucified*, 44–53.

Jerusalem—and the people of Israel whom the city represents—was the past, but Rome—and the church of the nations that that city represents—is now the present and future.

But this reading of the geographical structure of Acts leaves out a crucial feature: every time the story takes another step outward, it concludes that stage of the story by returning to Jerusalem. Paul encounters Jesus on the road to Damascus, *and then returns to Jerusalem* (9:26–29). Peter proclaims Jesus to Cornelius in Caesarea, *and then returns to Jerusalem* (11:2). A congregation arises in Antioch, *and then sends aid to Jerusalem* in a time of famine (11:27–30). Paul and Barnabas journey from Antioch to Asia Minor, *and then return afterward to Jerusalem* for the Jerusalem council (15:2). From Jerusalem Paul travels with Silas to Greece, *and then returns again to Jerusalem* (18:22).[11] Paul takes his final journey as a free man, *and then returns to Jerusalem*, where he is arrested (21:17—23:11).

For one who senses the dynamic ebb and flow of the narrative, with the ebb continuously expanding outward but always flowing back to its center, the end of the book comes as a shock. The tide has been halted in the middle of its movement. What is the message here? Since Luke and Acts are both likely written after 70 CE, the original readers knew that Jerusalem would be destroyed by Rome not long after Paul's entry to the gentile capital. As a result, Israel—and the Jesus community, which is inextricably tied to Israel—are in exile, and Rome—the new Babylon—symbolizes that exile. But the story of Israel ends not with exile, but with return and restoration. Therefore, the point of this geographical structure is to convey prophetic hope for Israel—the story is not over, but will only reach its conclusion when the tide flows back to its source, the place where it began: Jerusalem, the city of the great King.

The eschatological scenario of Romans 11 is vague and could be interpreted as anticipating a positive response to Jesus from a large number of individual Jews throughout the world, without any particular geographical focus. The narrative of Luke and Acts, on the other hand, sketches a broad eschatological outline whose contours are clean and legible. The Jewish people will once again have a national presence in the land of Israel and that presence will be centered in the city of Jerusalem. The leaders of that city will also be the leaders of the nation. Their

---

11. See the previous chapter, 155–56n8.

response to Jesus will represent and embody the response of "all Israel" throughout the world.

In Luke and Acts, the drama of Jesus's eschatological reconciliation with the Jewish people is enacted on the stage of the land of Israel, with Jerusalem in the spotlight. What might that mean for our theological interpretation of modern history?

## DISCERNING DIVINE PROVIDENCE IN MODERN HISTORY

As already stated, we can never confidently assert how prophetic texts will be fulfilled until the fulfillment is before our eyes. But in some cases, fulfillment might occur as an extended process rather than a singular event. In such instances, recognition of the fulfillment by disciples of Jesus will likewise be an extended process.

In *Jerusalem Crucified*, I point to two modern historical developments whose synchronicity and formal similarity are striking: the movement to establish an autonomous Jewish presence in the land of Israel and the movement to establish a corporate Jewish presence in the body of Jesus the Messiah.[12] Both began in the early to middle nineteenth century, picked up steam at the end of the nineteenth and beginning of the twentieth centuries, and crystallized institutionally in the middle of the twentieth century. Both involved attempts to recover realities lost in the Jewish wars with Rome at the end of the first and beginning of the second centuries. Both featured distorted extremes that dismissed as worthless all that had intervened in Jewish (or Christian) life between the biblical and modern eras. But both have also generated visions of exile and return in which restoration involves the transformation rather than the utter negation of the era of exile, with the redeemed bringing to Jerusalem social, cultural, and spiritual wealth gathered among the nations during the time of dispersion. Of course, these two movements are radically disproportionate in their impact on world affairs. One has gained worldwide attention while the other has remained relatively obscure. Nevertheless, the parallels between them are intriguing.

No historical figure displays the connection between these two historical developments more strikingly than Joseph Rabinowitz (1837–99). In the formative years of Zionism—the 1880s—Rabinowitz was caught

---

12. Kinzer, *Jerusalem Crucified*, 240–70.

up in the intellectual ferment created by the new movement. In 1882, he traveled to Palestine to investigate whether collective immigration to the land might be a solution to the ills plaguing the Jewish people. While gazing on the Holy City from the Mount of Olives, Rabinowitz was suddenly convinced that "*Yeshua Achinu*" (Jesus our brother) was the Messiah, and that he alone could save Israel.[13] He returned to Kishinev (Chisinau) in Bessarabia (Moldova), and sought to gather a group of Jewish disciples of Jesus whom he called "Israelites of the New Covenant." This fellowship would circumcise their sons, observe the Sabbath and the Jewish holidays, and guard their autonomy as a Jewish Jesus-believing community. Unable to win governmental authorization, Rabinowitz's group in Kishinev failed to survive his death in 1899. Nevertheless, he gained an international hearing for his program.[14] Following in his footsteps were other like-minded Jewish disciples of Jesus such as Isaac Lichtenstein in Hungary, Mark John Levy in the United States, and Paul Levertoff in Britain. Kai Kjaer-Hansen's biography of Rabinowitz refers to him in its subtitle as "the Herzl of Jewish Christianity," and the moniker points both to his significance within Jewish Christianity and to the connection between that movement and the Zionist enterprise.[15]

Each of these two movements creates conditions among the Jewish people that make possible a scenario of the sort anticipated by the prophetic teaching of Luke and Acts. There is no indication that this scenario will be consummated in either the next year or the next decade. We may be in the early stages of an extended process or we may be witnessing proleptic signs pointing to an era in the distant future. But, given the message of Luke and Acts, it would be rash to dismiss either of these historical developments as theologically insignificant.

13. Kjaer-Hansen, *Joseph Rabinowitz and the Messianic Movement*, 11–22.

14. Rabinowitz traveled to Germany, Hungary, England, Scotland, and the United States, attracting attention wherever he went (Kjaer-Hansen, *Joseph Rabinowitz*, 75–90, 171–78). He even became the subject of an essay by the great Russian philosopher Vladimir Solovyov, who wrote about Rabinowitz in 1885. Urging the Russian government to grant legal status to the nascent congregation of Kishinev, Solovyov wrote: "On what grounds and interest does our government remove independence from the Jewish commune which attained Christ by its own lawful path, receiving its Messiah on its and His own personal native soil, the soil of a historical, three-thousand-year-long tradition?" (Solovyov, *The Burning Bush*, 343).

15. Kjaer-Hansen's subtitle derives from a statement made by Hugh Schonfield in 1936: "The story of Rabinowitz is a remarkable one. He may without unfair comparison be described as the Herzl of Jewish Christianity" (Schonfield, *The History of Jewish Christianity*, 163).

## ESCHATOLOGICAL SIGNS IN POST-SUPERSESSIONIST PERSPECTIVE

The astonishing dual resurrection in the modern period of (1) a Jewish commonwealth in the land of Israel, and (2) a Jewish expression of the body of the Messiah, challenges Christians to rethink fundamental theological assumptions. These historical phenomena are not minor subplots preparing the way for a narrative climax whose content is unrelated to them. The return of the Messiah is that climax, and the returning Messiah is the King of *the Jews*. He comes to his own city via the Mount of Olives and his return is contingent upon his being welcomed there by its Jewish leaders and inhabitants. Yes, this is a story about all nations and all creation and a story about the church, which is their first fruits. But it is a universal story only by virtue of being first a story about a particular people and its land, a people who, like their King, constitute a "stone which the builders rejected." If the eschatological "conversion of the Jews" involves a reversal of the rejection of the stone that is Jesus, the eschatological "conversion of the Christians" involves a reversal of the rejection of the stone that is Israel. And each of these two reversals requires a reassessment of the stone that is the *ecclesia ex circumcisione*.

This is a post-supersessionist eschatology—a "Zionology"—that enriches rather than impoverishes Christology by underlining its Jewish character as "Messianology." But it effects that enrichment through its integration with ecclesiology/Israelology.

Such an eschatology need not produce or reinforce Christian evangelistic missions to the Jews. The Jewish people have their own holy historical vocation, which Christians should support rather than subvert. Moreover, just as the hiding of the Messiah's face from Israel was a providential divine act, so the revelation of his face will likewise be a matter of sovereign divine initiative (Rom 11:25–26). As Pope Benedict wrote, "Israel retains its own mission. Israel is in the hands of God, who will save it 'as a whole' at the proper time, when the number of the Gentiles is complete."[16]

However, as already noted, "the proper time" will likely be an extended period rather than a singular moment. Has that period begun? Or is it not at least visible from a distance through proleptic signs? With such a possibility in view, other words from Pope Benedict (uttered when he was still Cardinal Ratzinger) come to mind. Upon meeting privately with

---

16. Ratzinger, *Jesus of Nazareth, Part Two*, 46.

a contingent of Messianic Jews in 1997, the Prefect of the Congregation for the Doctrine of the Faith reportedly remarked: "If you are whom you say you are, this is an eschatological sign."

Given the eschatological teaching of Luke and Acts, I would propose that the regathering of the Jewish people to the land of Israel and the emergence of Jewish Christianity and Messianic Judaism are indeed twin eschatological signs demanding concentrated theological attention. Let us look to the Mount of Olives, and perhaps, like Joseph Rabinowitz, all Israel will one day meet its brother there.

APPENDIX A

# The Messianic Jewish Rabbinical Council's Vision for Messianic Judaism

> *The Messianic Jewish Rabbinical Council (MJRC) is a community of Messianic Jewish leaders that seeks to articulate and promote a cohesive vision for Messianic Judaism that is rooted in Torah, responsive to tradition, and faithful to the Messiah. It seeks to define, clarify, and foster normative standards of faith and halakhic practice for the emerging Messianic Jewish community. The MJRC was established in 2006, and Kinzer was among its founding members. This document was adopted by the MJRC in 2021. Kinzer composed the first draft and spearheaded the process of revision, which culminated in the adoption of this final version.*

THE PRIMARY PURPOSE OF the Messianic Jewish Rabbinical Council (MJRC) is to articulate and promote a cohesive vision for Messianic Judaism rooted in Torah, responsive to tradition, and faithful to Messiah Yeshua. Such a vision must (1) state how the MJRC sees the relationship between the Messianic Jewish movement and the Jewish people as a whole, the historical churches, and the Jews within those churches. It must also (2) define the Messianic Jewish relationship to the traditions transmitted and embodied by the Jewish people and the Christian church. Finally, a cohesive vision for Messianic Judaism must (3) include reflection on the potential eschatological significance of this movement. The following is an attempt to accomplish these three tasks by painting a portrait of Messianic Judaism not as it is, but as we work, pray, and long for it to be.

## 1. THE TWOFOLD YESHUA COMMUNITY

As the resurrected Messiah, Yeshua of Nazareth came to fulfill God's purpose for Israel, a purpose which included the redemption of the nations and the entire cosmos. Yeshua and his apostles established a community within Israel which confirmed God's eternal covenant with Israel while extending Israel's reach beyond its own social borders.

The community established by Yeshua has an essential twofold constitution: it is composed of Jews and gentiles. In order for the twofold character of the Yeshua community to be adequately expressed and preserved, it is necessary to foster distinct but united Jewish and gentile communal environments (though Jews will sometimes live in the gentile environments, and gentiles will sometimes live in the Jewish ones). Although the nature of this twofold community is articulated in the Apostolic Writings [i.e., the New Testament], it cannot be understood apart from God's relationship with Israel which is articulated in the *Tanakh* and which endures perpetually. For this reason, the Jewish Yeshua-community is called to live as an integral part of the Jewish people, mediating Yeshua's holiness to the rest of Israel (Rom 11:16), while the gentile Yeshua-community is called to serve as a messianic extension of Israel among the nations of the world. As such, the Jewish Yeshua-community has a vocation of being a principal source of unity and reconciliation in the differentiated people of God.

Historically this twofold constitution binding the gentile Yeshua-community to the people of Israel through the Jewish Yeshua-community was compromised with the disappearance of the Jewish Yeshua-community. The Jewish people and the gentile Yeshua-community (i.e., the historical Christian church) share responsibility for this loss, each in its own way. The people of Israel eventually denied the legitimacy of the messianic remnant and at times even vigorously suppressed it. In this way Israel undermined the visible mediation of Yeshua's sanctifying presence in its midst. Likewise, the historical Christian church denied the legitimacy of its Jewish communal partner and the enduring covenantal identity of Israel as a whole. Moreover, the Christian church far exceeded the people of Israel in suppressing Jewish expressions of Yeshua-faith, at times even resorting to violence. In this way, the Christian church undermined the visible mediation of Israel's presence in the body of the Messiah. In undermining the Jewish Yeshua-community, the Christian church also undermined its own source of differentiated and reconciled unity, which is rooted in the life of the covenant people of Israel. It thereby opened itself up to opposing extremes of centralized clerical domination, on the one hand, and schismatic fragmentation, on the other.

Pressed on both sides, the Jewish Yeshua-community faded into the mists of a distant past. Yeshua continued to dwell in the midst of Israel, but now his sanctifying presence was hidden and diluted. Similarly, Israel continued to dwell in the midst of the Christian church through the church's union with Yeshua, but the covenantal power of Israel's life with God was hidden and diluted.

The MJRC believes that the God of Israel, who raised Yeshua from the dead, has begun the work of resurrecting the Jewish Yeshua-community. The MJRC sees the awakening of Jewish identity among Jewish disciples of Yeshua—manifested most visibly in the Messianic Jewish movement—as the first-fruits of that resurrection. The Messianic Jewish movement is not the full expression of that resurrection, but it points forward to that future reality. The MJRC employs the term "Messianic Jew" to refer to Jewish members of that movement, and the term "Messianic Judaism" to refer to their corporate way of life.

At present only a minority of Jewish disciples of Yeshua participate in the Messianic Jewish community. The majority are members of Christian churches, and their faith is shaped by the theological, liturgical, and devotional traditions of those churches. Some continue to identify as Jews and seek ways to express that reality. If properly related to Messianic Jews and to the wider Jewish world, followers of Yeshua in the church who are awakening to their Jewish identity could become a sign and instrument of the Christian church's enduring connection to the Jewish people. Strictly speaking, the MJRC sees these Jewish disciples of Yeshua as practicing Jewish Christianity rather than Messianic Judaism, for their communities are not Jewish, and the pattern of life of their communities is largely unaffected by the ongoing tradition of the Jewish people. In their service to the gentile Yeshua-community, Jews in that community order their life in relation to the life of their gentile brothers and sisters, for whose benefit the community has been established. Though such Jews have a different orientation to Jewish communal life than Jews in the Jewish Yeshua-community, the MJRC affirms them as fellow Jews in the Messiah. At the same time, the MJRC views the participation of Jews in the Christian church as an exception to the normal vocation of Jewish disciples of Yeshua, which lies within the Jewish Yeshua-community.

At present the majority of participants in the Messianic Jewish community are gentiles. While such gentile members are not Messianic Jews, they have a share in Messianic Judaism insofar as they participate in and serve the Messianic Jewish community. Without their dedicated and often sacrificial support Messianic Judaism would not have come to birth or have grown to its present level of maturity. If properly related to the Christian tradition, affirming its gifts even as they heed a call to a Jewish rather than a Christian communal life, these gentile members can serve as a continual reminder of the Messianic Jewish debt to the Christian church. The MJRC appreciates their ongoing contribution. Nevertheless, the role of gentiles in the Messianic Jewish community should be ordered in relation to that of their Messianic Jewish brothers and sisters, just as the role of Jewish Christians in the church is ordered in relation to that of their gentile brothers and sisters. Gentile members of the Messianic Jewish community are called to serve and advance God's purposes for the Jewish members, who are central to that community. Moreover, the participation of gentile members of the Messianic Jewish community is an exception to the normal vocation of gentile Christians, which lies within the gentile Yeshua-community. In the future the MJRC hopes to see a Messianic Jewish community in which a majority of its members are Jewish.

## 2. TORAH, BESORAH, AND THE TWOFOLD TRADITION

The MJRC envisions Messianic Judaism as the corporate way of life practiced by Jews within the Jewish corporate expression of the twofold Yeshua-community. The MJRC believes that this way of life must be rooted in the Torah, guided by Jewish tradition, and oriented to the welfare of the Jewish people. When this is the case, the Jewish expression within the twofold Yeshua-community remains vitally connected with the ongoing life of the Jewish people. But the Messianic Jewish way of life is also to be animated by and centered upon the teaching, example, and redemptive self-offering of Messiah Yeshua, who is present among his disciples through the gift of his Spirit. Consequently, such a Messianic Judaism represents in visible form the hidden presence of the resurrected Messiah in the midst of the Jewish people and mediates corporately the resurrected visible presence of Israel in the midst of the twofold Yeshua-community.

The Messianic Jewish understanding of the Torah focuses upon God's eternally faithful love expressed in Israel's election (Deuteronomy

7:6–7) and in the mission of the Messiah who gave his life for Israel and the nations (John 3:16). That love is now embodied within the Yeshua-community through the presence of the Spirit (Romans 5:5), empowering its Jewish members to fulfill the Torah by rooting observance of all the *mitzvot* in Yeshua's own perfect fulfillment of the two great commandments of love of God and love of neighbor (Mark 12:28–34).

As those whose way of life visibly represents and mediates the sanctifying presence of the Messiah in the midst of the Jewish people, Messianic Jews have the vocation to live as part of that people and as descendants, heirs, transmitters, and practitioners of its interpretive tradition. Messianic Jews have received the Torah—and *Tanakh* as a whole—through generations of Jews who have gone before them, and their engagement with *Tanakh* is always also an engagement with those Jews.

Messianic Jews likewise represent and mediate the presence of Israel to the multinational extension of the covenant people established by the risen Messiah. As partners with the historical Christian church, Messianic Jews are beneficiaries of fundamental elements of its interpretive tradition. They have received the *Besorah* [i.e., the good news/gospel] which tells of the crucified and risen Messiah, fully divine and fully human—and the Apostolic Writings as a whole—through generations of Christians who have gone before them, and their engagement with this message and these texts is always also an engagement with those Christians.

Messianic Jewish fulfillment of the Torah—through Yeshua, in the Spirit, and centered on the two great *mitzvot*—takes concrete form in the practices of study (Torah), prayer (*avodah*), and deeds of loving-kindness (*gemilut chasadim*). As envisioned by the MJRC, Messianic Jewish study focuses especially on *Tanakh*, the Apostolic Writings, and the classic texts of the rabbinic tradition. Messianic Jewish prayer is rooted in Jewish liturgical practice, mediated by the heavenly priesthood of the risen Messiah and empowered by the Spirit. Messianic Jewish deeds of loving-kindness actualize the conviction that all human beings are created in the divine image and that the Messiah himself is especially present among the hungry, the thirsty, and the stranger; moreover, they also take the form of addressing the underlying cultural, social, economic, and political realities which produce or exacerbate such conditions of deprivation.

As descendants, heirs, and continuators of the entire tradition of the Jewish people, we look for unifying commonalities among the diverse expressions of Jewish life through the ages while respecting and learning from the distinctive contribution of each. As beneficiaries of fundamental elements of the tradition of the historical Christian church, we likewise look for unifying commonalities among the diverse expressions of ecclesial life through the ages while respecting and learning from the distinctive contribution of each.

## 3. MESSIANIC JUDAISM AND THE AGE TO COME

The awakening of Jewish identity among Jewish disciples of Yeshua occurred in the nineteenth and twentieth centuries in the midst of fervent expectation of Yeshua's imminent return. While the MJRC is skeptical of efforts to chart the details of events that will occur at the final turning of the ages, it acknowledges that the Messianic Jewish movement is an eschatological sign. This sign challenges the entire people of God to attain the differentiated and reconciled unity befitting the consummation of history and anticipates the return of the Messiah and the definitive establishment of his kingdom. Just as the return of Jews to the land of Israel over the past century signals a new phase in the eschatological frame of history, so the re-emergence of the Jewish Yeshua-community conveys the same message.

Messianic Judaism is not merely the restoration of an original biblical template for the people of God. The rebirth of the Jewish Yeshua-community is a new heavenly intervention in the world which intimates something of God's ultimate purpose for Israel and the nations. As participants in this movement—heirs of a tradition oriented to the messianic future and beneficiaries of a tradition in which that future has already been inaugurated—Messianic Jews are called to live their lives in this age with eyes focused on the age to come.

The MJRC understands Messianic Jewish study of Torah, observance of *mitzvot* (including the messianic *mitzvot* of *Tevilat Mashiach* [i.e., baptism] and *Zichron Mashiach* [i.e., the Eucharist]), and practices of prayer and deeds of loving-kindness as anticipations of the messianic age. The passionate desire for ultimate divine justice and peace expressed in the Prophets and Psalms has new meaning for Messianic Jews who taste now the powers of the age to come and who humbly attempt to embody that eschatological vision in provisional form through practices of justice, peace, and healing in the present age.

The MJRC vision of Messianic Judaism is rooted in God's eternally faithful love for Israel, the nations, and all creation in Yeshua. It is a love which perseveres and will not fail. The One who raised Yeshua from the dead and enthroned him at his right hand will send him once again to reign in Jerusalem. From there he will raise the dead, restore Israel, renew creation, and unify all things under the sovereignty of God. All who embrace the MJRC vision long for Yeshua's return and seek to advance it through lives lived in union with him in which the fragrance of the age to come ascends amidst a world still groaning in travail. Maran ata—Come Lord Yeshua!

APPENDIX B

# Collected Statements of The Helsinki Consultation on Jewish Continuity in the Body of Messiah

*The Helsinki Consultation on Jewish Continuity in the Body of Messiah grew out of Kinzer's friendship with Fr. Antoine Lévy, who first crossed paths with Kinzer in Jerusalem in 2008. Together, they envisioned a high-level theological dialogue that included voices from Jewish followers of Jesus who span the ecclesial spectrum. They invited a group of such scholars to Helsinki, Finland, in 2010 for both a public conference and a set of private meetings. The Helsinki Consultation met annually in different European cities for the next eight years, and each year endeavored to create a statement relevant to that year's particular conference theme. In 2018, the vision to expand the fellowship became a reality with the founding of Yachad BeYeshua (www.yachad-beyeshua.org). Since then, Yachad BeYeshua has gained traction as a membership organization, bringing together a remarkably diverse cross-section of Jewish followers of Jesus.*

## HELSINKI STATEMENT (2010)

WE THANK GOD FOR bringing us as Jews to the knowledge of Jesus the Messiah, and we express a debt of gratitude to those from the Nations who have transmitted the knowledge of Christ from generation to generation. While we seek to speak on behalf of those who share our Jewish identity and faith in Christ, we have no official mandate from our respective communities. In what follows we are expressing our own deeply held convictions.

At this unprecedented event, we have experienced the depth of our bond, and at the same time we have wrestled with the diversity of our ingrained theological and cultural constructs. In spite of church divisions, we have come together as Jews who believe in Jesus. We hope that sharing the fruit of our common efforts will benefit our brothers and sisters in Christ. We do not aim to issue a definitive declaration, but to initiate an ongoing process of discussion.

There are many Jewish people in the body of Christ. We believe that this reality reflects God's intention that Israel and the Nations live as mutual blessings to one another. In fact, the Church in its essence is the communion of Jews and those from the Nations called to faith in Christ.

In light of this truth, we think that the life of Jews in the body of Christ has theological significance for that body as a whole. Their presence serves as a constant reminder to the body that its existence is rooted in the ongoing story of the people of Israel. This story resounds throughout the celebration of the liturgical life of the community. We believe that this story finds its center in Israel's Messiah. We believe that Jews within the body are a living bond between the Church and the people of Israel. Accordingly, we would like to explore concrete ways in which Jewish people may live out their distinctive calling in the body of Christ.

Finally, we wish to express to our Jewish brothers and sisters who do not share our faith in Jesus the Messiah that we consider ourselves to be part of the Jewish people and are committed to its welfare.

## PARIS STATEMENT ON AM ISRAEL (2011)

The theme of this year's consultation was "*Am Israel*—our People." As the many papers demonstrated, the identity of the Jewish People is complex, consisting of historical, familial, ethnic, cultural, and spiritual components that are all essential and inseparable. The paradoxical nature of Jewish identity challenges us to avoid reductionist interpretation and to explore further the mystery of our people.

As Jewish believers in Jesus, we affirm our identity as part of both the people of Israel and of the body of Christ. We recognise the pain this affirmation may cause to some of those of our people who do not believe in Yeshua. We are also aware of the misunderstanding that can occur in the Church when we state that we continue to be part of the Jewish people.

Nevertheless, we believe that we are a living witness to the mysterious and invisible bond which persists between the Church and Israel. Our dual membership brings us into a unique relationship with one another, and also entails weighty responsibilities and formidable challenges. Our two communities have been separated but belong together. We bear witness to the tragedy of their division and herald the hope of their future reconciliation.

We are exploring how this unique relationship to one another as Jewish believers in Jesus might take visible form as a wider fellowship dedicated to the service of the Jewish people and the body of Messiah.

## BERLIN STATEMENT ON TORAH (2012)

We, the members of the Helsinki Consultation, bear living witness to the recent emergence of Jewish believers in Yeshua (Jesus) who affirm their Jewish identity and acknowledge its theological significance. We are increasingly recognizing the intrinsic connection between this identity and Torah, the dynamic reality that has shaped the life of the Jewish people throughout its historical journey. We are also increasingly challenged to understand the continuing significance of the Torah encountered in the light of the gospel within the life of the body of the Messiah.

The complex nature of Jewish existence reflects the multifaceted and paradoxical character of the Torah. Torah is both the historical revelation of God to Israel, and Israel's window to the eternity of God; once-for-all transmitted truth, and ever new process of discovery; the fashioner of human institutions, and the secret of the cosmic order; the absoluteness of the Divine Word, and the relativity of its human interpretation; the vulnerable letter of the written text, and its invulnerable spirit; defining mark of Israel's singular path and destiny, and wisdom for all nations of the earth.

From an early period, many Christians have not fully grasped the Torah's paradoxical unity. They have limited its relevance to what they deemed "moral precepts" whilst rejecting the so-called "civil" and "ceremonial" practices that are foundational to Jewish life. They have frequently viewed Torah through the dualistic lens of grace and law, contrasting faith and works, and thus overlooking the Torah's enduring value.

Recent scholarship has shed new light on the Jewish context of Yeshua and the early Yeshua-movement which challenges traditional Christian understanding of the Torah and brings renewed appreciation for its positive significance. Many now recognize that Yeshua, Sha'ul (Paul), and the other early Jewish followers of Yeshua were Torah-observant. This historical reality carries significant theological implications.

We as Jewish believers in Yeshua acknowledge the special bond that unites us with Israel's Torah. This bond with Israel's Torah witnesses in the Church to the irrevocability of God's gifts and call to Israel (Rom 11:29). For Yeshua said, "Think not that I have come to destroy the Torah, or the prophets: I have not come to destroy, but to fulfill" (Mt 5:17). We believe in the continuing validity of the Torah even as it is fulfilled in Christ. Moreover, we see Christ as the incarnate Torah, the eternal wisdom of the Father in human flesh. He alone lived out the Torah in perfect form, and he calls his disciples to walk in his ways.

As Jewish believers in Yeshua we are in the process of working out the meaning and concrete implications of this bond that we collectively experience. We find ourselves in a variety of different ecclesial and Jewish communal contexts, and we hold different understandings and definitions of Torah observance. Some of us consider the observance of *mitzvot* such as Shabbat, Jewish holidays, and the dietary laws as an essential component of fidelity to Torah. Yet we all understand that our attempt to live in radical discipleship to Yeshua (in conformity to teaching such as that found in the Sermon on the Mount) is the foundational principle of Torah observance. Furthermore, we all understand our faithfulness to Israel's Torah as a commitment to promote an awareness of the Jewish roots of the Church.

In the midst of our different approaches, we have experienced through our deliberations and fellowship the dynamic and unifying power of Christ as Torah. Continuing to reflect on the Torah's role in our lives, we desire to grow together as Jews and as disciples of Yeshua. We hope these insights will resonate with other Jewish believers in Yeshua, and we invite them to join us on our journey.

# EDE STATEMENT ON JEWISH AND CHRISTIAN TRADITION (2014)

As Jewish disciples of Yeshua we inherit and respect both Jewish and Christian traditions. Jewish tradition, rooted in the Torah and developed through the centuries, guides the life of our people Israel and remains a vital source of our identity. Christian tradition, rooted in Christ and unfolding over time, shapes the life of the body of Christ and is therefore an indispensable source for our shared faith and life in Messiah.

Tragically, Jewish denial of the legitimacy of Jewish belief in Yeshua as Messiah and Christian denial of the reality of his ongoing relationship with the Jewish people have been central in the development of these two traditions. We recognize the need to challenge these core denials.

Although the Messiahship of Yeshua is not recognized in Rabbinic tradition, we believe that the Spirit of Yeshua is at work within it. Conversely, Christian tradition, founded on Yeshua's teaching and redemptive work, has often propagated a distorted understanding of Christ by failing to acknowledge his Jewish identity and his ongoing relationship with the Jewish people and their tradition. As heirs of both traditions, our faith in Yeshua and our commitment to our people summon us to receive each tradition with filial deference and with the critical freedom of mature sons and daughters.

As Jews who believe in Yeshua, we represent a spectrum in our concrete expression of the Jewish and Christian traditions we have inherited. Each of us embodies in some way fidelity to the core practices of these traditions, such as Shabbat and the Lord's Supper. We experience an increasingly harmonious and natural integration of these two traditions as we search for an authentic way of being Jewish disciples of Yeshua. At the same time, the tensions that exist between Jewish and Christian traditions pulsate within us. As diverse as our practices might be (and diversity is a mark of both traditions), these practices express our shared commitment to honor the Lord Yeshua and identify as members of the Jewish people.

Therefore, we undertake to bear witness to and transmit a life of faithfulness to Torah and Messiah in which Jewish and Christian tradition are not opposed but rather mutually enriching. We believe this witness has significance for the entire people of God, both Israel and the Church. We aim to foster and embody a living community in which, even as both traditions are respected and upheld, the historical division between them is challenged and transcended.

## MOSCOW STATEMENT ON JEWISH EXPRESSION IN THE BODY OF MESSIAH (2015)

The theological significance of the Jewish presence in the body of the Messiah has been the object of a growing reflection over recent years. This must be seen in connection with the increasing visibility that this presence has taken in the Messianic Jewish movement and in various churches. This visibility has expressed itself in many forms. Two main forms of corporate expression have prevailed until now. The first is based on a reconnection with the legacy of Jewish tradition outside the boundaries of the institutional churches. The second combines the rediscovery of the significance of Jewish identity with the striving to promote it from within the context of the institutional churches.

As the first form faces the challenge of forging a creative synthesis between faith in Yeshua (Jesus) and Jewish tradition, the second faces that of fighting against remnants of anti-Jewish discourse and behavior. Both share the experience of rejection by mainstream Jews while both maintain that their faith in Yeshua strengthens their Jewish identity and deepens their appreciation of the riches conveyed by Jewish tradition. We, members of the Helsinki Consultation, discern in both forms God's providence presiding over the destiny of the body of the Messiah and leading it, through ways that are often puzzling for human minds, to its final goal, the unity of Israel and the Nations in Messiah Yeshua.

## KRAKOW STATEMENT ON THE WOUNDS OF MEMORY (2017)

We have gathered in Krakow, Poland surrounded by witnesses to both a beautiful and tragic past. So too we have been reminded of King Casimir's welcome of the Jews, the rich achievements of Jewish culture, and its engagement with Polish society over many centuries, including the presence of Jews within the Church.

It is precisely in this ambivalent context of blessing and woundedness that we have sought to pursue our reflections on our place as Jewish believers in Yeshua in the living body of the Messiah. As Jews, we remember with our people the deep wounds received from the hands of Christians, sometimes with the assent of church authorities. We also remember that many Christians have been prey to persecutions across the ages, most acutely in the last century. We remember too that we Jews can be agents of violence and cause of suffering. Finally, we remember that we are part of the body of the Christ, who is the source and agent of all reconciliation. It is the paradox and mystery of our faith that healing and forgiveness come forth from the wounds of the Messiah on the cross.

Remembering has led us back to the wound that is the separation between the Church and the major part of the Jewish people. This has hindered the full realization of the body of Christ. As Jewish disciples of Jesus, we are profoundly affected by this separation. We are aware that our dual identity has sometimes proven a stumbling block on the path to reconciliation and unity. The misguided zeal of some Jewish followers of Jesus has historically even furthered mutual rejection between members of the Church and the Jewish people. But we have also witnessed great figures among the Jewish followers of Jesus who have fought anti-Judaism, antisemitism, and their legacy, and who have worked tirelessly for reconciliation. They understood how healing the wounds of memory demands that the Church affirm the ongoing election of the Jewish people and the richness of its tradition. They believed also that the Church should welcome the expression of Jewish identity within her life.

Inspired by these great witnesses, we are convinced that a corporate Jewish expression is essential to the integrity of the entire body of the Messiah. The acceptance of this Jewish presence in its midst is itself an aspect of needed repentance from anti-Judaism and antisemitism, and a decision to break with its destructive legacy. This acceptance will also contribute to disclosing the authentic nature of the body of Christ, which is rooted in Israel's election and the Jewishness of its Messiah. We Jewish followers of Yeshua seek to be instruments of Christ's power for this healing of the wounds of memory and for reconciliation within his divided body.

# Bibliography

Allison, Dale C., Jr. "Jesus and the Victory of Apocalyptic." In *Jesus and the Restoration of Israel*, edited Carey C. Newman, 126–41. Downers Grove, IL: InterVarsity, 1999.
———. "Matt. 23:39 = Luke 13:35b as a Conditional Prophecy." *Journal for the Study of the New Testament* 18 (1983) 75–84.
Aquinas, Thomas. *Summa Theologica of St. Thomas Aquinas*. Vol. 2. Translated by the Fathers of the English Dominican Province. Westminster, MD: Christian Classics, 1981.
Ariel, Yaakov. *Evangelizing the Chosen People: Mission to the Jews in America, 1880–2000*. Chapel Hill: University of North Carolina Press, 2000.
Arndt, William F., and F. Wilbur Gingrich. *A Greek-English Lexicon of the New Testament*. Chicago: University of Chicago Press, 1979.
Augustine, Aurelius. *The Works of St. Augustine: Letters 1–99*. Translated by Roland Teske, SJ. Hyde Park, NY: New City, 2001.
Azar, Michael G. "'Supersessionism': The Political Origins of a Theological Neologism." *Studies in Christian-Jewish Relations* 16.1 (2021) 1–25.
Baker, Cynthia M. *Jew*. New Brunswick, NJ: Rutgers University Press, 2017.
Balthasar, Hans Urs von. *Martin Buber and Christianity: A Dialogue between Israel & the Church*. Translated by Alexander Dru. New York: Macmillan, 1960.
Bauckham, Richard. "James and the Gentiles (Acts 15.13–21)." In *History, Literature, and Society in the Book of Acts*, edited by Ben Witherington III, 154–84. Cambridge: Cambridge University Press, 1996.
———. "James and the Jerusalem Church." In *The Book of Acts in Its First Century Setting*, edited by Richard Bauckham, 452–75. Grand Rapids: Eerdmans, 1995.
———. "James and the Jerusalem Council Decision." In *Introduction to Messianic Judaism: Its Ecclesial Context and Biblical Foundations*, edited by David Rudolph and Joel Willitts, 178–86. Grand Rapids: Zondervan, 2013.
———. "James, Peter, and the Gentiles." In *The Missions of James, Peter, and Paul: Tensions in Early Christianity*, edited by Bruce Chilton and Craig Evans, 91–142. Leiden: Brill, 2004.
———. *Jude and the Relatives of Jesus in the Early Church*. Edinburgh: T. & T. Clark, 1990.
Beasley-Murray, George R. *John*. Word Biblical Commentary 36. Waco, TX: Word Books, 1987.
Behr-Sigel, Elisabeth. *Lev Gillet: A Monk of the Eastern Church*. Translated by Helen Wright. Oxford: Fellowship of St. Alban and St. Sergius, 1999.

## BIBLIOGRAPHY

Ben-Shimon, Kamoun. "The Murder Midrash." *Jerusalem Report* XXI.12, September 27, 2010, 14–17.

Boccaccini, Gabriele, and Carlos A. Segovia, eds. *Paul the Jew: Rereading the Apostle as a Figure of Second Temple Judaism*. Minneapolis: Fortress, 2016.

Boyarin, Daniel. *Border Lines: The Partition of Judaeo-Christianity*. Philadelphia: University of Pennsylvania Press, 2004.

———. *Carnal Israel*. Berkeley: University of California Press, 1993.

———. *Dying for God*. Stanford, CA: Stanford University Press, 1999.

———. *The Jewish Gospels: The Story of the Jewish Christ*. New York: New Press, 2012.

———. *A Radical Jew*. Berkeley: University of California Press, 1994.

Brawley, Robert L. *Luke-Acts and the Jews: Conflict, Apology, and Conciliation*. Atlanta: Scholars, 1987.

Burge, Gary M. *Jesus and the Land: The New Testament Challenge to "Holy Land" Theology*. Grand Rapids: Baker, 2010.

Burns, Joshua Ezra. *The Christian Schism in Jewish History and Jewish Memory*. Cambridge: Cambridge University Press, 2016.

Campbell, William S. *Romans: A Social Identity Commentary*. London: T. & T. Clark, 2023.

Casey, Thomas G., and Justin Taylor, eds. *Paul's Jewish Matrix*. Rome: Gregorian and Biblical Press, 2011.

Cohen, Jeremy. *Living Letters of the Law: Ideas of the Jew in Medieval Christianity*. Berkeley: University of California Press, 1999.

Cohn-Sherbok, Dan. *Messianic Judaism*. London: Cassell, 2000.

Connelly, John. *From Enemy to Brother: The Revolution in Catholic Teaching on the Jews 1933–1965*. Cambridge: Harvard University Press, 2012.

Conzelmann, Hans. *The Theology of St. Luke*. Translated by Geoffrey Buswell. 1961. Reprint, Philadelphia: Fortress, 1982.

Cunningham, Philip A. *Seeking Shalom: The Journey to Right Relationship between Catholics and Jews*. Grand Rapids: Eerdmans, 2015.

Dan, Joseph. *The Ancient Jewish Mysticism*. Tel Aviv: MOD, 1993.

Duchesne, Jean, ed. *Jean-Marie Lustiger on Christians and Jews*. New York: Paulist, 2010.

Dunn, James D. G. *The Partings of the Ways: Between Christianity and Judaism and Their Significance for the Character of Christianity*. Philadelphia: Trinity, 1991.

Endelman, Todd M. *Leaving the Jewish Fold: Conversion and Radical Assimilation in Modern Jewish History*. Princeton: Princeton University Press, 2015.

Edersheim, Alfred. *The Life and Times of Jesus the Messiah*. 1886. Reprint, Grand Rapids: Eerdmans, 1971.

Eusebius. *Ecclesiastical History*. Translated by Kirsopp Lake. Cambridge: Harvard University Press, 1926.

Fox, Everett. *The Five Books of Moses*. New York: Schocken, 1995.

Fredriksen, Paula. *Paul: The Pagans' Apostle*. New Haven, CT: Yale University Press, 2017.

Friedman, Elias. *Jewish Identity*. New York: Miriam, 1987.

Gaon, Saadia. *Book of Beliefs and Opinions*. Translated by Samuel Rosenblatt. New Haven, CT: Yale University Press, 1948.

Garber, Zev, and Kenneth Hanson. *Judaism and Jesus*. Newcastle, UK: Cambridge Scholars, 2020.

Gillet, Lev. *Communion in the Messiah: Studies in the Relationship between Judaism and Christianity*. 1942. Reprint, Eugene, OR: Wipf and Stock, 2014.
Gordon, Benjamin D. "On the Sanctity of Mixtures: Two Halakic Sayings in Romans 11:16–24." *Journal of Biblical Literature* 135.2 (2016) 356–59.
Goshen-Gottstein, Alon. "The Body as Image of God in Rabbinic Literature." *Harvard Theological Review* 87.2 (1994) 171–95.
Gunton, Colin. *The Promise of Trinitarian Theology*. London: T. & T. Clark, 1991.
Hamant, Yves. *Alexander Men: A Witness for Contemporary Russia*. Translated by Fr. Steven Bigham. Torrance, CA: Oakwood, 1995.
Harink, Douglas. "Accountabilities, Tensions, Transformations with Lou Martyn and Mark Kinzer on a Theological Journey." In *Covenant and the People of God: Essays in Honor of Mark S. Kinzer*, edited by Jonathan Kaplan et al., 54–65. Eugene, OR: Pickwick, 2023.
Harvey, Richard S. *Luther and the Jews: Putting Right the Lies*. Eugene, OR: Cascade, 2017.
Hays, Richard B. *First Corinthians*. Louisville, KY: John Knox, 1997.
Hesslein, Kayko Driedger. *Dual Citizenship: Two-Natures Christologies and the Jewish Jesus*. London: T. & T. Clark, 2015.
Hurtado, Larry W. *Lord Jesus Christ*. Grand Rapids: Eerdmans, 2003.
Idel, Moshe. *Ben: Sonship and Jewish Mysticism*. London: Continuum, 2007.
Jacobs, Louis. "Belief in a Personal God: The Position of Liberal Supernaturalism." In *Contemporary Jewish Theology: A Reader*, edited by Elliot N. Dorff and Louis E. Newman, 98–111. Oxford: Oxford University Press, 1999.
Jackson-McCabe, Matt, ed. *Jewish Christianity Reconsidered: Rethinking Ancient Groups and Texts*. Minneapolis: Fortress, 2007.
———. *Jewish Christianity: The Making of the Christianity-Judaism Divide*. New Haven, CT: Yale University Press, 2020.
Jenson, Robert W. "Toward a Christian Theology of Judaism." In *Jews and Christians: People of God*, edited by Carl E. Braaten and Robert W. Jenson, 1–13. Grand Rapids: Eerdmans, 2003.
Jervell, Jacob. *Luke and the People of God: A New Look at Luke-Acts*. Minneapolis: Augsburg, 1972.
Jocz, Jakob. *The Jewish People and Jesus Christ after Auschwitz: A Study in the Controversy between Church and Synagogue*. Grand Rapids: Baker, 1981.
John Paul II, Pope. *Spiritual Pilgrimage*. Edited by Eugene J. Fischer and Leon Klenicky. New York: Crossroad, 1995.
Jones, F. Stanley. *Pseudoclementina Elchasaiticaque Inter Judaeochristiana: Collected Studies*. Leuven: Peeters, 2012.
———, ed. *The Rediscovery of Jewish Christianity: From Toland to Baur*. Atlanta: Society of Biblical Literature, 2012.
Juel, Donald. *Luke-Acts: The Promise of History*. Atlanta: John Knox: 1983.
Juster, Dan. *Jewish Roots: Understanding Your Jewish Faith*. Shippensburg, PA: Destiny Image, 2013.
Kaplan, Jonathan, et al., eds. *Covenant and the People of God: Essays in Honor of Mark S. Kinzer*. Eugene, OR: Pickwick, 2023.
Kelly, J. N. D. *Early Christian Doctrines*. New York: Harper & Row, 1978.
Kereszty, Roch. "Messianic Jews and the Catholic Church: Reflections on the Ecclesiology of Mark S. Kinzer." *Communio* 42.3 (2015) 413–519.

Kinzer, Mark S. *Israel's Messiah and the People of God: A Vision for Messianic Jewish Covenant Fidelity*. Edited by Jennifer M. Rosner. Eugene, OR: Cascade, 2011.

———. *Jerusalem Crucified, Jerusalem Risen: The Resurrected Messiah, the Jewish People, and the Land of Promise*. Eugene, OR: Cascade, 2018.

———. "A Messianic Jewish Approach to Jewish Catholicism: Responding to Antoine Levy's *Jewish Church*." *Pro Ecclesia* 31.3 (2022) 350–88.

———. *Postmissionary Messianic Judaism: Redefining Christian Engagement with the Jewish People*. Grand Rapids: Brazos, 2005.

———. *Searching Her Own Mystery: Nostra Aetate, the Jewish People, and the Identity of the Church*. Eugene, OR: Cascade, 2015.

Kinzer, Mark S., et al., eds. *Jesus der Messias Israels? Messianisches Judentum und christliche Theologie im Gespräch*. Freiburg: Herder, 2023.

———. *Jesus—the Messiah of Israel? Messianic Judaism and Christian Theology in Conversation*. New York: Crossroad, 2024.

Kjaer-Hansen, Kai. *Joseph Rabinowitz and the Messianic Movement*. Grand Rapids: Eerdmans, 1995.

Kornblatt, Judith Deutsch. *Doubly Chosen: Jewish Identity, The Soviet Intelligentsia, and the Russian Orthodox Church*. Madison: University of Wisconsin Press, 2004.

Levering, Matthew. *Christ's Fulfillment of Torah and Temple: Salvation according to Thomas Aquinas*. Notre Dame, IN: University of Notre Dame Press, 2002.

Levertoff, Paul Philip. *Love and the Messianic Age*. 1923. Reprint, Marshfield, MO: Vine of David, 2009.

———. *The Religious Thought of the Chasidim*. Translated by Brian Reed. Jerusalem: Vine of David, 2018.

Lévy, Antoine. *Jewish Church: A Catholic Approach to Messianic Judaism*. Minneapolis: Lexington, 2021.

Lindbeck, George. *The Church in a Postliberal Age*. Grand Rapids: Eerdmans, 2002.

———. *The Nature of Doctrine: Religion and Theology in a Postliberal Age*. Philadelphia: Westminster, 1984.

Loader, William. *Jesus' Attitude towards the Law: A Study of the Gospels*. Grand Rapids: Eerdmans, 1997.

Lustiger, Jean-Marie. *The Promise*. Translated by Rebecca Howell Balinski et al. Grand Rapids: Eerdmans, 2007.

Magid, Shaul. *Hasidism Incarnate: Hasidism, Christianity, and the Construction of Modern Judaism*. Stanford, CA: Stanford University Press, 2015.

Maoz, Baruch. *Judaism Is Not Jewish*. Ross-shire, UK: Mentor, 2003.

Marshall, Bruce D. *Trinity and Truth*. Cambridge: Cambridge University Press, 2000.

Marshall, I. Howard. *The Acts of the Apostles: An Introduction and Commentary*. Grand Rapids: Eerdmans, 1980.

Matt, Daniel Chanan. *Zohar: The Book of Enlightenment*. Ramsey, NJ: Paulist, 1983.

———. *The Zohar, Pritzker Edition*. Vol. 4. Stanford, CA: Stanford University Press, 2007.

Matt, Hershel Jonah. *Walking Humbly with God*. Edited by Daniel C. Matt. Hoboken, NJ: Ktav, 1993.

McDermott, Gerald R., ed. *The New Christian Zionism: Fresh Perspectives on Israel & the Land*. Downers Grove, IL: IVP Academic, 2016.

———, ed. *Understanding the Jewish Roots of Christianity: Biblical, Historical, and Theological Essays on the Relationship between Judaism and Christianity*. Bellingham, WA: Lexham, 2021.

McRay, John. *Paul: His Life and Teaching*. Grand Rapids: Baker, 2003.
Melnick, Jim, et al., eds. *Upholding God's Word, Reaching God's Chosen: A Festschrift in Honor of Dr. Mitchell L. Glaser*. New York: KIFM, 2022.
Meyer, Barbara U. *Jesus the Jew in Christian Memory: Theological and Philosophical Explorations*. Cambridge: Cambridge University Press, 2020.
Meyer, Lester V. "Remnant." In *Anchor Bible Dictionary*, vol. 5, edited by David Noel Freedman, 669–71. New York: Doubleday, 1992.
Miller, John W. *How the Bible Came to Be: Exploring the Narrative and Message*. New York: Paulist, 2004.
Mulder, Michael, Koert van Bekkum, and Arco den Heijer, eds. *Israel as a Hermeneutical Challenge*. Leiden: Brill, forthcoming.
Nanos, Mark D. *Reading Corinthians and Philippians within Judaism*. Eugene, OR: Cascade, 2017.
———. *Reading Paul within Judaism*. Eugene, OR: Cascade, 2017.
Nanos, Mark D., and Magnus Zetterholm, eds. *Paul within Judaism: Restoring the First-Century Context to the Apostle*. Minneapolis: Fortress, 2015.
Neusner, Jacob. *The Incarnation of God*. Atlanta: Scholars, 1992.
———. *Recovering Judaism: The Universal Dimension of Judaism*. Minneapolis: Fortress, 2001.
Novak, David. *Jewish-Christian Dialogue: A Jewish Justification*. Oxford: Oxford University Press, 1989.
Novenson, Matthew V. *The Grammar of Messianism: An Ancient Jewish Political Idiom and Its Users*. Oxford: Oxford University Press, 2017.
Ochs, Peter, ed. *The Return to Scripture in Judaism and Christianity: Essays in Postcritical Scriptural Interpretation*. New York: Paulist, 1993.
Oepke, Albrecht. "*apokathistēmi, apokatastasis*." In *Theological Dictionary of the New Testament*, volume 1, translated by Geoffrey W. Bromiley, 388. Grand Rapids: Eerdmans, 1964.
Oliver, Isaac W. "The First 'Paul within Judaism' Perspective? The Incorporation of Non-Jews into the Ekklesia according to the Acts of the Apostles." Delivered at the Annual Meeting of the Society of Biblical Literature, Boston, November 19, 2017. Available at https://bradley.academia.edu/IsaacWOliverakadeOliveira.
———. *Torah Praxis after 70 CE: Reading Matthew and Luke-Acts as Jewish Texts*. Tübingen: Mohr Siebeck, 2013.
Painter, John. *Just James*. Minneapolis: Fortress, 1999.
Park, Wongi. *The Politics of Race and Ethnicity in Matthew's Passion Narrative*. Cham, Switzerland: Palgrave Macmillan, 2019.
Parkes, James. *The Conflict of the Church and the Synagogue*. 1934. Reprint, New York: Atheneum, 1981.
Pitre, Brant. *Jesus and the Jewish Roots of Mary*. New York: Image, 2018.
———. *Jesus and the Jewish Roots of the Eucharist*. New York: Image, 2011.
Presbyterian Church (USA). *The Constitution of the Presbyterian Church (U.S.A.) Part I—Book of Confessions*. New York: Office of the General Assembly, 1983.
Pro Ecclesia. "Symposium on Totus Christus." *Pro Ecclesia* 29.1 (2020) 3–67.
Puskas, Charles B. *The Conclusion of Luke-Acts: The Significance of Acts 28:16–31*. Eugene, OR: Pickwick, 2009.
Raffelt, Albert, ed. *Der Stern der Erlösung*. Freiburg: Universitätsbibliothek, 2002.

Rashi. *Rashi: Commentary on the Torah, Vol. 5. Devarim/Deuteronomy*. Translated by Israel Isser Zvi Herczeg. New York: Mesorah, 2001.

Ratzinger, Joseph (Pope Benedict XVI). *Jesus of Nazareth, Part Two*. San Francisco: Ignatius, 2011.

Rausch, David A. *Messianic Judaism: Its History, Theology, and Polity*. New York: Mellen, 1982.

Rosenzweig, Franz. *The Star of Redemption*. Translated by Barbara E. Galli. Madison: University of Wisconsin Press, 2005.

Rudolph, David. "Messianic Judaism in Antiquity and in the Modern Era." In *Introduction to Messianic Judaism: Its Ecclesial Context and Biblical Foundations*, edited by D. Rudolph and J. Willitts, 21–36. Grand Rapids: Zondervan, 2013.

Ruether, Rosemary R. *Faith and Fratricide: The Theological Roots of Anti-Semitism*. New York: Seabury, 1974.

Runesson, Anders. "Who Parted from Whom? The Myth of the So-Called Parting of the Ways between Judaism and Christianity." In *Chosen to Follow: Jewish Believers through History and Today*, edited by K. H. Hoyland and J. W. Nielsen, 53–72. Jerusalem: Caspari Center, 2012.

Sacks, Jonathan, trans. *The Koren Siddur*. Jerusalem: Koren, 2009.

Sandgren, Leo Dupree. *Vines Intertwined: A History of Jews and Christians from the Babylonian Exile to the Advent of Islam*. Peabody, MA: Hendrickson, 2010.

Schaff, Philip, and Henry Wace, eds. *The Seven Ecumenical Councils: Nicene and Post-Nicene Fathers of the Christian Church, Second Series*. Vol. 14. Grand Rapids: Eerdmans, 1983.

Schlink, Edmund. *Theology of the Lutheran Confessions*. Translated by P. F. Koehneke and H. J. A. Bouman. Philadelphia: Fortress, 1961.

Scholem, Gershom. *Kabbalah*. Jerusalem: Keter, 1974.

———. *On the Mystical Shape of the Godhead*. New York: Schocken, 1991.

Schonfield, Hugh J. *The History of Jewish Christianity: From the First to the Twentieth Century*. London: Duckworth, 1936.

Schumacher, Thomas. "The Addressees of Ephesians and the Question of the Distinction between Jews and Gentiles." In *Covenant and the People of God: Essays in Honor of Mark S. Kinzer*, edited by Jonathan Kaplan et al., 233–47. Eugene, OR: Pickwick, 2023.

Skarsaune, Oskar. *In the Shadow of the Temple*. Downers Grove, IL: IVP Academic, 2002.

Skarsaune, Oskar, and Reidar Hvalvik, eds. *Jewish Believers in Jesus: The Early Centuries*. Peabody, MA: Hendrickson, 2007.

Solovyov, Vladimir. *The Burning Bush: Writings on Jews and Judaism*. Translated by Gregory Yuri Glazov. Notre Dame, IN: University of Notre Dame Press, 2016.

Sommer, Benjamin D. *The Bodies of God and the World of Ancient Israel*. Cambridge: Cambridge University Press, 2009.

Soulen, R. Kendall. *The God of Israel and Christian Theology*. Minneapolis: Fortress, 1996.

———. *Irrevocable: The Name of God and the Unity of the Christian Bible*. Minneapolis: Fortress, 2022.

Spitzer, Lee B. "Covenant Partners: Messianic Jews, Jewish Christians, and Bilateral Ecclesiology." In *Covenant and the People of God: Essays in Honor of Mark S. Kinzer*, edited by Jonathan Kaplan et al. 268–80. Eugene, OR: Pickwick, 2023.

Stern, David. *Messianic Jewish Manifesto*. Jerusalem: Jewish New Testament, 1991.
Tannehill, Robert C. *Luke*. Nashville: Abingdon, 1996.
―――. *The Narrative Unity of Luke-Acts*. Vol. 2. Minneapolis: Fortress, 1990.
Tapie, Matthew A. *Aquinas on Israel and the Church: The Question of Supersessionism in the Theology of Thomas Aquinas*. Eugene, OR: Pickwick, 2014.
Tappert, Theodore G., trans and ed. *The Book of Concord: The Confessions of the Evangelical Lutheran Church*. Philadelphia: Fortress, 1959.
Taylor Coolman, Holly. "Jewish Church: A New (and Ancient) Agenda for Catholic Theology." In *Covenant and the People of God: Essays in Honor of Mark S. Kinzer*, edited by Jonathan Kaplan et al., 18–31. Eugene, OR: Pickwick, 2023.
Taylor, Justin. "Paul and the Jewish Leaders of Rome: Acts 28:17–31." In *Paul's Jewish Matrix*, edited by Thomas G. Casey and Justin Taylor, 311–26. Rome: Gregorian and Biblical Press, 2011.
Thiessen, Matthew. *A Jewish Paul: The Messiah's Herald to the Gentiles*. Grand Rapids: Baker, 2023.
―――. *Paul and the Gentile Problem*. Oxford: Oxford University Press, 2016.
Tomson, Peter J. *"If this be from Heaven . . .": Jesus and the New Testament Authors in Their Relationship to Judaism*. Sheffield, UK: Sheffield Academic, 2001.
―――. *Paul and the Jewish Law*. Minneapolis: Fortress, 1990.
Torrance, Thomas F. *The Christian Doctrine of God: One Being Three Persons*. Edinburgh: T. & T. Clark, 1996.
―――. *Theology in Reconciliation*. 1975. Reprint, Eugene, OR: Wipf & Stock, 1996.
Trobisch, David. *The First Edition of the New Testament*. Oxford: Oxford University Press, 2000.
Tucker, J. Brian. *Reading Romans after Supersessionism*. Eugene, OR: Cascade, 2018.
Tyson, Joseph B., ed. *Luke-Acts and the Jewish People: Eight Critical Perspectives*. Minneapolis: Augsburg, 1988.
―――. *Luke, Judaism, and the Scholars: Critical Approaches to Luke-Acts*. Columbia: University of South Carolina Press, 1999.
Ulitskaya, Ludmila. *Daniel Stein, Interpreter*. Translated by Arch Tait. New York: Overlook Duckworth, 2011.
Van Buren, Paul M. *A Theology of the Jewish-Christian Reality, Part 1: Discerning the Way*. San Francisco: Harper & Row, 1980.
Vanhoozer, Kevin J. *The Drama of Doctrine: A Canonical Linguistic Approach to Christian Theology*. Louisville, KY: WJK, 2005.
Weigel, George. *Witness to Hope: The Biography of Pope John Paul II*. New York: HarperCollins, 2001.
Weinandy, Thomas G. "The Jews and the Body of Christ: An Essay in Hope." *Pro Ecclesia* 27.4 (2018) 412–24.
Wilken, Robert L. *The Land Called Holy: Palestine in Christian History and Thought*. New Haven, CT: Yale University Press, 1992.
Willebrands, Johannes Cardinal. *Church and Jewish People: New Considerations*. New York: Paulist, 1992.
Wilson, S. G. *Luke and the Law*. Cambridge: Cambridge University Press, 1983.
Winter, Ralph D. "The Two Structures of God's Redemptive Mission." In *Perspectives on the World Christian Movement: A Reader*, edited by Ralph D. Winter and Steven C. Hawthorne, 244–53. 4th ed. Littleton, CO: William Carey, 2013.

Witherington, Ben, III. *The Acts of the Apostles: A Socio-Rhetorical Commentary*. Grand Rapids: Eerdmans, 1998.

Wolfson, Elliot R. "Judaism and Incarnation: The Imaginal Body of God." In *Christianity in Jewish Terms*, edited by Tikva Frymer-Kensky et al, 239–54. Boulder, CO: Westview, 2000.

———. *Open Secret: Postmessianic Messianism and the Mystical Revision of Menahem Mendel Schneerson*. New York: Columbia University Press, 2009.

Wright, N. T. *Jesus and the Victory of God*. London: SPCK, 1996.

Wyschogrod, Michael. *Abraham's Promise: Judaism and Jewish-Christian Relations*. Edited by R. Kendall Soulen. Grand Rapids: Eerdmans, 2004.

———. *The Body of Faith*. Northvale, NJ: Aronson, 1996.

Yoder, John Howard. *The Jewish-Christian Schism Revisited*. Grand Rapids: Eerdmans, 2003.

Yoshiko Reed, Annette. *Jewish-Christianity and the History of Judaism*. Minneapolis: Fortress, 2022.

Zellentin, Holger M. *Law beyond Israel: From the Bible to the Qur'an*. Oxford: Oxford University Press, 2022.

Zizioulas, John. *Being as Communion*. Crestwood, NY: St. Vladimir's Seminary Press, 1985.

# Name/Subject Index

Arianism, 25–26, 30–32, 35
Association of Hebrew Catholics, 59–60, 82

Barth, Karl, 87
Boyarin, Daniel, 43–44, 76–77, 92
Burge, Gary, 151–53, 157–58, 164–65, 175

Catholicism, Jewish 60, 82n28, 86
Chasidism, 42, 44–45, 46
christology, Chalcedonian, 127; high, 178; as Messianology, 4–5, 15–39, 63n37, 137–38
Cornelius episode, 53–55, 155, 166
Cunningham, Philip, 74, 76

discipleship, differentiated, xx, 112; Jewish, 113–18, 127–30
Dunn, James, 78–81

ecclesiology, bilateral, xvi, xx, xxi, 15–39, 57n14, 65n44, 127; in light of Israel's election, 51–150
*ekklesia*, catholicity of, 70, 84–85, 98–99; *ex circumcisione*, 17, 29n26, 61, 64, 84–86; *ex gentibus*, 17, 29n26, 61, 64, 66, 84–86; gentilization of, 52–58; Jewish priestly vocation within, 100–111; rebirth of Jewish, 62–70
election, xxv 23n5, 24, 76–77, 96–97, 105, 129–30, 192–93, 202

eschatology, and God's oneness, 45–46, 93; expansion to include gentiles, 97–100, 105–7, 108–9; and land of Israel, xxiii-xxv, 151–175; and people of Israel, xxiii-xxv, 4–5, 14, 55, 70–71, 176–87; post-supersessionist, 186–87

Friedman, Elias, 59–60, 82

Garber, Zev, 40–42, 45, 46, 47
*Gifts and Calling of God Are Irrevocable*, 84–85
Gillet, Lev, 132–39, 141

Hanson, Kenneth, 40–42, 45, 46, 47

Idel, Moshe, 43–44
Incarnation, 4, 26–27, 30, 40–47, 97, 98

James the apostle, as model for covenant fidelity xxii, 55–57, 103–8
Jenson, Robert, 4–5, 7
Jewish-Christianity, 52n4, 78–9, 137–38, 157, 191
Jerusalem, assembly, 64–65, 66, 67n49, 78, 101–6; centrality of, xxiii-xxiv, 152–75, 179–84; Council of, 54–57, 61–62, 66, 69, 155, 183; destruction of, xxiii, 11, 52, 57–58, 158–63, 172;

Jerusalem, assembly (*continued*)
restoration of xxiii, 52, 61, 77, 158, 162, 163, 172–74, 179–82, 184, 195

kabbalah, 32–33, 37–38, 42, 44–45
Karaites, 30–31

land of Israel, xxiii-xxv, 151–64, 175, 176–87; Jewish national home in, 52, 58–59, 70, 184–87, 194
Levertoff, Paul, 81, 141, 185
Lindbeck, George, 25, 63n36
Lustiger, Jean-Marie, 60, 69, 82, 83–85, 141
logos, 4, 16, 32, 34n23, 37, 41–42, 43, 77

Maimonides, 31, 41–43, 46, 91–92
Magid, Shaul, 44–45
Maritain, Jacques, 134
Marshall, Bruce, 4–5, 7
Men, Alexander, 60, 81–82, 141
Messianic Jewish Rabbinical Council (MJRC), xxii, 121, 124, 189–95
monotheism, "absolute" 40–48

Nicaea, Council of, 21–23; creed, 15–30, 33–39, 93, 98, 100; in Messianic Jewish perspective, 22–23, 33–37
Novak, David, 44

Oral Torah, 123n7, 125–26

Parks, James, 79–80
parting of the ways, 21, 74–79, 86–87, 127
Paul the apostle, as model for covenant fidelity xxii, 55–57, 103–8
Pentecost, 53–55, 156–57

Peter the apostle, as model for covenant fidelity xxii, 55–57, 103–8
Pontius Pilate, 9–11, 12

Rabinowitz, Joseph, 59, 81–82, 184–85
Revelation, 53n5, 133; in Christ, 14, 53, 77, 86; God's self-, 32, 89; Jesus to Jews, 14, 186; in Torah, 13, 52–53, 86, 198
Rosenzweig, Franz 67, 89–92, 99, 132

Saadia Gaon, 30–32
Saint James, Association of, 59, 82
Scholem, Gershon, 31–32
*Shema*, 17, 27, 30, 41–42, 45–46, 93–95
Soulen, Kendall. 23–24
Solovyov, Vladimir, 81–82, 185n14
Supersessionism, xxiv, 22–23, 93; post-, 177–78; structural, 23–24

Temple, 43, 104–5, 154, 159–61, 172, 179; destruction of, 123, 179
Torah observance, 17, 44, 109; Catholic understanding of, 63; denigration of, 17, 63–64; for Jewish followers of Jesus, xx, xxii, 18, 38–39, 114–16, 121, 123–24, 193, 199; Protestant understanding of, 63–64

Van Buren, Paul, 52–53

Wolfson, Elliot, 44–45
Wyschogrod, Michael, 56–57, 92, 126

*Yachad BeYeshua*, xx–xxi, xxii, 110, 130, 137, 196
Yoder, John Howard, 75–76

Zionism, xxiii, xxiv, 58–59, 152, 174, 184–85
Zohar, 32, 45–46

# Ancient Document Index

## HEBREW SCRIPTURES

**Exodus**

| | |
|---|---|
| 19:6 | 97n15 |
| 23 | 44 |

**Leviticus**

| | |
|---|---|
| 17–18 | 55, 57 |

**Numbers**

| | |
|---|---|
| 15:18–20 | 101n19 |

**Deuteronomy**

| | |
|---|---|
| 6:4 | 45 |
| 7:6 | 96 |
| 7:6–7 | 192–93 |

**1 Chronicles**

| | |
|---|---|
| 17:21 | 94 |

**Psalms**

| | |
|---|---|
| 2 | 28 |
| 2:7 | 28 |
| 95:7 | 181n9 |
| 118 | 179 |

**Proverbs**

| | |
|---|---|
| 8:22–31 | 28n15 |

**Isaiah**

| | |
|---|---|
| 6 | 164, 168–69, 169n25, 170 |
| 35:10 | 164 |
| 40 | 167n23, 168n24 |
| 40:1 | 167n23 |
| 40:3 | 166 |
| 40:4–5 | 166 |
| 40:5 | 166–67, 168 |
| 49 | 168 |
| 49:5–6 | 167, 168 |
| 49:5–6a | 168 |
| 49:5–6b | 168 |
| 49:6 | xxiii–iv, 165 |
| 53 | 134 |

**Jeremiah**

| | |
|---|---|
| 16:15 | 162n17 |
| 24:6 | 162n17 |

**Ezekiel**

| | |
|---|---|
| 1:26 | 31 |

**Daniel**

| | |
|---|---|
| 7:9 | 31 |
| 9:27 | 159–60 |
| 11:31 | 159–60 |
| 12:11 | 159–60 |

**Hosea**

| | |
|---|---|
| 11:11 | 162n17 |

## Amos

| | |
|---|---|
| 9:11–12 | 55 |

## Zechariah

| | |
|---|---|
| 14:2–5 | 174 |
| 14:8–9 | 175 |

# NEW TESTAMENT

## Matthew

| | |
|---|---|
| 2:1–12 | 154 |
| 20:20–28 | 12 |
| 23:34–36 | 158 |
| 23:37–39 | 158 |

## Mark

| | |
|---|---|
| 4:41 | 16 |
| 8:29 | 16 |
| 10:35–45 | 12 |
| 12:28–34 | 193 |
| 13 | 160n14 |
| 13:2 | 58 |
| 13:14–20 | 159 |
| 15:32 | 9 |

## Luke

| | |
|---|---|
| 1:5–23 | 154 |
| 1:68 | 162 |
| 1:69–79 | 162 |
| 1:71 | 162 |
| 1:72 | 162 |
| 1:73 | 162 |
| 1:77 | 162 |
| 1:79 | 162 |
| 2:1–70 | 154 |
| 2:25 | 167n23 |
| 2:28 | 162 |
| 2:29–32 | 167 |
| 2:32 | 168 |
| 2:38 | 162 |
| 2:41–5 | 154 |
| 3:4–6 | 166 |
| 3:16 | 53 |
| 3:22 | 28 |
| 9:51—18:14 | 154 |
| 9:51 | 154 |
| 13 | 180 |
| 13:22 | 154 |
| 13:31–33 | 158 |
| 13:33–35 | 179 |
| 13:34 | 158 |
| 13:35 | 163, 170, 174 |
| 13:38 | 179 |
| 17:11 | 154 |
| 19:37 | 179–80 |
| 19:38 | 174 |
| 19:41–44 | 159, 163, 174 |
| 21:5–36 | 159 |
| 21:20–24 | 160–61 |
| 21:24 | 161, 168, 172, 173 |
| 23:27 | 159 |
| 23:28–31 | 159 |
| 24:49 | 154 |
| 24:53 | 154 |

## John

| | |
|---|---|
| 1:1–5 | 28 |
| 1:14 | 28 |
| 1:18 | 28 |
| 1:49 | 9 |
| 3:16–17 | 10n16 |
| 3:16 | 28, 193 |
| 3:18 | 28 |
| 4:42 | 10n16 |
| 6:46 | 28 |
| 12:13 | 9 |
| 12:31 | 10n16 |
| 12:47 | 10n16 |
| 14:6 | 89 |
| 14:25–26 | 126 |
| 16:12–14 | 126 |
| 17:5 | 28 |
| 18:36 | 10n16 |
| 19:19–22 | 10 |
| 19:21 | 9 |
| 20:28 | 36n25 |

## Acts

| | |
|---|---|
| 1–12 | 65 |
| 1 | 153 |
| 1:5 | 53 |
| 1:6–8 | xxiii, 152, 153, 163, 165, 166, 172–74 |
| 1:6 | 165n21, 172, 173, 180, 181, 181n8 |
| 1:7–8 | 173 |
| 1:7 | 180 |
| 1:8 | 153, 155, 156, 157 |
| 1:9–12 | 173 |
| 2:4 | 53 |
| 2:5 | 156 |
| 2:9–11 | 156, 157 |
| 2:11 | 53 |
| 2:46 | 155 |
| 3:1–10 | 155 |
| 3:17–21 | 161, 172–73, 180–81 |
| 3:19–21 | 163, 170 |
| 3:20 | 179 |
| 3:21 | 162, 173, 181n8 |
| 4:1–2 | 155 |
| 5:12 | 155 |
| 5:20–21 | 155 |
| 5:42 | 155 |
| 8:1 | 155n7 |
| 8:4–25 | 155n7 |
| 9:1–19 | 166 |
| 9:1–2 | 155n7 |
| 9:4 | 68 |
| 9:10 | 155n7 |
| 9:19 | 155n7 |
| 9:26–29 | 155, 183 |
| 10–11 | 54n7 |
| 10 | 53, 105, 155 |
| 10:1–48 | 166 |
| 10:46 | 53 |
| 11 | 155 |
| 11:1–18 | 54n7 |
| 11:2 | 183 |
| 11:4–16 | 166 |
| 11:12 | 155 |
| 11:15–17 | 53 |
| 11:16 | 53 |
| 11:19–21 | 54 |
| 11:19 | 155 |
| 11:27–30 | 155, 183 |
| 13:1–3 | 54, 155 |
| 13:4—14:26 | 155 |
| 13:16–41 | 165 |
| 13:33 | 28 |
| 13:42–43 | 165 |
| 13:46–47 | 165, 168 |
| 13:47 | xxiii, 166 |
| 15 | 54n7, 55n8, 56 |
| 15:1–29 | 54n7 |
| 15:1–21 | 54 |
| 15:2 | 155, 183 |
| 15:7–9 | 166 |
| 15:13–18 | 106 |
| 15:1 | 54 |
| 15:7a | 53 |
| 15:8–9 | 55 |
| 15:12 | 55 |
| 15:14 | 56 |
| 15:20 | 56 |
| 15:28–29 | 56 |
| 16:4 | 56 |
| 16:9–10 | 155, 165 |
| 18:5–7 | 165 |
| 18:22 | 155, 155n8, 183 |
| 21:17—23:11 | 156, 183 |
| 21:25 | 56 |
| 22:6–16 | 166 |
| 26:12–18 | 166 |
| 26:22–23 | 168 |
| 28:17–20 | 171 |
| 28:17 | 156, 169 |
| 28:20 | 169 |
| 28:23–31 | 164 |
| 28:23b–25a | 169 |
| 28:25b–27 | 170 |
| 28:25b–28 | 164 |
| 28:28 | xxiii, 164, 165n21, 166, 167, 170 |

## Romans

| | |
|---|---|
| 1:3 | 103 |
| 1:5 | 65, 105 |
| 1:7 | 101 |
| 1:13–15 | 105 |
| 5:5 | 193 |

## Romans (continued)

| | |
|---|---|
| 9:4–5 | 103 |
| 10:9 | 16 |
| 11 | 101, 178, 182, 183 |
| 11:1 | 100 |
| 11:5–7 | 100–101 |
| 11:13–14 | 105 |
| 11:15 | 100 |
| 11:16–24 | 58 |
| 11:16 | 70, 100, 101, 190 |
| 11:25–26 | 70, 186 |
| 11:29 | 199 |
| 15 | 103 |
| 15:15–16 | 102, 105 |
| 15:16 | 65 |
| 15:25–33 | 105 |
| 15:25–27 | 58, 102 |
| 15:25–26 | 101 |
| 15:31 | 101 |

## 1 Corinthians

| | |
|---|---|
| 1:2 | 101 |
| 1:12 | 105 |
| 3:22 | 105 |
| 8:5–6 | 26 |
| 9:5 | 105 |
| 12:3 | 16 |
| 16:1–4 | 105 |
| 16:1 | 101 |

## 2 Corinthians

| | |
|---|---|
| 3:17 | 126 |
| 8:4 | 101 |
| 9:1–15 | 105 |
| 9:1 | 101 |
| 9:12 | 101 |
| 11:22–24 | 105n26 |

## Galatians

| | |
|---|---|
| 1:15–16 | 65 |
| 1:16 | 105 |
| 2:7–10 | 65 |
| 2:7–9 | 105 |
| 2:9 | 105 |
| 2:10 | 105 |
| 2:11–14 | 106 |

## Ephesians

| | |
|---|---|
| 1:3–4 | 97 |
| 1:11–12 | 97 |
| 2 | 99 |
| 2:11–12 | 97 |
| 2:17 | 99 |
| 2:19–21 | 97–98 |
| 4:4–6 | 98 |

## Philippians

| | |
|---|---|
| 2:11 | 16 |

## Hebrews

| | |
|---|---|
| 1:3 | 23, 28n16 |
| 1:5 | 28 |

## James

| | |
|---|---|
| 1:18 | 102 |

## 1 Peter

| | |
|---|---|
| 5:13 | 106 |

## 1 John

| | |
|---|---|
| 4:9 | 28 |

## Revelation

| | |
|---|---|
| 17–18 | 67 |

# RABBINIC WRITINGS

## Mishna

| | |
|---|---|
| Berachot 2:2 | 45, 95n13 |
| Avot 2:21 | 111 |

## Babylonian Talmud

| | |
|---|---|
| Berachot 6a | 94 |
| Bava Metzia 59b | 13 |
| Sanhedrin 98a | 181n9 |

## Midrash

Exodus Rabah 28:6    13
Exodus Rabah 47:1    13

www.ingramcontent.com/pod-product-compliance
Lightning Source LLC
Chambersburg PA
CBHW022009220426
43663CB00007B/1020